Z250 .P47 2004

Perfect, Christopher.

Rookledge's classic
international typefinder
2004.

2006 01 23

DISCARD

W9-BDU-270

0 1341 0824668 4

nkledge's classic international typefinder

DISCARD

3199 Lakeshore Blvd. West
Toronto, ON   M8V 1K8
...ge Library

Rookledge's **classic** international typefinder

Laurence King Publishing

in association with **Harper Design International** an imprint of **HarperCollins**Publishers

pe

Humber College Library

160201

the essential handbook of typeface recognition and selection

by **Christopher Perfect** and **Gordon Rookledge**

revised by Phil Baines & with a foreword by Adrian Frutiger

Imprint

Published in 2004 by Laurence King Publishing Ltd
71 Great Russell Street
London WC1B 3BP
United Kingdom
Tel +44 20 7430 8850
Fax +44 20 7430 8880
e-mail enquiries@laurenceking.co.uk
www.laurenceking.co.uk

Distributed in North and South America by
Harper Design International
an imprint of HarperCollins*Publishers*
10 East 53rd Street
New York, NY 10022
Fax: (212) 207-7654

First edition published in 1983 by Sarema Press
(Publishers) Ltd, UK (hardback); second printing 1984
Sarema Press (Publishers) Ltd (paperback); first published in the USA in 1984 by Frederick C Beil, Publisher
Inc. (hardback)/PBC International Inc. (paperback);
republished in 1990 by Sarema Press (Publishers) Ltd
(hardback & paperback editions); reprinted in 1991 by
Sarema Press (Publishers) Ltd (hardback); published in
the USA in 1991 by Moyer Bell Ltd, New York (paperback).

Copyright © 2004 Gordon Rookledge

Original design and artwork by the Perfect Design
Company Limited, London.

All rights reserved. No part of this publication may be
reproduced or transmitted in any form or by any means,
electronic or mechanical, including photocopy, recording
or any information storage and retrieval system, without
prior permission in writing from the publisher.

Great care has been taken throughout this book to
ensure accuracy but the publisher cannot accept respon-
sibility for errors that may occur.

A catalogue record for this book is available from the
British Library.

ISBN 1 85669 406 2

Printed in Singapore

Acknowledgements to the first edition

We are indebted to the principal collaborators who
helped formulate the content of this book: Eiichi Kono
MA(RCA) MSTD and Alfred Lubran FRSA. Without
their considerable efforts and skill its publication would
not have been possible.

Our thanks are also due to the staff of The Perfect
Design Company Limited, especially Fiona Barton and
Matthew Kirby, as well as Leslie Carvalho and Andrew
Bennett for their painstaking skills in the preparation of
the artwork; to the staff of Gavin Martin Limited and
Brian Thompson for print production; to Mel Hobbs and
his staff at Text Filmsetters for supplying a large percent-
age of the typeface specimens and for getting the most
out of a Linotron 202 typesetting machine.

Also to the following companies and individuals who
supplied typeface specimens and information: Alphabet
Limited, Apex Typesetting Limited, Apex Photosetting
Limited, H. Berthold AG, Character Photosetting
Limited, Diagraphic Typesetters Limited, Face Ronchetti
Limited, Filmcomposition, Linotype-Paul Limited,
Margaret Calvert, The Monotype Corporation, Pinnacle
Phototype Limited and Stempel Haas.

Christopher Perfect
Gordon Rookledge
1983

*To Jennie, Sarah, Gavin and Emma for all their patience and
understanding over the years. (G R)*

For my wife, Tessa. (C P)

CONTENTS

**Preface to the first edition by
Herbert Spencer RDI Dr RCA**

As with other inspired innovations – such as the safety pin, the paper clip, the zip-fastener, and the ball-point pen – now that *Rookledge's International Typefinder* is here one wonders how it was possible to function for so long without it. Though it may lack the universal significance of some of the other innovations I mentioned, for the graphic designer and typographer this publication is without doubt a real milestone.

Fundamental changes in printing technology and the rapid development of alternative media for distributing ideas and information during the past twenty-five years have released a torrent of new type designs – some good, a few excellent, and, inevitably, many bad.

This book will be used, first, as an invaluable working tool enabling the designer quickly to identify and to select particular typefaces for his immediate purposes. However, for the student this publication will serve another – and, in the long term, perhaps an even more important – function: by highlighting and indicating the essential characteristics of each typeface shown it will *educate* the user to distinguish between good and bad designs, between sound and sloppy solutions, between the imaginative and the merely perverse – in fact, to separate the grain from the chaff. And for that the publisher and editor will deserve the gratitude of all readers as well as of all designers.

This typefinder, then, is a publication of major importance. The task of assembling and arranging the enormous number of specimens it contains must have been a daunting one. It was Gordon Rookledge who recognised the need for such a book and it is due to his enthusiasm, persistence and tenacity that the idea has become a reality. Christopher Perfect has worked with exceptional editorial dedication and design skill to define and evolve the original concept for this book, and, in collaboration with Eiichi Kono, to bring the project to fruition. Both of them, publisher and editor, are to be congratulated on having fashioned not just a tool but a powerful weapon in the fight for better, more effective, typography.

Introduction to the first edition

The recognition and selection of typefaces is a regular everyday task for the practising graphic designer and typographer. Yet, up until now, no single reference source has been available to assist in these processes. This book has been produced especially to fill this gap, serving as an invaluable working tool for everyone who works with type.

It is the editor's experience that other than expert or highly-experienced typographers, the majority of creative people have difficulty in recognising and identifying individual typefaces. Therefore, the primary purpose of the book is to satisfy this need and simplify this essential task as fully as possible.

A secondary purpose is to help in the process of typeface selection. The graphic designer often has difficulty in obtaining good, comprehensive reference material despite an abundance of typefounders' and typesetters' catalogues. It is the aim of this book to make this job easier and to contribute to the educational experience in the process.

This book is divided into two parts, *Text* and *Decorative* (non-continuous text) typefaces. The classification system used in each part is entirely new and does not follow previous established type classifications. The typefaces selected were all available at the time of compilation of the book and all the major international typefounders' current lists were consulted so as to make the choice as comprehensive as possible. Readers should note that 'bastard' versions of well-known typefaces have not been included but are cross-referenced in the index. The possible number of *Decorative* typefaces is endless so, with limited space, selection has been confined to a cross-section of the more commonly-used designs. (NB. It is not the purpose of this book to act as a complete typeface dictionary or specimen book.)

The listing of *Text* typefaces are all, as far as possible, in the normal weight of type for text setting (i.e. regular roman). It was not the editor's intention to include the many other variations of one typeface family (e.g. light, bold, italic, condensed etc.) as it is the regular weight which is most commonly used and which establishes the 'style' characteristics of a particular typeface. In order to obtain information on the range of different weights and variations of a typeface it is suggested that readers should consult their own typesetters.

Whilst the selection and compilation of the typefaces in this book were carried out with great care some may have been omitted which readers feel should be included. Your suggestions, submitted through the publisher, will be welcome.

Christopher Perfect
Gordon Rookledge

PREFACE
By Adrian Frutiger

The capital letters of our alphabet are already 2000 years old. Their basic forms were carved into triumphal monuments by the stone-masons of Ancient Rome. Our lower-case letters have not fundamentally changed for 1000 years, since monastic scribes first began to form words in the Carolingian miniscule script, rounding off the letters with flowing penmanship.

Letter-forms, whether carved, handwritten or printed, have always reflected the spirit of their times, being constantly renewed by individual scribes and typefounders, and not least by the techniques of typesetting and printing.

During recent decades, the advent of phototypesetting and rub-off lettering has brought a vast increase in the number of new typefaces. These resources contain both the best and the worst of type and their multitude can be bewildering to the user. To clarify the matter, this mass of typefaces has repeatedly been classified according to historical periods, styles or typesetting techniques. Nowadays, such simple classifications are no longer sufficient, owing to the large number of variations, often unhelpful, of individual letter-forms.

Publication of the typefinder has brought a completely new aid to the world of typography. For the first time, it provides a logical grouping of all existing alphabets, together with clear descriptions of individual letters. The tangle of typefaces has been combed out so as to produce new divisions and classifications of alphabets that were previously jumbled together in piles of heavy specimen books.

For the creative typographer, whose job is to present words to the reader in a correct and completely legible form, the present work is a completely new aid, enabling him to appreciate typefaces in a new dimension and dress the printed message in the right clothing.

Modern reproduction techniques have not made it any easier to deal with type. Specification of the page image is increasingly falling into the hands of untrained people. We hope that the present reference book will be distributed beyond the strictly professional community to reach the uninitiated user of type and serve as an aid to decision-making. In this sense I see the new, enlarged edition of the typefinder as the clearest guide, with the very worthy task of preserving the authenticity of the printed word.

The authors and publisher of this authoritative work have earned the gratitude of the entire graphic world, and indirectly of the reading public as a whole. I hope that it will be accepted as a world standard.

Adrian Frutiger
Paris, January 1990

INTRODUCTION

It is seven years since Rookledge's International typefinder was first published as a single reference work for the correct identification of typefaces. During this time it has proved an invaluable tool for everyone who works with type. For this new edition the opportunity has been taken to expand the scope of the book as well as correct a few minor errors in the original.

The three main parts of the original typefinder have been retained. They are as follows:
1. An at-a-glance guide to typeface classification, with a substantial typeface catalogue grouped according to eight classifications for comparative study.
2. Letter-by-letter recognition (earmark) tables with cross-references to the typeface catalogue.
3. A fully cross-referenced index, bibliography and notes for further reading.

The original typefinder leads the user to the correct identification of a typeface specimen by a process of visual inspection and elimination. The first step in the process is the fitting of the face into one of eight basic categories, using the classification guide. This edition keeps this successful method but prefaces each category with an introduction examining the historical background to each category of typeface design.

The first edition contained 700 typefaces, this new edition updates these with the addition of selected faces released since that date.

The final new feature for this edition is an eight page section devoted to some of the leading people behind the typefaces. Alphabetically arranged, it provides biographical notes on over fifty type designers from Gutenberg to the present day. Entries are cross-referenced to the typefaces included in the typefinder. This section of the typefinder is an abridged list from Rookledge's International Handbook of Type Designers, to be published by Sarema Press later this year (1990).

Whilst the selection and compilation of the typefaces in this book were carried out with great care some may have been omitted which readers feel should be included. Your suggestions, submitted through the publisher, will be welcome.

Phil Baines
Gordon Rookledge
London, February 1990

pt. I:

text
typefaces

SLOPING E-BAR
(VENETIAN SERIF)

e

ANGLED STRESS OBLIQUE SERIFS
(OLD STYLE SERIF)

od

VERTICAL STRESS OBLIQUE SERIFS
(TRANSITIONAL SERIF)

od

VERTICAL STRESS STRAIGHT SERIFS
(NEW TRANSITIONAL)

od

ABRUPT CONTRAST STRAIGHT SERIFS
(MODERN SERIF)

od

SLAB SERIF

I I

WEDGE SERIF
(HYBRID SERIF)

I I

SANS SERIF

G G

TEXT TYPEFACE CATEGORIES

THIS PART OF the book contains typefaces which are commonly used for continuous text setting. The characteristic features of each of the eight typeface categories are described below and are illustrated on the opposite page.

The classification system used in this book is entirely new and is based on the grouping of typefaces according to specific design features. This will sometimes mean that typefaces of a similar historical origin fall into different categories. This book, therefore, does not follow established classifications such as the British Standards Typeface Nomenclature and Classification System (BS 2961). (NB. a comparison to this can be found in the Appendix at the back of the book.)

Each category is further divided into smaller groups according to more specific design features which are explained at the beginning of each section. Typeface specimens are then arranged alphabetically within each group and have an individual specimen number which is cross-referenced to both the index and 'Earmark' Tables starting on p. 97.

NB. There is a small overlap between the *Text* and *Decorative* parts of the book. For instance, some *Decorative* typefaces in special circumstances may be used for continuous text setting and vice-versa.

Categories 1 to 5 are all variations of the roman serif design and begin with:

1. Sloping e-Bar (Venetian Serif). *Nos. 1-34*
Typefaces in this category all have a sloping bar on the lower case e. All roman serif typefaces with this feature, *plus those which have slab or wedge serif characteristics*, will be found here. Generally, these typefaces are of a heavy appearance and have poor contrast between thick and thin strokes. They usually have oblique ascender serifs.

2. Angled Stress/Oblique Serifs (Old Style Serif) *Nos. 35-53*
Typefaces in this group are characterised by an angled stress on the bowls of letters (e.g. the lower case o) and have oblique serifs on the ascenders of lower case letters. The foot serif on the lower case d is also oblique. There is a stronger contrast between the thick and thin strokes of letters than in Category 1.

3. Vertical Stress/Oblique Serifs (Transitional Serif) *Nos. 54-110*
Typefaces in this category have vertical stress (or nearly so) on the bowls of letters (such as the lower case o) but still have distinct oblique serifs on the ascenders. The serif foot of the lower case d is usually horizontal but sometimes slightly oblique. The contrast between the thick and thin strokes of letters is generally more pronounced than in Category 2. All typefaces have bracketed serifs.

4. Vertical Stress/Straight Serifs (New Transitional Serif) *Nos. 111-150*
All typefaces in this group have a definite vertical stress and serifs are normally all horizontal (straight). However, a small number have slightly oblique serifs. These typefaces generally have little contrast between the thick and thin strokes and the serifs are usually bracketed.

5. Abrupt Contrast/Straight Serifs (Modern Serif) *Nos. 151-187*
These typefaces feature a strong and abrupt contrast between the thick and thin strokes of letters and all serifs are horizontal (straight). The overall stress is clearly vertical. Serifs can be line (unbracketed) or slightly bracketed and typefaces can vary in colour from light to black face.

6. Slab Serif. *Nos. 188-217*
These typefaces are characterised by a generally heavy appearance with thick 'slab' serifs often the same thickness as the main stem of the letters. Serifs can be square (unbracketed) or bracketed. *(NB. Slab serif style typefaces with a sloping bar on the lower case e will be found in Category 1.)*

7. Wedge Serif (Hybrid Serif). *Nos. 218-240*
This category contains typefaces which are not always clearly serif or sans serif (i.e. hybrids).

It includes typefaces both of a general serif-style but with only a thickening at the terminals of letters and sans serif-style typefaces with very small line serifs on the terminals. It includes other groups with wedge-shaped serifs and half serifs. *(NB. Wedge serif-style typefaces with a sloping bar on the lower case e are to be found in Category 1.)*

8. Sans Serif. *Nos. 245-304*
Typefaces with no serifs. Generally, with little or no difference between strokes (i.e. monoline.) These typefaces are primarily divided according to whether the capital G has a spur or not and if it has, whether it is of a wide, medium or narrow design. The category also includes groups of typefaces of a special shape (such as rounded).

The Typefinding Process

1. To identify a typeface, first decide into which of the main categories shown opposite the typeface specimen you wish to identify belongs.

2. By using the thumb index on the edge of the page turn to the appropriate category introduction page.

3. From the 'contents' list given there select the specific group within the category to which your specimen relates.

4. Read off the specimen numbers given for this group and find them in the following listings of typeface specimens.

5. Decide which of the typefaces in the group it equates to with the help of asterisks which show letters with special or 'style' characteristics.

Text Typeface 'Earmark' Tables

These will be found at the end of this part of the book, beginning on p. 97, and offer an alternative but companion method of identifying *Text* typefaces by comparing to 'earmarks' or features on individual letters. The tables are divided into two parts, 'Common' and 'Special Earmarks', and letters are arranged in a continuous sequence from a to z in both capital and lower case forms (plus ampersand and figures.)

Type categories

General characteristics

1. Sloping e-Bar (Venetian Serif) *Nos 1-34*

e.g. **6** Kennerley, **19** Centaur, **30** ITC Souvenir, and **32** Italian Old Style (Monotype).

little contrast | e-bar sloped | angled or vertical stress | oblique ascender serif (not always) | oblique lower case serif (not always) | foot serif often oblique (not always)

e o l d n

SLOPING E-BAR (VENETIAN SERIF) — **e**

2. Angled Stress/Oblique Serifs (Old Style Serif) *Nos 35-53*

e.g. **35** Bembo, **39** Plantin, **44** Trump Mediaeval and **53** Times New Roman (Monotype).

medium contrast | e-bar horizontal | angled stress | oblique ascender serif | oblique lower case serif | oblique foot serif

e o l d n

ANGLED STRESS OBLIQUE SERIFS (OLD STYLE SERIF) — **od**

3. Vertical Stress/Oblique Serifs (Transitional Serif) *Nos 54-110*

e.g. **61** Caslon 540, **78** Baskerville 169 (Monotype), **92** Garamond (Stempel) and **105** Romulus.

good contrast | e-bar horizontal | stress vertical (or nearly so) | oblique serifs | oblique lower case serif | foot serif usually level (not always)

e o l d n

VERTICAL STRESS OBLIQUE SERIFS (TRANSITIONAL SERIF) — **od**

4. Vertical Stress/Straight Serifs (New Transitional Serif) *Nos. 151-187*

e.g. **111** Joanna, **119** Century Schoolbook, **123** Cheltenham, and **138** Melior.

little contrast | e-bar horizontal | vertical stress | straight serifs (some slightly oblique) | straight serif in lower case (some oblique)

e o l d n

VERTICAL STRESS STRAIGHT SERIFS (NEW TRANSITIONAL) — **od**

5. Abrupt Contrast/Straight Serifs (Modern Serif) *Nos 151-187*

e.g. **153** Bauer Bodoni, **161** Walbaum (Linotype), **174** Caledonia and **185** Scotch Roman.

abrupt contrast | e-bar horizontal | vertical stress | line or bracketed serifs | straight serifs | straight serifs

e o l d n

ABRUPT CONTRAST STRAIGHT SERIFS (MODERN SERIF) — **od**

6. Slab Serif *Nos 188-217*

e.g. **197** Rockwell, **203** Schadow Antiqua, **209** Clarendon (Linotype), and **214** ITC American Typewriter.

little or no contrast | square slab serifs | bracketed serifs | rounded serif

Ig single storey **g** double storey **Ig** single storey **g** double storey **I**

SLAB SERIF — **II**

7. Wedge Serif (Hybrid Serif) *Nos 218-240*

e.g. **218** Albertus, **233** Meridien, **236** Copperplate Gothic and **240** Romic.

poor contrast | wedge-ended serifs | wedge-shaped serifs | fine line terminals | half serif only

I l I l I

WEDGE SERIF (HYBRID SERIF) — **II**

8. Sans Serif *Nos 245-304*

e.g. **254** Futura, **259** Gill Sans, **267** Univers 55 and **279** Helvetica.

little or no contrast | wide | medium | narrow | wide | medium | narrow | special shape (rounded)

G G G no spur **G G G** spur **G**

SANS SERIF — **GG**

I. SLOPING e-BAR
(Venetian Serif) Nos 1-34

Typefaces in this category all have a sloping bar on the lower case e. All roman serif typefaces with this feature, *plus those which have slab or wedge characteristics*, will be found here. Generally, these typefaces are of a heavy appearance and have poor contrast between thick and thin strokes. They usually have oblique ascender serifs.

When printing from moveable metal type was first perfected by Gutenberg and his partners in Mainz, Germany, in 1455, the letterforms they used were of course those of the middle ages, a heavy black script called textura. German printers moved to Italy, the centre of the Renaissance, and within ten years a new style of type appeared which became known as *roman*. Although imperfect, it was the type of a new age.

Venice became the centre of fine printing and it was there that the Frenchman Nicholas Jenson designed and cut his famous type in about 1470. The letters have a calligraphic (oblique) stress but the change from thick to thin strokes is gradual whilst the serifs are strong and steeply sloped. The most obvious characteristic is the sloping bar to the lower case e.

A generation later, the types of Manutius ousted Jenson's which were then largely ignored by all but a few experts for four centuries. When William Morris, the leader of the Arts and Crafts movement, turned his attention to typography it was to Jenson that he looked for inspiration. His **Golden** type of 1892 was based on Jenson's type of 1470.

In this century there have been several notable revivals such as E. F. Detterer's **Eusebius** (for Ludlow) and Bruce Rodgers' **Centaur** of 1915 (Monotype 1929).

I. SLOPING e-BAR
(Venetian Serif) Nos 1-34

Specimen nos	Basic characteristics	Secondary characteristics	
1-5	O steeply inclined axis on bowls of letters		e.g. **5** Windsor
6-12	O less steeply inclined axis	q short descenders long serifs	e.g. **7** Lavenham
13	,,	q short descenders short serifs	e.g. **13** Della Robbia
14-18	,,	q longer descenders weak contrast	e.g. **17** Schneidler Old Style
19-21	,,	q longer descenders strong contrast	e.g. **19** Centaur
22-27	o vertical axis	r roman serifs	e.g. **25** Lutetia
28-31	,,	r wedge serifs	e.g. **30** ITC Souvenir
32	o inclined axis	d roman and slab serifs (mixed)	e.g. **32** Italian Old Style (Monotype)
33-34	o vertical or slightly inclined axis	d slab serifs on ascenders	e.g. **34** Jenson Old Style

NB. Typefaces in each group are arranged in alphabetical order.

SLOPING E-BAR
(VENETIAN SERIF)

e

Bellini
Erasmus
Hollandse Mediaeval
Pastonchi
Windsor
Kennerley
Lavenham
Raleigh
Surrey Old Style
Trajanus

steeply inclined axis

1 Bellini

ABCDEFGHIJKLMNOPQRSTUVWXYZ&

2 Erasmus

ABCDEFGHIJKLMNOPQRSTUVWXYZ&

3 Hollandse Mediaeval

ABCDEFGHIJKLMNOPQRSTUVWXYZ&

4 Pastonchi

ABCDEFGHIJKLMNOPQRSTUVWXYZ&

5 Windsor

ABCDEFGHIJKLMNOPQRSTUVWXYZ&

less steeply inclined axis
short descenders
long serifs

6 Kennerley

ABCDEFGHIJKLMNOPQRSTUVWXYZ&

7 Lavenham

ABCDEFGHIJKLMNOPQRSTUVWXYZ&

8 Raleigh

ABCDEFGHIJKLMNOPQRSTUVWXYZ&

9 Surrey Old Style

ABCDEFGHIJKLMNOPQRSTUVWXYZ&

10 Trajanus

ABCDEFGHIJKLMNOPQRSTUVWXYZ&

* These letters show special or 'style' characteristics. (NB. J, Q, & and g will usually vary from one typeface to another).

**SLOPING E-BAR
(VENETIAN SERIF)**

*Bellini
Erasmus
Hollandse Mediaeval
Pastonchi
Windsor
Kennerley
Lavenham
Raleigh
Surrey Old Style
Trajanus*

Bellini **1**

abcdefghijklmnopqrstuvwxyz1234567890

Erasmus **2**

abcdefghijklmnopqrstuvwxyz1234567890

Hollandse Mediaeval **3**

abcdefghijklmnopqrstuvwxyz1234567890

Pastonchi **4**

abcdefghijklmnopqrstuvwxyz1234567890

Windsor **5**

abcdefghijklmnopqrstuvwxyz 1234567890

Kennerley **6**

abcdefghijklmnopqrstuvwxyz1234567890

Lavenham **7**

abcdefghijklmnopqrstuvwxyz1234567890

Raleigh **8**

abcdefghijklmnopqrstuvwxyz1234567890

Surrey Old Style **9**

abcdefghijklmnopqrstuvwxyz1234567890

Trajanus **10**

abcdefghijklmnopqrstuvwxyz1234567890

NB. On lower case letters generally look at the x height and length of ascenders and descenders.

SLOPING E-BAR
(VENETIAN SERIF)

Verona
Worcester Round
Della Robbia
Bauer Text
Cloister
Jenson
Schneidler Old Style
Seneca
Centaur
Horley Old Style

11 Verona

ABCDEFGHIJKLMNOPQRSTUVWXYZ&

12 Worcester Round

ABCDEFGHIJKLMNOPQRSTUVWXYZ&

less steeply
inclined
axis
short
descenders
short serifs

13 Della Robbia

ABCDEFGHIJKLMNOPQRSTUVWXYZ&

less steeply
inclined
axis
longer
descenders
weak
contrast

14 Bauer Text

ABCDEFGHIJKLMNOPQRSTUVWXYZ&

15 Cloister

ABCDEFGHIJKLMNOPQRSTUVWXYZ&

16 Jenson

ABCDEFGHIJKLMNOPQRSTUVWXYZ

17 Schneidler Old Style

ABCDEFGHIJKLMNOPQRSTUVWXYZ&

18 Seneca

ABCDEFGHIJKLMNOPQRSTUVWXYZ&

less steeply
inclined
axis
longer
descenders
strong
contrast

19 Centaur

ABCDEFGHIJKLMNOPQRSTUVWXYZ&

20 Horley Old Style

ABCDEFGHIJKLMNOPQRSTUVWXYZ&

* These letters show special or 'style' characteristics. (NB. J, Q, & and g will usually vary from one typeface to another).

Verona
Worcester Round
Della Robbia
Bauer Text
Cloister
Jenson
Schneidler Old Style
Seneca
Centaur
Horley Old Style

Verona 11

abcdefghijklmnopqrstuvwxyz 1234567890

Worcester Round 12

abcdefghijklmnopqrstuvwxyz1234567890

Della Robbia 13

abcdefghijklmnopqrstuvwxyz1234567890

Bauer Text 14

abcdefghijklmnopqrstuvwxyz1234567890

Cloister 15

abcdefghijklmnopqrstuvwxyz1234567890

Jenson 16

abcdefghijklmnopqrstuvwxyz 1234567890

Schneidler Old Style 17

abcdefghijklmnopqrstuvwxyz1234567890

Seneca 18

abcdefghijklmnopqrstuvwxyz1234567890

Centaur 19

abcdefghijklmnopqrstuvwxyz1234567890

Horley Old Style 20

abcdefghijklmnopqrstuvwxyz1234567890

NB. On lower case letters generally look at the x height and length of ascenders and descenders.

21-30

**SLOPING E-BAR
(VENETIAN SERIF)**

Deepdene
Brighton
Clearface Bold 157
(Monotype)
ITC Clearface
Lutetia
Stratford
ITC Tiffany
ITC Benguiat
Seagull
ITC Souvenir

21 Deepdene

ABCDEFGHIJKLMNOPQRSTUVWXYZ&

*vertical
axis
roman
serifs*

22 Brighton

ABCDEFGHIJKLMNOPQRSTUVWXYZ&

23 Clearface Bold 157 (Monotype)

ABCDEFGHIJKLMNOPQRSTUVWXYZ&

24 ITC Clearface

ABCDEFGHIJKLMNOPQRSTUVWXYZ&

25 Lutetia

ABCDEFGHIJKLMNOPQRSTUVWXYZ&

26 Stratford

ABCDEFGHIJKLMNOPQRSTUVWXYZ&

27 ITC Tiffany

ABCDEFGHIJKLMNOPQRSTUVWXYZ&

*vertical axis
wedge serifs*

28 ITC Benguiat

ABCDEFGHIJKLMNOPQRSTUVWXYZ&

29 Seagull

ABCDEFGHIJKLMNOPQRSTUVWXYZ&

30 ITC Souvenir

ABCDEFGHIJKLMNOPQRSTUVWXYZ&

* These letters show special or 'style' characteristics. (NB. J, Q, & and g will usually vary from one typeface to another).

Deepdene
Brighton
Clearface Bold 157
(Monotype)
ITC Clearface
Lutetia
Stratford
ITC Tiffany
ITC Benguiat
Seagull
ITC Souvenir

Deepdene **21**

abcdefghijklmnopqrstuvwxyz1234567890

Brighton **22**

abcdefghijklmnopqrstuvwxyz**1234567890**

Clearface Bold 157 (Monotype) **23**

abcdefghijklmnopqrstuvwxyz1234567890

ITC Clearface **24**

abcdefghijklmnopqrstuvwxyz1234567890

Lutetia **25**

abcdefghijklmnopqrstuvwxyz1234567890

Stratford **26**

abcdefghijklmnopqrstuvwxyz1234567890

ITC Tiffany **27**

abcdefghijklmnopqrstuvwxyz1234567890

ITC Benguiat **28**

abcdefghijklmnopqrstuvwxyz1234567890

Seagull **29**

abcdefghijklmnopqrstuvwxyz1234567890

ITC Souvenir **30**

abcdefghijklmnopqrstuvwxyz1234567890

NB. On lower case letters generally look at the x height and length of ascenders and descenders.

SLOPING E-BAR
(VENETIAN SERIF)

Vendôme
Italian Old Style
(Monotype)
ITC Italia
Jenson Old Style
Guardi 55 (Linotype)

31 Vendôme

ABCDEFGHIJKLMNOPQRSTUVWXYZ&

inclined axis
roman and slab serifs

32 Italian Old Style (Monotype)

ABCDEFGHIJKLMNOPQRSTUVWXYZ&

vertical or slightly inclined axis
slab serifs on ascenders

33 ITC Italia

ABCDEFGHIJKLMNOPQRSTUVWXYZ&

34 Jenson Old Style

ABCDEFGHIJKLMNOPQRSTUVWXYZ&

new entry

34A Guardi 55 (Linotype)

ABCDEFGHIJKLMNOPQRSTUVWXYZ&

* These letters show special or 'style' characteristics. (NB. J, Q, & and g will usually vary from one typeface to another).

Vendôme **31**

abcdefghijklmnopqrstuvwxyz1234567890

Italian Old Style (Monotype) **32**

abcdefghijklmnopqrstuvwxyz1234567890

ITC Italia **33**

abcdefghijklmnopqrstuvwxyz1234567890

Jenson Old Style **34**

abcdefghijklmnopqrstuvwxyz1234567890

Guardi 55 (Linotype) **34A**

abcdefghijklmnopqrstuvwxyz 1234567890

NB. On lower case letters generally look at the x height and length of ascenders and descenders.

SLOPING E-BAR (VENETIAN SERIF)

Vendôme
Italian Old Style
(Monotype)
ITC Italia
Jenson Old Style
Guardi 55 (Linotype)

2. ANGLED STRESS/OBLIQUE SERIFS
(Old Style Serif) Nos 35-53

Typefaces in this group are characterised by an angled stress on the bowls of letters (e.g. the lower case o) and have oblique serifs on the ascenders of the lower case letters. The foot of the lower case d is also oblique. There is a stronger contrast between the thick and thin strokes of letters than in Category 1.

In 1495 the great Renaissance publisher and printer Aldus Manutius published *Erotomata* using a new set of types which were a development from the earlier *venetian* types of Nicholas Jenson and which became the basic model for European type design for the next two hundred and fifty years. Printers of each generation from Manutius to Caslon used this basic letter form with differences in emphasis only.

The design followed the underlying principles of Jenson's type, a calligraphic stress and oblique serifs and the most obvious difference is a straight cross-bar to the lower case e, but Aldus' type had a better balanced set of capitals and lower case and the fit of the letters together was more even. These factors and Aldus' position as a pioneer of cheap and accurate editions ensured their success.

91-95/96   The design was further refined in France from 1540 onwards by Claude **Garamond*** and
66   later, Jean Jannon and Robert **Granjon**. French types were bought by Dutch printers such as
39, 107   Christopher **Plantin** and Christoffel **Van Dijck** (who darkened the design a little), and their types in turn were bought by English printers, notably Dr. Fell of Cambridge. William
59-61/99   **Caslon** was the first English typefounder to satisfy the home market, and his types (started in 1725), the last of this category, followed Dutch models.

35   In this century, the *old style* has enjoyed enormous success following the various 'revivals' of designs such as Garamond, **Bembo**, Granjon, &c. In addition, the most
52/53   successful book typeface yet produced, Stanley Morison's **Times New Roman**, is a version of this style.

*The types in the typefinder are arranged for easy recognition and identification first and foremost, thus faces such as Garamond, Van Dijck and Granjon, which academically/historically are *old style*, are included for typefinding purposes in category 3.

A note about italics.
The first italic typeface is usually accepted as that of Aldus Manutius, first used in 1501; mean and cramped it was designed to save space in pocket editions. Other early italics took as their models the cursive formal hand of the Italian writing masters such as Arrighi in Rome and Tagliente in Venice. Although only a lower-case matched with roman capitals the italic was originally used as an independent face. Today it is regarded generally as an accompaniment to a roman and is little used alone.

2. ANGLED STRESS/OBLIQUE SERIFS
(Old Style Serif) Nos 35-53

Specimen nos	Basic characteristics	Secondary characteristics	
35-41	o d angled stress / definite oblique serifs / (including foot serif)	W crossed centre strokes	e.g. **35** Bembo
42-44	,,	W centre strokes joining at cap height (or nearly so)	e.g. **44** Trump Mediaeval
45-46	,,	W no centre serif	e.g. **45** Berling
47-53	,,	W stepped centre strokes	e.g. **53** Times New Roman

NB. *Typefaces in each group are arranged in alphabetical order.*

capital W with centre strokes joining at cap height (or nearly so)
M parallel (or nearly so)

54 Fry's Baskerville

ABCDEFGHIJKLMNOPQRSTUVWXYZ&

55 Binny Old Style

ABCDEFGHIJKLMNOPQRSTUVWXYZ&

56 Bookman

ABCDEFGHIJKLMNOPQRSTUVWXYZ&

57 ITC Bookman

ABCDEFGHIJKLMNOPQRSTUVWXYZ&

58 Bulmer

ABCDEFGHIJKLMNOPQRSTUVWXYZ&

59 Caslon Old Face No 2

ABCDEFGHIJKLMNOPQRSTUVWXYZ&

60 Caslon 128 (Monotype)

ABCDEFGHIJKLMNOPQRSTUVWXYZ&

61 Caslon 540

ABCDEFGHIJKLMNOPQRSTUVWXYZ&

62 Century Old Style

ABCDEFGHIJKLMNOPQRSTUVWXYZ&

63 Chiswell Old Face

ABCDEFGHIJKLMNOPQRSTUVWXYZ&

* These letters show special or 'style' characteristics. (NB. J, Q, & and g will usually vary from one typeface to another).

VERTICAL STRESS OBLIQUE SERIFS (TRANSITIONAL SERIF)

Fry's Baskerville
Binny Old Style
Bookman
ITC Bookman
Bulmer
Caslon Old Face No 2
Caslon 128 (Monotype)
Caslon 540
Century Old Style
Chiswell Old Face

Fry's Baskerville **54**

abcdefghijklmnopqrstuvwxyz1234567890

Binny Old Style **55**

abcdefghijklmnopqrstuvwxyz1234567890

Bookman **56**

abcdefghijklmnopqrstuvwxyz1234567890

ITC Bookman **57**

abcdefghijklmnopqrstuvwxyz1234567890

Bulmer **58**

abcdefghijklmnopqrstuvwxyz1234567890

Caslon Old Face No 2 **59**

abcdefghijklmnopqrstuvwxyz1234567890

Caslon 128 (Monotype) **60**

abcdefghijklmnopqrstuvwxyz1234567890

Caslon 540 **61**

abcdefghijklmnopqrstuvwxyz1234567890

Century Old Style **62**

abcdefghijklmnopqrstuvwxyz1234567890

Chiswell Old Face **63**

abcdefghijklmnopqrstuvwxyz 1234567890

**VERTICAL STRESS
OBLIQUE SERIFS
(TRANSITIONAL SERIF)**

od

Fry's Baskerville
Binny Old Style
Bookman
ITC Bookman
Bulmer
Caslon Old Face No 2
Caslon 128 (Monotype)
Caslon 540
Century Old Style
Chiswell Old Face

NB. On lower case letters generally look at the x height and length of ascenders and descenders.

64 Concorde Nova

ABCDEFGHIJKLMNOPQRSTUVWXYZ&

65 Fontana

ABCDEFGHIJKLMNOPQRSTUVWXYZ&

66 Granjon

ABCDEFGHIJKLMNOPQRSTUVWXYZ&

67 Imprint

ABCDEFGHIJKLMNOPQRSTUVWXYZ&

68 Monticello

ABCDEFGHIJKLMNOPQRSTUVWXYZ&

69 Old Style No 2

ABCDEFGHIJKLMNOPQRSTUVWXYZ&

70 Old Style No 7

ABCDEFGHIJKLMNOPQRSTUVWXYZ&

71 Olympian

ABCDEFGHIJKLMNOPQRSTUVWXYZ&

72 Ronaldson

ABCDEFGHIJKLMNOPQRSTUVWXYZ&

73 Ehrhardt

ABCDEFGHIJKLMNOPQRSTUVWXYZ&

**VERTICAL STRESS
OBLIQUE SERIFS
(TRANSITIONAL SERIF)**

od

Concorde Nova
Fontana
Granjon
Imprint
Monticello
Old Style No 2
Old Style No 7
Olympian
Ronaldson
Ehrhardt

*capital W
with centre
strokes joining
at cap height
(or nearly so)
M definitely
splayed*

* These letters show special or 'style' characteristics. (NB. J, Q, & and g will usually vary from one typeface to another).

Concorde Nova **64**

abcdefghijklmnopqrstuvwxyz1234567890

Fontana **65**

abcdefghijklmnopqrstuvwxyz1234567890

Granjon **66**

abcdefghijklmnopqrstuvwxyz1234567890

Imprint **67**

abcdefghijklmnopqrstuvwxyz1234567890

Monticello **68**

abcdefghijklmnopqrstuvwxyz1234567890

Old Style No 2 **69**

abcdefghijklmnopqrstuvwxyz1234567890

Old Style No 7 **70**

abcdefghijklmnopqrstuvwxyz1234567890

Olympian **71**

abcdefghijklmnopqrstuvwxyz1234567890

Ronaldson **72**

abcdefghijklmnopqrstuvwxyz1234567890

Ehrhardt **73**

abcdefghijklmnopqrstuvwxyz1234567890

VERTICAL STRESS OBLIQUE SERIFS (TRANSITIONAL SERIF)

Concorde Nova
Fontana
Granjon
Imprint
Monticello
Old Style No 2
Old Style No 7
Olympian
Ronaldson
Ehrhardt

NB. On lower case letters generally look at the x height and length of ascenders and descenders.

74-83

74 Galliard

ABCDEFGHIJKLMNOPQRSTUVWXYZ&

capital W with no centre serif

75 Aldus

ABCDEFGHIJKLMNOPQRSTUVWXYZ&

76 Aster

ABCDEFGHIJKLMNOPQRSTUVWXYZ&

VERTICAL STRESS OBLIQUE SERIFS (TRANSITIONAL SERIF)

Galliard
Aldus
Aster
Baskerville (Berthold)
Baskerville 169 (Monotype)
Baskerville (Linotype)
Baskerville No. 2
Cartier
Congress
Lectura

77 Baskerville (Berthold)

ABCDEFGHIJKLMNOPQRSTUVWXYZ&

78 Baskerville 169 (Monotype)

ABCDEFGHIJKLMNOPQRSTUVWXYZ&

79 Baskerville (Linotype)

ABCDEFGHIJKLMNOPQRSTUVWXYZ&

80 Baskerville No 2

ABCDEFGHIJKLMNOPQRSTUVWXYZ&

81 Cartier

ABCDEFGHIJKLMNOPQRSTUVWXYZ&

82 Congress

ABCDEFGHIJKLMNOPQRSTUVWXYZ&

83 Lectura

ABCDEFGHIJKLMNOPQRSTUVWXYZ&

* These letters show special or 'style' characteristics. (NB. J, Q, & and g will usually vary from one typeface to another).

Galliard **74**

* * * * * *
abcdefghijklmnopqrstuvwxyz1234567890

Aldus **75**

* * * * * *
abcdefghijklmnopqrstuvwxyz1234567890

Aster **76**

* * * * *
abcdefghijklmnopqrstuvwxyz1234567890

Baskerville (Berthold) **77**

* * * * *
abcdefghijklmnopqrstuvwxyz 1234567890

Baskerville 169 (Monotype) **78**

* * * * *
abcdefghijklmnopqrstuvwxyz1234567890

Baskerville (Linotype) **79**

* * * * *
abcdefghijklmnopqrstuvwxyz1234567890

Baskerville No 2 **80**

* * * *
abcdefghijklmnopqrstuvwxyz1234567890

Cartier **81**

* * *
abcdefghijklmnopqrstuvwxyz1234567890

Congress **82**

* * * *
abcdefghijklmnopqrstuvwxyz1234567890

Lectura **83**

* * * *
abcdefghijklmnopqrstuvwxyz1234567890

VERTICAL STRESS
OBLIQUE SERIFS
(TRANSITIONAL SERIF)

od

Galliard
Aldus
Aster
Baskerville (Berthold)
Baskerville 169
(Monotype)
Baskerville (Linotype)
Baskerville No. 2
Cartier
Congress
Lectura

NB. On lower case letters generally look at the x height and length of ascenders and descenders.

84 Palatino

ABCDEFGHIJKLMNOPQRSTUVWXYZ&

85 Poppl Pontifex

ABCDEFGHIJKLMNOPQRSTUVWXYZ&

86 Times Europa

ABCDEFGHIJKLMNOPQRSTUVWXYZ&

VERTICAL STRESS OBLIQUE SERIFS (TRANSITIONAL SERIF)

od

Palatino
Poppl Pontifex
Times Europa
Quadriga Antiqua
Sabon
Barbou
Fournier
Garamond 156 (Monotype)
Garamond (Stempel)
Garamond 3 (Linotype)

capital W with crossed centre strokes
M with serifs at cap height
lower case w with centre strokes joining at cap height

87 Quadriga Antiqua

ABCDEFGHIJKLMNOPQRSTUVWXYZ&

88 Sabon

ABCDEFGHIJKLMNOPQRSTUVWXYZ&

capital W with crossed strokes
M with serifs on tops
lower case w with crossed centre strokes

89 Barbou

ABCDEFGHIJKLMNOPQRSTUVWXYZ&

capital W with crossed centre strokes
M with serifs on tops
lower case w with stepped centre strokes

90 Fournier

ABCDEFGHIJKLMNOPQRSTUVWXYZ&

91 Garamond 156 (Monotype)

ABCDEFGHIJKLMNOPQRSTUVWXYZ&

92 Garamond (Stempel)

ABCDEFGHIJKLMNOPQRSTUVWXYZ&

93 Garamond 3 (Linotype)

ABCDEFGHIJKLMNOPQRSTUVWXYZ&

These letters show special or 'style' characteristics. (NB. J, Q, & and g will usually vary from one typeface to another).

Palatino **84**

abcdefghijklmnopqrstuvwxyz1234567890

Poppl Pontifex **85**

abcdefghijklmnopqrstuvwxyz1234567890

Times Europa **86**

abcdefghijklmnopqrstuvwxyz1234567890

Quadriga Antiqua **87**

abcdefghijklmnopqrstuvwxyz1234567890

Sabon **88**

abcdefghijklmnopqrstuvwxyz1234567890

Barbou **89**

abcdefghijklmnopqrstuvwxyz 1234567890

Fournier **90**

abcdefghijklmnopqrstuvwxyz1234567890

Garamond 156 (Monotype) **91**

abcdefghijklmnopqrstuvwxyz1234567890

Garamond (Stempel) **92**

abcdefghijklmnopqrstuvwxyz1234567890

Garamond 3 (Linotype) **93**

abcdefghijklmnopqrstuvwxyz1234567890

**VERTICAL STRESS
OBLIQUE SERIFS
(TRANSITIONAL SERIF)**

od

Palatino
Poppl Pontifex
Times Europa
Quadriga Antiqua
Sabon
Barbou
Fournier
Garamond 156
(Monotype)
Garamond
(Stempel)
Garamond 3
(Linotype)

NB. On lower case letters generally look at the x height and length of ascenders and descenders.

94 Garamond (Berthold)

ABCDEFGHIJKLMNOPQRSTUVWXYZ&

95 ITC Garamond

ABCDEFGHIJKLMNOPQRSTUVWXYZ&

96 Garamont (Amsterdam)

ABCDEFGHIJKLMNOPQRSTUVWXYZ&

VERTICAL STRESS
OBLIQUE SERIFS
(TRANSITIONAL SERIF)

Garamond
(Berthold)

ITC Garamond

Garamont
(Amsterdam)

Spectrum

Weiss

Caslon 3

Concorde

ITC Cushing

Dante

Gazette

*capital W
with crossed
centre strokes*

*M with
no serifs at
cap height*

*capital W
with stepped
centre strokes*

*M parallel
(or nearly so)*

97 Spectrum

ABCDEFGHIJKLMNOPQRSTUVWXYZ&

98 Weiss

ABCDEFGHIJKLMNOPQRSTUVWXYZ&

99 Caslon 3

ABCDEFGHIJKLMNOPQRSTUVWXYZ&

100 Concorde

ABCDEFGHIJKLMNOPQRSTUVWXYZ&

101 ITC Cushing

ABCDEFGHIJKLMNOPQRSTUVWXYZ&

102 Dante

ABCDEFGHIJKLMNOPQRSTUVWXYZ&

103 Gazette

ABCDEFGHIJKLMNOPQRSTUVWXYZ&

These letters show special or 'style' characteristics. (NB. J, Q, & and g will usually vary from one typeface to another).

Garamond (Berthold) **94**

abcdefghijklmnopqrstuvwxyz1234567890

ITC Garamond **95**

abcdefghijklmnopqrstuvwxyz1234567890

Garamont (Amsterdam) **96**

abcdefghijklmnopqrstuvwxyz1234567890

Spectrum **97**

abcdefghijklmnopqrstuvwxyz1234567890

Weiss **98**

abcdefghijklmnopqrstuvwxyz1234567890

Caslon 3 **99**

abcdefghijklmnopqrstuvwxyz1234567890

Concorde **100**

abcdefghijklmnopqrstuvwxyz1234567890

ITC Cushing **101**

abcdefghijklmnopqrstuvwxyz1234567890

Dante **102**

abcdefghijklmnopqrstuvwxyz1234567890

Gazette **103**

abcdefghijklmnopqrstuvwxyz1234567890

VERTICAL STRESS
OBLIQUE SERIFS
(TRANSITIONAL SERIF)

Garamond
(Berthold)
ITC Garamond
Garamont
(Amsterdam)
Spectrum
Weiss
Caslon 3
Concorde
ITC Cushing
Dante
Gazette

NB. On lower case letters generally look at the x height and length of ascenders and descenders.

104 ITC Isbell

ABCDEFGHIJKLMNOPQRSTUVWXYZ&

105 Romulus

ABCDEFGHIJKLMNOPQRSTUVWXYZ&

106 Rotation

ABCDEFGHIJKLMNOPQRSTUVWXYZ&

VERTICAL STRESS OBLIQUE SERIFS (TRANSITIONAL SERIF)

107 Van Dijck

ABCDEFGHIJKLMNOPQRSTUVWXYZ&

capital W with stepped centre strokes
M definitely splayed

ITC Isbell
Romulus
Rotation
Van Dijck
De Roos
Janson
Rundfunk

108 De Roos

ABCDEFGHIJKLMNOPQRSTUVWXYZ&

109 Janson

ABCDEFGHIJKLMNOPQRSTUVWXYZ&

110 Rundfunk

ABCDEFGHIJKLMNOPQRSTUVWXYZ&

* These letters show special or 'style' characteristics. (NB. J, Q, & and g will usually vary from one typeface to another).

ITC Isbell **104**

*   *   * * *   * *
abcdefghijklmnopqrstuvwxyz1234567890

Romulus **105**

  *   *   *   *
abcdefghijklmnopqrstuvwxyz1234567890

Rotation **106**

  *   *   *   *
abcdefghijklmnopqrstuvwxyz1234567890

Van Dijck **107**

        *   *   *
abcdefghijklmnopqrstuvwxyz1234567890

De Roos **108**

* *   * *   * *
abcdefghijklmnopqrstuvwxyz 1234567890

Janson **109**

          *   *
abcdefghijklmnopqrstuvwxyz1234567890

Rundfunk **110**

  *   *   *
abcdefghijklmnopqrstuvwxyz1234567890

VERTICAL STRESS
OBLIQUE SERIFS
(TRANSITIONAL SERIF)

ITC Isbell
Romulus
Rotation
Van Dijck
De Roos
Janson
Rundfunk

NB. On lower case letters generally look at the x height and length of ascenders and descenders.

4. VERTICAL STRESS/STRAIGHT SERIFS
(New Transitional Serif) Nos 111-150

All typefaces in this group* have a definite vertical stress and serifs are normally all horizontal (straight). However, a small number have slightly oblique serifs. These typefaces generally have little contrast between the thick and thin strokes and serifs are usually bracketed.

*These typefaces appear together because of stylistic similarities which will aid identification and recognition. They are nearly all late nineteenth or twentieth century designs which draw on several historical precedents for their inspiration and (with the exception of nos. 118-122: see footnote, p.64) cannot be easily grouped elsewhere.

4. VERTICAL STRESS/STRAIGHT SERIFS
(New Transitional Serif) Nos 111-150

Specimen nos	Basic characteristics	Secondary characteristics	
111-112	r d *horizontal line serifs (or nearly so)*	n *line serifs*	e.g. 111 Joanna
113-117	r d *horizontal bracketed serifs (or nearly so)* W *centre strokes joining at cap height*	n *light face*	e.g. 117 Primer
118-122	,,	,, n *black face*	e.g. 121 Ionic 5
123-127	,,	W *crossed centre strokes*	e.g. 123 Cheltenham
128-132	,,	W *stepped centre strokes*	e.g. 130 Columbia
133-140	,,	W *no centre serif*	e.g. 138 Melior
141-146	r d *some definite oblique bracketed serifs*	n *weak contrast*	e.g. 146 Textype
147-150	,,	n *good contrast*	e.g. 147 Cochin

NB. *Typefaces in each group are arranged in alphabetical order.*

VERTICAL STRESS
STRAIGHT SERIFS
(NEW TRANSITIONAL)

horizontal line serifs (or nearly so)

III Joanna

ABCDEFGHIJKLMNOPQRSTUVWXYZ&

II2 Maximus

ABCDEFGHIJKLMNOPQRSTUVWXYZ&

horizontal bracketed serifs (or nearly so)

capital W with centre strokes joining at cap height (or nearly so)

light face

II3 Breughel 55

ABCDEFGHIJKLMNOPQRSTUVWXYZ&

II4 Century Expanded

ABCDEFGHIJKLMNOPQRSTUVWXYZ&

II5 Excelsior

ABCDEFGHIJKLMNOPQRSTUVWXYZ&

II6 Perpetua

ABCDEFGHIJKLMNOPQRSTUVWXYZ&

II7 Primer

ABCDEFGHIJKLMNOPQRSTUVWXYZ&

horizontal bracketed serifs (or nearly so)

capital W with centre strokes joining at cap height (or nearly so)

black face

II8 Aurora

ABCDEFGHIJKLMNOPQRSTUVWXYZ

II9 Century Schoolbook

ABCDEFGHIJKLMNOPQRSTUVWXYZ&

I20 Corona

ABCDEFGHIJKLMNOPQRSTUVWXYZ&

* These letters show special or 'style' characteristics. (NB. J, Q, & and g will usually vary from one typeface to another).

**VERTICAL STRESS
STRAIGHT SERIFS
(NEW TRANSITIONAL)**

Joanna
Maximus
Breughel 55
Century Expanded
Excelsior
Perpetua
Primer
Aurora
Century Schoolbook
Corona

Joanna III

abcdefghijklmnopqrstuvwxyz1234567890

Maximus II2

abcdefghijklmnopqrstuvwxyz1234567890

Breughel 55 II3

abcdefghijklmnopqrstuvwxyz1234567890

Century Expanded II4

abcdefghijklmnopqrstuvwxyz1234567890

Excelsior II5

abcdefghijklmnopqrstuvwxyz1234567890

Perpetua II6

abcdefghijklmnopqrstuvwxyz1234567890

Primer II7

abcdefghijklmnopqrstuvwxyz1234567890

Aurora II8

abcdefghijklmnopqrstuvwxyz1234567890

Century Schoolbook II9

abcdefghijklmnopqrstuvwxyz1234567890

Corona I20

abcdefghijklmnopqrstuvwxyz1234567890

**VERTICAL STRESS
STRAIGHT SERIFS
(NEW TRANSITIONAL)**

Joanna
Maximus
Breughel 55
Century Expanded
Excelsior
Perpetua
Primer
Aurora
Century Schoolbook
Corona

NB. On lower case letters generally look at the x height and length of ascenders and descenders.

121 Ionic 5

ABCDEFGHIJKLMNOPQRSTUVWXYZ&

122 Nimrod

ABCDEFGHIJKLMNOPQRSTUVWXYZ&

horizontal bracketed serifs (or nearly so) capital W with crossed centre strokes

123 Cheltenham

ABCDEFGHIJKLMNOPQRSTUVWXYZ&

124 Cheltenham Nova

ABCDEFGHIJKLMNOPQRSTUVWXYZ&

**VERTICAL STRESS
STRAIGHT SERIFS
(NEW TRANSITIONAL)**

125 Comenius

ABCDEFGHIJKLMNOPQRSTUVWXYZ&

Ionic 5
Nimrod
Cheltenham
Cheltenham Nova
Comenius
Gloucester Old Style
Sorbonne
Bramley
ITC Cheltenham
Columbia

126 Gloucester Old Style

ABCDEFGHIJKLMNOPQRSTUVWXYZ&

127 Sorbonne

ABCDEFGHIJKLMNOPQRSTUVWXYZ&

horizontal bracketed serifs (or nearly so) capital W with stepped centre strokes

128 Bramley

ABCDEFGHIJKLMNOPQRSTUVWXYZ&

129 ITC Cheltenham

ABCDEFGHIJKLMNOPQRSTUVWXYZ&

130 Columbia

ABCDEFGHIJKLMNOPQRSTUVWXYZ&

* These letters show special or 'style' characteristics. (NB. J, Q, & and g will usually vary from one typeface to another).

Ionic 5 121

* * * * *
abcdefghijklmnopqrstuvwxyz1234567890

Nimrod 122

* * * * *
abcdefghijklmnopqrstuvwxyz1234567890

Cheltenham 123

* * * * * * * * * * *
abcdefghijklmnopqrstuvwxyz1234567890

Cheltenham Nova 124

* * * * * * * * *
abcdefghijklmnopqrstuvwxyz1234567890

Comenius 125

* * * * * * * *
abcdefghijklmnopqrstuvwxyz1234567890

Gloucester Old Style 126

* * * * * * * *
abcdefghijklmnopqrstuvwxyz1234567890

Sorbonne 127

* * * *
abcdefghijklmnopqrstuvwxyz1234567890

Bramley 128

* * * * *
abcdefghijklmnopqrstuvwxyz1234567890

ITC Cheltenham 129

* * * * * *
abcdefghijklmnopqrstuvwxyz1234567890

Columbia 130

* * * *
abcdefghijklmnopqrstuvwxyz1234567890

VERTICAL STRESS
STRAIGHT SERIFS
(NEW TRANSITIONAL)

od

Ionic 5
Nimrod
Cheltenham
Cheltenham Nova
Comenius
Gloucester Old Style
Sorbonne
Bramley
ITC Cheltenham
Columbia

NB. On lower case letters generally look at the x height and length of ascenders and descenders.

131 French Round Face

* * * * * * *
ABCDEFGHIJKLMNOPQRSTUVWXYZ&

132 Goudy Modern

* * * *
ABCDEFGHIJKLMNOPQRSTUVWXYZ&

horizontal serifs (or nearly so) no centre serif on capital W

133 Apollo

* * * * *
ABCDEFGHIJKLMNOPQRSTUVWXYZ&

134 Athenaeum

* * * * * * *
ABCDEFGHIJKLMNOPQRSTUVWXYZ&

**VERTICAL STRESS
STRAIGHT SERIFS
(NEW TRANSITIONAL)**

French Round Face
Goudy Modern
Apollo
Athenaeum
Diotima
Franklin Antiqua
Impressum
Melior
Orion
Renault

135 Diotima

* * * * *
ABCDEFGHIJKLMNOPQRSTUVWXYZ&

136 Franklin Antiqua

* * *
ABCDEFGHIJKLMNOPQRSTUVWXYZ&

137 Impressum

* * * *
ABCDEFGHIJKLMNOPQRSTUVWXYZ&

138 Melior

* * * * *
ABCDEFGHIJKLMNOPQRSTUVWXYZ&

139 Orion

* * * *
ABCDEFGHIJKLMNOPQRSTUVWXYZ&

140 Renault

* *
ABCDEFGHIJKLMNOPQRSTUVWXYZ&

* These letters show special or 'style' characteristics. (NB. J, Q, & and g will usually vary from one typeface to another).

French Round Face 131

* * * * * * * *
abcdefghijklmnopqrstuvwxyz1234567890

Goudy Modern 132

* * * *
abcdefghijklmnopqrstuvwxyz1234567890

Apollo 133

* * * * * * *
abcdefghijklmnopqrstuvwxyz1234567890

Athenaeum 134

* *
abcdefghijklmnopqrstuvwxyz1234567890

Diotima 135

* * * * *
abcdefghijklmnopqrstuvwxyz1234567890

Franklin Antiqua 136

* * *
abcdefghijklmnopqrstuvwxyz1234567890

Impressum 137

* * * *
abcdefghijklmnopqrstuvwxyz1234567890

Melior 138

* * * * *
abcdefghijklmnopqrstuvwxyz1234567890

Orion 139

* *
abcdefghijklmnopqrstuvwxyz1234567890

Renault 140

* * *
abcdefghijklmnopqrstuvwxyz1234567890

**VERTICAL STRESS
STRAIGHT SERIFS
(NEW TRANSITIONAL)**

French Round Face
Goudy Modern
Apollo
Athenaeum
Diotima
Franklin Antiqua
Impressum
Melior
Orion
Renault

NB. On lower case letters generally look at the x height and length of ascenders and descenders.

some definite
oblique bracketed
serifs
weak contrast

141 Dominante

ABCDEFGHIJKLMNOPQRSTUVWXYZ&

142 Lo-type

ABCDEFGHIJKLMNOPQRSTUVWXYZ&

143 Menhart

ABCDEFGHIJKLMNOPQRSTUVWXYZ&

144 Paragon

ABCDEFGHIJKLMNOPQRSTUVWXYZ

145 Primus Antiqua

ABCDEFGHIJKLMNOPQRSTUVWXYZ&

146 Textype

ABCDEFGHIJKLMNOPQRSTUVWXYZ&

some definite
oblique bracketed
serifs
good contrast

147 Cochin

ABCDEFGHIJKLMNOPQRSTUVWXYZ&

148 Electra

ABCDEFGHIJKLMNOPQRSTUVWXYZ&

149 Iridium

ABCDEFGHIJKLMNOPQRSTUVWXYZ&

150 ITC Zapf International

ABCDEFGHIJKLMNOPQRSTUVWXYZ&

**VERTICAL STRESS
STRAIGHT SERIFS
(NEW TRANSITIONAL)**

Dominante
Lo-Type
Menhart
Paragon
Primus Antiqua
Textype
Cochin
Electra
Iridium
ITC Zapf
International

* These letters show special or 'style' characteristics. (NB. J, Q, & and g will usually vary from one typeface to another).

Dominante 141

* * * * *
abcdefghijklmnopqrstuvwxyz1234567890

Lo-type 142

* * * *
abcdefghijklmnopqrstuvwxyz1234567890

Menhart 143

* * * * *
abcdefghijklmnopqrstuvwxyz1234567890

Paragon 144

* * * *
abcdefghijklmnopqrstuvwxyz1234567890

Primus Antiqua 145

* * * * *
abcdefghijklmnopqrstuvwxyz1234567890

Textype 146

* * * * *
abcdefghijklmnopqrstuvwxyz1234567890

Cochin 147

* * * * *
abcdefghijklmnopqrstuvwxyz1234567890

Electra 148

* * * * * *
abcdefghijklmnopqrstuvwxyz1234567890

Iridium 149

* * * *
abcdefghijklmnopqrstuvwxyz1234567890

ITC Zapf International 150

* * * *
abcdefghijklmnopqrstuvwxyz1234567890

**VERTICAL STRESS
STRAIGHT SERIFS
(NEW TRANSITIONAL)**

Dominante
Lo-Type
Menhart
Paragon
Primus Antiqua
Textype
Cochin
Electra
Iridium
ITC Zapf
International

NB. On lower case letters generally look at the x height and length of ascenders and descenders.

5. ABRUPT CONTRAST/STRAIGHT SERIFS
(Modern Serif) Nos 151-187

These typefaces feature a strong and abrupt contrast between the thick and thin strokes of letters and all serifs are horizontals (straight). The overall stress is nearly vertical. Serifs can be line (unbracketed) or slightly bracketed and typefaces can vary in colour from light to black face.

58,172,185/186   After Baskerville, designers took the trends of greater contrast and vertical stress a stage further. In Britain, influenced as much by contemporary copper-plates as by Baskerville's types, William Martin (Bulmer; c. 1790) and Richard Austin (Bell; 1788, Scotch Roman; c. 1812) condensed the basic letterform and sharpened the serifs.

156

153/154/162/163
161/167/168/187   On the Continent the trend was taken further and the types of Firmin Didot (c. 1784), Giovanni Batista Bodoni (1798) and Justus Erich Walbaum (c. 1800) took the design to its limits as a text face. The thin strokes and serifs were now simply hairlines and demanded the most exacting presswork and high quality paper to achieve the desired, almost dazzling effect. The resultant characters were 'designed' rather than 'drawn' and the abrupt vertical stress makes them difficult to read in any quantity without generous leading. Unfortunately the *modern* design became the standard typeface for much of the nineteenth century and these defects were ignored. Insensitive *modern* typefaces and poor typography (loose letter and word spacing in particular) led to William Morris's typographic revolution of the 1890's.*

Although not used much as book types today the *moderns* (particularly Bodoni and Walbaum) continue to be popular for display and magazine work where their brilliance can be better appreciated.

*See also the introduction to category 1, p.14.

5. ABRUPT CONTRAST/STRAIGHT SERIFS
(Modern Serif) Nos 151-187

Specimen nos	Basic characteristics		Secondary characteristics	
151-161	N	*line serifs*	n *light face*	e.g. **161** Walbaum (Linotype)
162-169	,,		n *black face*	e.g. **162** Bodoni 135 (Monotype)
170-187	N	*bracketed serifs*		e.g. **185** Scotch Roman (Monotype)

NB. *Typefaces in each group are arranged in alphabetical order.*

line serifs
light face

151 Auriga

ABCDEFGHIJKLMNOPQRSTUVWXYZ&

152 Basilia

ABCDEFGHIJKLMNOPQRSTUVWXYZ&

153 Bauer Bodoni

ABCDEFGHIJKLMNOPQRSTUVWXYZ&

154 Bodoni Book (Linotype)

ABCDEFGHIJKLMNOPQRSTUVWXYZ&

155 Corvinus

ABCDEFGHIJKLMNOPQRSTUVWXYZ &

ABRUPT CONTRAST STRAIGHT SERIFS (MODERN SERIF)

Auriga
Basilia
Bauer Bodoni
Bodoni Book
(Linotype)
Corvinus
Didot
Egmont
Fairfield
Tiemann
Torino

156 Didot

ABCDEFGHIJKLMNOPQRSTUVWXYZ&

157 Egmont

ABCDEFGHIJKLMNOPQRSTUVWXYZ&

158 Fairfield

ABCDEFGHIJKLMNOPQRSTUVWXYZ&

159 Tiemann

ABCDEFGHIJKLMNOPQRSTUVWXYZ&

160 Torino

ABCDEFGHIJKLMNOPQRSTUVWXYZ&

* These letters show special or 'style' characteristics. (NB. J, Q, & and g will usually vary from one typeface to another).

Auriga 151

* * * * *
abcdefghijklmnopqrstuvwxyz1234567890

Basilia 152

* * *
abcdefghijklmnopqrstuvwxyz1234567890

Bauer Bodoni 153

* * * * *
abcdefghijklmnopqrstuvwxyz1234567890

Bodoni Book (Linotype) 154

* * *
abcdefghijklmnopqrstuvwxyz1234567890

Corvinus 155

* * * * *
abcdefghijklmnopqrstuvwxyz1234567890

Didot 156

* * * * * *
abcdefghijklmnopqrstuvwxyz1234567890

Egmont 157

* * * * *
abcdefghijklmnopqrstuvwxyz1234567890

Fairfield 158

* * * *
abcdefghijklmnopqrstuvwxyz1234567890

Tiemann 159

* * *
abcdefghijklmnopqrstuvwxyz1234567890

Torino 160

* * * *
abcdefghijklmnopqrstuvwxyz1234567890

ABRUPT CONTRAST STRAIGHT SERIFS (MODERN SERIF)

od

Auriga
Basilia
Bauer Bodoni
Bodoni Book
(Linotype)
Corvinus
Didot
Egmont
Fairfield
Tiemann
Torino

NB. On lower case letters generally look at the x height and length of ascenders and descenders.

161 Walbaum (Linotype)

* * * * * * *
ABCDEFGHIJKLMNOPQRSTUVWXYZ&

line serifs
black face

162 Bodoni 135 (Monotype)

* * *
ABCDEFGHIJKLMNOPQRSTUVWXYZ&

163 Bodoni (Haas)

* * *
ABCDEFGHIJKLMNOPQRSTUVWXYZ&

164 Craw Modern

* * *
ABCDEFGHIJKLMNOPQRSTUVWXYZ&

165 ITC Fenice

* * * * * *
ABCDEFGHIJKLMNOPQRSTUVWXYZ&

**ABRUPT CONTRAST
STRAIGHT SERIFS**
(MODERN SERIF)

od

Walbaum (Linotype)
Bodoni 135 (Monotype)
Bodoni (Haas)
Craw Modern
ITC Fenice
Modern (Linotype)
Walbaum Book
(Berthold)
Walbaum (Monotype)
ITC Zapf Book
Albion 42

166 Modern (Linotype)

* * * * * *
ABCDEFGHIJKLMNOPQRSTUVWXYZ&

167 Walbaum Book (Berthold)

* * * * *
ABCDEFGHIJKLMNOPQRSTUVWXYZ&

168 Walbaum (Monotype)

* * * * * *
ABCDEFGHIJKLMNOPQRSTUVWXYZ&

169 ITC Zapf Book

* * * * *
ABCDEFGHIJKLMNOPQRSTUVWXYZ&

bracketed
serifs

170 Albion 42

* *
ABCDEFGHIJKLMNOPQRSTUVWXYZ&

* These letters show special or 'style' characteristics. (NB. J, Q, & and g will usually vary from one typeface to another).

Walbaum (Linotype) **161**

abcdefghijklmnopqrstuvwxyz1234567890

Bodoni 135 (Monotype) **162**

abcdefghijklmnopqrstuvwxyz1234567890

Bodoni (Haas) **163**

abcdefghijklmnopqrstuvwxyz1234567890

Craw Modern **164**

abcdefghijklmnopqrstuvwxyz1234567890

ITC Fenice **165**

abcdefghijklmnopqrstuvwxyz1234567890

Modern (Linotype) **166**

abcdefghijklmnopqrstuvwxyz1234567890

Walbaum Book (Berthold) **167**

abcdefghijklmnopqrstuvwxyz1234567890

Walbaum (Monotype) **168**

abcdefghijklmnopqrstuvwxyz1234567890

ITC Zapf Book **169**

abcdefghijklmnopqrstuvwxyz1234567890

Albion 42 **170**

abcdefghijklmnopqrstuvwxyz1234567890

ABRUPT CONTRAST STRAIGHT SERIFS (MODERN SERIF)

od

Walbaum (Linotype)
Bodoni 135 (Monotype)
Bodoni (Haas)
Craw Modern
ITC Fenice
Modern (Linotype)
Walbaum Book (Berthold)
Walbaum (Monotype)
ITC Zapf Book
Albion 42

NB. On lower case letters generally look at the x height and length of ascenders and descenders.

171 Augustea

ABCDEFGHIJKLMNOPQRSTUVWXYZ&

172 Bell

ABCDEFGHIJKLMNOPQRSTUVWXYZ&

173 Bruce Old Style

ABCDEFGHIJKLMNOPQRSTUVWXYZ&

174 Caledonia

ABCDEFGHIJKLMNOPQRSTUVWXYZ&

175 ITC Century

ABCDEFGHIJKLMNOPQRSTUVWXYZ&

ABRUPT CONTRAST STRAIGHT SERIFS (MODERN SERIF)

Augustea
Bell
Bruce Old Style
Caledonia
ITC Century
Century Nova
De Vinne
Madison
Modern No 20
Neo Didot

176 Century Nova

ABCDEFGHIJKLMNOPQRSTUVWXYZ&

177 De Vinne

ABCDEFGHIJKLMNOPQRSTUVWXYZ&

178 Madison

ABCDEFGHIJKLMNOPQRSTUVWXYZ&

179 Modern No 20

ABCDEFGHIJKLMNOPQRSTUVWXYZ&

180 Neo Didot

ABCDEFGHIJKLMNOPQRSTUVWXYZ&

These letters show special or 'style' characteristics. (NB. J, Q, & and g will usually vary from one typeface to another).

Augustea 171

* * * * * *
abcdefghijklmnopqrstuvwxyz1234567890

Bell 172

* * * * * *
abcdefghijklmnopqrstuvwxyz1234567890

Bruce Old Style 173

* * * * *
abcdefghijklmnopqrstuvwxyz1234567890

Caledonia 174

* * * * *
abcdefghijklmnopqrstuvwxyz1234567890

ITC Century 175

* * * * * * *
abcdefghijklmnopqrstuvwxyz1234567890

Century Nova 176

* * * * * * *
abcdefghijklmnopqrstuvwxyz1234567890

De Vinne 177

* * * *
abcdefghijklmnopqrstuvwxyz1234567890

Madison 178

* * * *
abcdefghijklmnopqrstuvwxyz1234567890

Modern No 20 179

* * * *
abcdefghijklmnopqrstuvwxyz1234567890

Neo Didot 180

* * *
abcdefghijklmnopqrstuvwxyz1234567890

ABRUPT CONTRAST STRAIGHT SERIFS (MODERN SERIF)

Augustea
Bell
Bruce Old Style
Caledonia
ITC Century
Century Nova
De Vinne
Madison
Modern No 20
Neo Didot

NB. On lower case letters generally look at the x height and length of ascenders and descenders.

181 Paganini

ABCDEFGHIJKLMNOPQRSTUVWXYZ&

182 Photina

ABCDEFGHIJKLMNOPQRSTUVWXYZ&

183 Pilgrim

ABCDEFGHIJKLMNOPQRSTUVWXYZ&

184 Promotor

ABCDEFGHIJKLMNOPQRSTUVWXYZ&

185 Scotch Roman (Monotype)

ABCDEFGHIJKLMNOPQRSTUVWXYZ&

186 Scotch 2 (Linotype)

ABCDEFGHIJKLMNOPQRSTUVWXYZ&

187 Walbaum Standard (Berthold)

ABCDEFGHIJKLMNOPQRSTUVWXYZ&

*new
entries*

187A Centennial 55 (Linotype)

ABCDEFGHIJKLMNOPQRSTUVWXYZ&

187B Versailles 55 (Linotype)

ABCDEFGHIJKLMNOPQRSTUVWXYZ&

187C Wilke 55 (Linotype)

ABCDEFGHIJKLMNOPQRSTUVWXYZ&

ABRUPT CONTRAST STRAIGHT SERIFS (MODERN SERIF)

Paganini
Photina
Pilgrim
Promotor
Scotch Roman (Monotype)
Scotch 2 (Linotype)
Walbaum Standard (Berthold)
Centennial 55 (Linotype)
Versailles 55 (Linotype)
Wilke 55 (Linotype)

* These letters show special or 'style' characteristics. (NB. J, Q, & and g will usually vary from one typeface to another).

62

Paganini **181**

* * * *
abcdefghijklmnopqrstuvwxyz1234567890

Photina **182**

* * * * * * * *
abcdefghijklmnopqrstuvwxyz1234567890

Pilgrim **183**

* * * * *
abcdefghijklmnopqrstuvwxyz1234567890

Promotor **184**

* * * * * *
abcdefghijklmnopqrstuvwxyz1234567890

Scotch Roman (Monotype) **185**

* * * * * *
abcdefghijklmnopqrstuvwxyz1234567890

Scotch 2 (Linotype) **186**

* * * * * *
abcdefghijklmnopqrstuvwxyz1234567890

Walbaum Standard (Berthold) **187**

* * * *
abcdefghijklmnopqrstuvwxyz1234567890

Centennial 55 (Linotype) **187A**

*
abcdefghijklmnopqrstuvwxyz1234567890

Versailles 55 (Linotype) **187B**

* * * *
abcdefghijklmnopqrstuvwxyz1234567890

Wilke 55 (Linotype) **187C**

* *
abcdefghijklmnopqrstuvwxyz1234567890

NB. On lower case letters generally look at the x height and length of ascenders and descenders.

ABRUPT CONTRAST STRAIGHT SERIFS (MODERN SERIF)

od

Paganini
Photina
Pilgrim
Promotor
Scotch Roman
(Monotype)
Scotch 2 (Linotype)
Walbaum Standard
(Berthold)
Centennial 55
(Linotype)
Versailles 55
(Linotype)
Wilke 55 (Linotype)

6. SLAB SERIF
(Egyptians and Clarendons) Nos 188-217

The typefaces in this section are characterised by a generally heavy appearance with thick 'slab' serifs often the same thickness as the main stem of the letters. When the serifs are square (unbracketed) the type is known as an *egyptian*, and when bracketed, as a *clarendon*. (NB Slab serif style typefaces with a sloping cross-bar to the lower case e will be found in Category 1, nos. 1-34).

Egyptian typefaces first appeared in Britain in the early nineteenth century. Figgins **Egyptian** of 1817, perhaps the first original design of advertising type, was quickly followed by versions from other founders. They were heavy with almost even weight and were designed not for legibility or sensitivity, but impact and aggression, they could not be ignored. Most of the *egyptians* shown in this section are polite twentieth century text versions of the basic design. Faces such as **Beton, Memphis** and **Rockwell** date from the 1920's and '30's and are contemporary with *sans serifs* such as **Erbar** and **Futura**, sharing with them geometric construction and a single storey lower case 'g'. **Calvert** (Margaret Calvert 1980), on the other hand, shows more irregularity in character, width and construction, and has an idiosyncratic serif treatment. Versions of the heavy Victorian originals can be found in Part 2 of this book, nos. 453-458.

189,196,197
253,254
190

Clarendons take their name from the first version of this typestyle, cut by Benjamin Fox of the Fann Street Foundry in 1845. They are not as heavy and exaggerated as the *egyptians* and the serifs are strongly bracketed. The first *clarendons* were condensed and designed as a bold face to accompany the *modern* typefaces then in use. Subsequently, expanded versions appeared and later still different weights, but all are characterised by a large x-height (for legibility), a strong horizontal emphasis, and an almost architectural sturdiness. These qualities make them ideal for printing on poor quality paper and the basic design has proved the most successful for newspaper types and also typewriters.*

*Because of other design features, some *clarendons* are to be found in category 4 of this book (nos. 118-122) including one of the most popular newspaper typefaces currently available, Robin Nicholas' **Nimrod, (122)**.

6. SLAB SERIF
(Egyptians and Clarendons) Nos 188-217

Specimen nos	Basic characteristics		Secondary characteristics	
188-200	I	square slab	g single storey	e.g. **197** Rockwell
201-203	,,		g double storey	e.g. **203** Schadow Antiqua
204-205	I	bracketed slab	g single storey	e.g. **205** Egyptian 505
206-213	,,		g double storey	e.g. **209** Clarendon (Linotype)
214-217	I	rounded slab		e.g. **214** ITC American Typewriter

NB. *Typefaces in each group are arranged in alphabetical order.*

SLAB SERIF

square
slab
single
storey g

188 A & S Gallatin

ABCDEFGHIJKLMNOPQRSTUVWXYZ&

189 Beton

ABCDEFGHIJKLMNOPQRSTUVWXYZ&

190 Calvert

ABCDEFGHIJKLMNOPQRSTUVWXYZ&

191 Candida

ABCDEFGHIJKLMNOPQRSTUVWXYZ&

192 City

ABCDEFGHIJKLMNOPQRSTUVWXYZ&

193 Glypha 55

ABCDEFGHIJKLMNOPQRSTUVWXYZ&

194 ITC Lubalin Graph

ABCDEFGHIJKLMNOPQRSTUVWXYZ&

195 ITC Lubalin Graph Extra Light

ABCDEFGHIJKLMNOPQRSTUVWXYZ&

196 Memphis

ABCDEFGHIJKLMNOPQRSTUVWXYZ&

197 Rockwell

ABCDEFGHIJKLMNOPQRSTUVWXYZ&

SLAB SERIF

A & S Gallatin
Beton
Calvert
Candida
City
Glypha 55
ITC Lubalin Graph
ITC Lubalin Graph
Extra Light
Memphis
Rockwell

These letters show special or 'style' characteristics. (NB. J, Q, & and g will usually vary from one typeface to another).

66

A & S Gallatin **188**

abcdefghijklmnopqrstuvwxyz1234567890

Beton **189**

abcdefghijklmnopqrstuvwxyz1234567890

Calvert **190**

abcdefghijklmnopqrstuvwxyz1234567890

Candida **191**

abcdefghijklmnopqrstuvwxyz1234567890

City **192**

abcdefghijklmnopqrstuvwxyz1234567890

Glypha 55 **193**

abcdefghijklmnopqrstuvwxyz1234567890

ITC Lubalin Graph **194**

abcdefghijklmnopqrstuvwxyz1234567890

ITC Lubalin Graph Extra Light **195**

abcdefghijklmnopqrstuvwxyz1234567890

Memphis **196**

abcdefghijklmnopqrstuvwxyz1234567890

Rockwell **197**

abcdefghijklmnopqrstuvwxyz1234567890

SLAB SERIF

11

A & S Gallatin
Beton
Calvert
Candida
City
Glypha 55
ITC Lubalin Graph
ITC Lubalin Graph
Extra Light
Memphis
Rockwell

NB. On lower case letters generally look at the x height and length of ascenders and descenders.

198 Serifa 55

ABCDEFGHIJKLMNOPQRSTUVWXYZ&

199 Stymie (ATF)

ABCDEFGHIJKLMNOPQRSTUVWXYZ&

200 ITC Stymie Hairline

ABCDEFGHIJKLMNOPQRSTUVWXYZ&

square slab double storey g

201 Antique No 5

ABCDEFGHIJKLMNOPQRSTUVWXYZ&

202 Egyptian 173

ABCDEFGHIJKLMNOPQRSTUVWXYZ&

203 Schadow Antiqua

ABCDEFGHIJKLMNOPQRSTUVWXYZ&

bracketed slab single storey g

204 Aachen

ABCDEFGHIJKLMNOPQRSTUVWXYZ&

205 Egyptian 505

ABCDEFGHIJKLMNOPQRSTUVWXYZ&

bracketed slab double storey g

206 Antique No 3

ABCDEFGHIJKLMNOPQRSTUVWXYZ&

207 Consort

ABCDEFGHIJKLMNOPQRSTUVWXYZ&

* *These letters show special or 'style' characteristics. (NB. J, Q, & and g will usually vary from one typeface to another).*

SLAB SERIF

11

Serifa 55
Stymie (ATF)
ITC Stymie Hairline
Antique No 5
Egyptian 173
Schadow Antiqua
Aachen
Egyptian 505
Antique No 3
Consort

Serifa 55 **198**

* * * *   *   *

abcdefghijklmnopqrstuvwxyz1234567890

Stymie (ATF) **199**

* * *   *

abcdefghijklmnopqrstuvwxyz1234567890

ITC Stymie Hairline **200**

* * *   *

abcdefghijklmnopqrstuvwxyz1234567890

Antique No 5 **201**

* * *   *

abcdefghijklmnopqrstuvwxyz1234567890

Egyptian 173 **202**

* * *   *   *

abcdefghijklmnopqrstuvwxyz1234567890

Schadow Antiqua **203**

* * * *   *

abcdefghijklmnopqrstuvwxyz1234567890

Aachen **204**

* * *   *

abcdefghijklmnopqrstuvwxyz1234567890

Egyptian 505 **205**

* * *   *   * *

abcdefghijklmnopqrstuvwxyz1234567890

Antique No 3 **206**

* * *   *   * *

abcdefghijklmnopqrstuvwxyz1234567890

Consort **207**

* * *   * *

abcdefghijklmnopqrstuvwxyz1234567890

SLAB SERIF

II

Serifa 55
Stymie (ATF)
ITC Stymie Hairline
Antique No 5
Egyptian 173
Schadow Antiqua
Aachen
Egyptian 505
Antique No 3
Consort

NB. On lower case letters generally look at the x height and length of ascenders and descenders.

208 Clarendon 12 (Monotype)

ABCDEFGHIJKLMNOPQRSTUVWXYZ&

209 Clarendon (Linotype)

ABCDEFGHIJKLMNOPQRSTUVWXYZ&

210 Egyptienne F 55

ABCDEFGHIJKLMNOPQRSTUVWXYZ&

211 New Clarendon

ABCDEFGHIJKLMNOPQRSTUVWXYZ&

212 Egizio

ABCDEFGHIJKLMNOPQRSTUVWXYZ&

213 Fortune

ABCDEFGHIJKLMNOPQRSTUVWXYZ&

rounded slab

214 ITC American Typewriter

ABCDEFGHIJKLMNOPQRSTUVWXYZ&

215 Clarinda Typewriter

ABCDEFGHIJKLMNOPQRSTUVWXYZ&

216 Linotype Typewriter

ABCDEFGHIJKLMNOPQRSTUVWXYZ&

217 Monotype Typewriter 105

ABCDEFGHIJKLMNOPQRSTUVWXYZ

These letters show special or 'style' characteristics. (NB. J, Q, & and g will usually vary from one typeface to another).

SLAB SERIF

11

Clarendon 12 (Monotype)
Clarendon (Linotype)
Egyptienne F 55
New Clarendon
Egizio
Fortune
ITC American Typewriter
Clarinda Typewriter
Linotype Typewriter
Monotype Typewriter 105

Clarendon 12 (Monotype) **208**

abcdefghijklmnopqrstuvwxyz1234567890

Clarendon (Linotype) **209**

abcdefghijklmnopqrstuvwxyz1234567890

Egyptienne F 55 **210**

abcdefghijklmnopqrstuvwxyz1234567890

New Clarendon **211**

abcdefghijklmnopqrstuvwxyz1234567890

Egizio **212**

abcdefghijklmnopqrstuvwxyz1234567890

Fortune **213**

abcdefghijklmnopqrstuvwxyz1234567890

ITC American Typewriter **214**

abcdefghijklmnopqrstuvwxyz1234567890

Clarinda Typewriter **215**

abcdefghijklmnopqrstuvwxyz1234567890

Linotype Typewriter **216**

abcdefghijklmnopqrstuvwxyz1234567890

Monotype Typewriter 105 **217**

abcdefghijklmnopqrstuvwxyz1234567890

SLAB SERIF

II

Clarendon 12 (Monotype)
Clarendon (Linotype)
Egyptienne F 55
New Clarendon
Egizio
Fortune
ITC American Typewriter
Clarinda Typewriter
Linotype Typewriter
Monotype Typewriter 105

NB. On lower case letters generally look at the x height and length of ascenders and descenders.

7. WEDGE SERIF
(Hybrid Serif), Nos 218-240

This category contains typefaces* which are not always clearly serif or sans serif (i.e. hybrids). It includes typefaces both of general serif-style but with only a thickening at the terminals of letters and sans serif style typefaces with very small line serifs on the terminals. It includes other groups with wedge-shaped serifs and half serifs. (N.B. Wedge serif style typefaces with a sloping bar on the lower case e are to be found in category 1.)

*Nos. 230-235 belong (stylistically) to a sub-group of *egyptians* (see introduction to category 5, p.64) called *latins*, they are not of the correct age. All the other typefaces are grouped here for identification and recognition purposes as they cannot be grouped elsewhere. Some bolder versions of these hybrids are also included in part 2, category 6, Modified Serif.

7. WEDGE SERIF
(Hybrid Serif), Nos 218-240

Specimen nos	Basic characteristics	
218-229	I *or* I	wedge-ended or small wedge serifs	e.g. **218** Albertus, **229** Romana
230-235	I	wedge-shaped serifs	e.g. **233** Meridien
236-238	I	line-ended serifs	e.g. **236** Copperplate Gothic
239-240	I	half serifs	e.g. **240** Romic

NB. *Typefaces in each group are arranged in alphabetical order.*

WEDGE SERIF
(HYBRID SERIF)

wedge-ended or small wedge serifs

218 Albertus

* * * * * * * *
ABCDEFGHIJKLMNOPQRSTUVWXYZ&

219 Americana

* * * *
ABCDEFGHIJKLMNOPQRSTUVWXYZ&

220 Flange

* * * * *
ABCDEFGHIJKLMNOPQRSTUVWXYZ&

221 French Old Style

* * * * * * * *
ABCDEFGHI JKLMNOPQRSTUVWXYZ&

222 ITC Friz Quadrata

* * * * *
ABCDEFGHIJKLMNOPQRSTUVWXYZ&

223 Icone

* * * * *
ABCDEFGHIJKLMNOPQRSTUVWXYZ&

224 ITC Korinna

* * *
ABCDEFGHIJKLMNOPQRSTUVWXYZ&

225 ITC Newtext

* * * *
ABCDEFGHIJKLMNOPQRSTUVWXYZ&

226 ITC Novarese

* * * *
ABCDEFGHIJKLMNOPQRSTUVWXYZ&

227 Poppl-Laudatio

* * * * *
ABCDEFGHIJKLMNOPQRSTUVWXYZ&

Albertus
Americana
Flange
French Old Style
ITC Friz Quadrata
Icone
ITC Korinna
ITC Newtext
ITC Novarese
Poppl-Laudatio

WEDGE SERIF (HYBRID SERIF)

11

* These letters show special or 'style' characteristics. (NB. J, Q, & and g will usually vary from one typeface to another).

Albertus **218**

abcdefghijklmnopqrstuvwxyz1234567890

Americana **219**

abcdefghijklmnopqrstuvwxyz1234567890

Flange **220**

abcdefghijklmnopqrstuvwxyz1234567890

French Old Style **221**

abcdefghijklmnopqrstuvwxyz1234567890

ITC Friz Quadrata **222**

abcdefghijklmnopqrstuvwxyz1234567890

Icone **223**

abcdefghijklmnopqrstuvwxyz1234567890

ITC Korinna **224**

abcdefghijklmnopqrstuvwxyz1234567890

ITC Newtext **225**

abcdefghijklmnopqrstuvwxyz1234567890

ITC Novarese **226**

abcdefghijklmnopqrstuvwxyz1234567890

Poppl-Laudatio **227**

abcdefghijklmnopqrstuvwxyz1234567890

Albertus
Americana
Flange
French Old Style
ITC Friz Quadrata
Icone
ITC Korinna
ITC Newtext
ITC Novarese
Poppl-Laudatio

WEDGE SERIF (HYBRID SERIF)

11

NB. On lower case letters generally look at the x height and length of ascenders and descenders.

228 ITC Quorum

ABCDEFGHIJKLMNOPQRSTUVWXYZ&

229 Romana

ABCDEFGHIJKLMNOPQRSTUVWXYZ&

wedge-shaped serifs

230 ITC Barcelona

ABCDEFGHIJKLMNOPQRSTUVWXYZ&

231 Biltmore

ABCDEFGHIJKLMNOPQRSTUVWXYZ&

232 ITC LSC Book

ABCDEFGHIJKLMNOPQRSTUVWXYZ&

233 Meridien

ABCDEFGHIJKLMNOPQRSTUVWXYZ&

234 Octavian

ABCDEFGHIJKLMNOPQRSTUVWXYZ&

235 Pegasus

ABCDEFGHIJKLMNOPQRSTUVWXYZ&

line-ended serifs

236 Copperplate Gothic

ABCDEFGHIJKLMNOPQRSTUVWXYZ&

237 ITC Serif Gothic

ABCDEFGHIJKLMNOPQRSTUVWXYZ&

ITC Quorum
Romana
ITC Barcelona
Biltmore
ITC LSC Book
Meridien
Octavian
Pegasus
Copperplate Gothic
ITC Serif Gothic

**WEDGE SERIF
(HYBRID SERIF)**

* These letters show special or 'style' characteristics. (NB. J, Q, & and g will usually vary from one typeface to another).

ITC Quorum **228**

abcdefghijklmnopqrstuvwxyz**1234567890**

Romana **229**

abcdefghijklmnopqrstuvwxyz1234567890

ITC Barcelona **230**

abcdefghijklmnopqrstuvwxyz1234567890

Biltmore **231**

abcdefghijklmnopqrstuvwxyz1234567890

ITC LSC Book **232**

abcdefghijklmnopqrstuvwxyz**1234567890**

Meridien **233**

abcdefghijklmnopqrstuvwxyz1234567890

Octavian **234**

abcdefghijklmnopqrstuvwxyz1234567890

Pegasus **235**

abcdefghijklmnopqrstuvwxyz1234567890

small capitals

Copperplate Gothic **236**

ABCDEFGHIJKLMNOPQRSTUVWXYZ**1234567890**

ITC Serif Gothic **237**

abcdefghijklmnopqrstuvwxyz1234567890

ITC Quorum
Romana
ITC Barcelona
Biltmore
ITC LSC Book
Meridien
Octavian
Pegasus
Copperplate Gothic
ITC Serif Gothic

WEDGE SERIF
(HYBRID SERIF)

11

NB. On lower case letters generally look at the x height and length of ascenders and descenders.

238 Spartan 140 (Monotype)

ABCDEFGHIJKLMNOPQRSTUVWXYZ&

half serifs

239 Parsons

ABCDEFGHIJKLMNOPQRSTUVWXYZ&

240 Romic

ABCDEFGHIJKLMNOPQRSTUVWXYZ&

new entries

240A Cantoria (Monotype)

ABCDEFGHIJKLMNOPQRSTUVWXYZ&

240B Footlight (Monotype)

ABCDEFGHIJKLMNOPQRSTUVWXYZ&

* These letters show special or 'style' characteristics. (NB. J, Q, & and g will usually vary from one typeface to another).

Spartan 140
(Monotype)
Parsons
Romic
Cantoria (Monotype)
Footlight
(Monotype)

WEDGE SERIF
(HYBRID SERIF)

11

Spartan 140 (Monotype) **238**

1234567890 <small>no lower case</small>

Parsons **239**

abcdefghijklmnopqrstuvwxyz1234567890

Romic **240**

abcdefghijklmnopqrstuvwxyz1234567890

Cantoria (Monotype) **240A**

abcdefghijklmnopqrstuvwxyz1234567890

Footlight (Monotype) **240B**

abcdefghijklmnopqrstuvwxyz1234567890

NB. Nos 241-244 have been deleted.

NB. On lower case letters generally look at the x height and length of ascenders and descenders.

Spartan 140
(Monotype)
Parsons
Romic
Cantoria (Monotype)
Footlight
(Monotype)

**WEDGE SERIF
(HYBRID SERIF)**

II

8. SANS SERIF
(sometimes called Grotesque), Nos 245-304

Typefaces with no serifs. Generally, with little or no difference between strokes (i.e. monoline). These typefaces are primarily divided according to whether the capital G has a spur on it or not, and if it has, if it is wide, medium or narrow. The category also includes groups of typefaces of a special shape (such as rounded).

The first *sans serifs* appeared in England in the early nineteenth century – Caslon's so-called **Egyptian** of 1816: a clumsy, unbalanced set of capitals probably intended for headings and emphasis only – but it was the German founders who developed the lower case in the 1830's.

British *sans serifs* of the nineteenth century tended to be heavy, have capitals of equal width and *modern*-face features to the G, R, g and t. These can be clearly seen on **Grot 9/ Headline Bold**. The German faces in contrast, reformed the style, the capitals differ in width and the strokes taper. Berthold's **Akzidenz Grotesk/Standard** of 1898 is typical and has been highly influential in the last forty years. American *sans serifs* drew on both sources, often using British forms with German stroke treatment. Morris Fuller Benton's **News Gothic** of 1908 typifies the approach.

During the first half of this century the development of the sans serif took two routes. In England in 1916, London Transport began using a *sans serif* especially designed for them by Edward Johnston, it was a break with previous *sans serifs* because it was based on classical letterforms. His approach was very closely followed by his pupil and friend Eric Gill with **Gill Sans** in 1928. In Germany, designs were influenced by the teachings of the Bauhaus and developed along geometric lines. Paul Renner's **Futura** of 1928 is the most popular of this kind and has been widely copied.

After World War II, the idea of a *sans serif* typeface with a whole family of related weights arose on the Continent, especially in Switzerland where Bauhaus principles had been modified to something akin to pattern making. Adrian Frutiger's **Univers** series begun in 1952 is the most ambitious of these typeface families, having twenty-one weights all carefully worked out and mathematically related from the outset. Max Miedinger's **New Haas Grotesque/Helvetica**, 1957, was based on Akzidenz Grotesque and has become the most popular and commercially successful *sans serif*. Although it now has a large family of weights, these were not all planned from the outset.

273

287

259/348/424/425/427/ 428/476/482/527 254

267/481/498

279/422/493/494/477/ 529/530/620/624

More recent developments have concentrated on introducing a little more 'personality' into the typeface and do not fall into any one category outlined above. 'Personality' can be difficult to handle. Both Roger Excoffon's **Antique Olive** of 1962 and Aldo Novarese's **Eurostile** of 1964/5 have too much for their own good and now look very dated. On the other hand, **Frutiger**, 1977 and Ong Chong Wah's **Abadi** of 1988 are more subtle and more successful.

271/473/483,
291/292

266, 304A

8. SANS SERIF
(sometimes called Grotesque), Nos 245-304

Specimen nos	Basic characteristics	Secondary characteristics	
245-248	**G** wide, no spur	**E** wide	e.g. **245** Adonis
249-257	**G** wide, no spur	**E** narrow	e.g. **254** Futura
258-265	**G** medium width, no spur	**G** round base	e.g. **259** Gill Sans
266-267	,,	**G** flatter base	e.g. **267** Univers 55
268-269	,,	**G** no bar, stressed strokes	e.g. **268** Optima
270	,,	**G** no bar, unstressed strokes	e.g. **270** Syntax
271-272	**G** narrow, no spur (or bar)		e.g. **271** Antique Olive
273	**G** wide, with spur		e.g. **273** Akzidenz Grotesk
274-283	**G** medium width, with spur		e.g. **279** Helvetica
284-289	**G** narrow, with spur		e.g. **287** News Gothic

NB. Typefaces in each group are arranged in alphabetical order.

290-294   Gg   *(sans serif)*
square   e.g. **291** Eurostile

295   Gg   *sloped*   e.g. **295** ITC Eras

296-301   Gg   *rounded*   e.g. **296** ITC Bauhaus

302-304   G   *electronic or*
machine-read   e.g. **303** OCR-A

N.B. *Typefaces in each group are arranged in alphabetical order.*

SANS SERIF

GG

wide capital G no spur
wide capital E.

245 Adonis

ABCDEFGHIJKLMNOPQRSTUVWXYZ&

246 Doric

ABCDEFGHIJKLMNOPQRSTUVWXYZ&

247 2-Line Block Gothic

ABCDEFGHIJKLMNOPQRSTUVWXYZ&

248 4-Line Block Gothic

ABCDEFGHIJKLMNOPQRSTUVWXYZ&

wide capital G no spur
narrow capital E.

249 Adsans

ABCDEFGHIJKLMNOPQRSTUVWXYZ&

250 ITC Avant Garde Gothic

ABCDEFGHIJKLMNOPQRSTUVWXYZ&

251 Bernhard Gothic

ABCDEFGHIJKLMNOPQRSTUVWXYZ&

252 20th Century

ABCDEFGHIJKLMNOPQRSTUVWXYZ&

253 Erbar

ABCDEFGHIJKLMNOPQRSTUVWXYZ&

254 Futura

ABCDEFGHIJKLMNOPQRSTUVWXYZ&

Adonis
Doric
2-Line Block Gothic
4-Line Block Gothic
Adsans
ITC Avant Garde Gothic
Bernhard Gothic
20th Century
Erbar
Futura

SANS SERIF

* These letters show special or 'style' characteristics. (Nb. J, Q, & and g will usually vary from one typeface to another).

Adonis **245**

abcdefghijklmnopqrstuvwxyz1234567890

Doric **246**

abcdefghijklmnopqrstuvwxyz1234567890

small capitals (no lower case)   2-Line Block Gothic **247**

ABCDEFGHIJKLMNOPQRSTUVWXYZ1234567890

small capitals (no lower case)   4-Line Block Gothic **248**

ABCDEFGHIJKLMNOPQRSTUVWXYZ1234567890

Adsans **249**

abcdefghijklmnopqrstuvwxyz1234567890

ITC Avant Garde Gothic **250**

abcdefghijklmnopqrstuvwxyz1234567890

Bernhard Gothic **251**

abcdefghijklmnopqrstuvwxyz1234567890

20th Century **252**

abcdefghijklmnopqrstuvwxyz1234567890

Erbar **253**

abcdefghijklmnopqrstuvwxyz1234567890

Futura **254**

abcdefghijklmnopqrstuvwxyz1234567890

Adonis
Doric
2-Line Block Gothic
4-Line Block Gothic
Adsans
ITC Avant Garde Gothic
Bernhard Gothic
20th Century
Erbar
Futura

SANS SERIF

NB. On lower case letters generally look at the x height and length of ascenders and descenders.

255 Neuzeit-Grotesk

ABCDEFGHIJKLMNOPQRSTUVWXYZ&

256 Nobel

ABCDEFGHIJKLMNOPQRSTUVWXYZ&

257 Spartan

ABCDEFGHIJKLMNOPQRSTUVWXYZ&

*medium
width
capital G
no spur
round base*

258 Cable (Klingspor)

ABCDEFGHIJKLMNOPQRSTUVWXYZ&

259 Gill Sans

ABCDEFGHIJKLMNOPQRSTUVWXYZ&

260 Granby

ABCDEFGHIJKLMNOPQRSTUVWXYZ&

261 Grotesque 215

ABCDEFGHIJKLMNOPQRSTUVWXYZ&

262 ITC Kabel

ABCDEFGHIJKLMNOPQRSTUVWXYZ&

263 Metro

ABCDEFGHIJKLMNOPQRSTUVWXYZ&

264 Tempo

ABCDEFGHIJKLMNOPQRSTUVWXYZ&

Neuzeit Grotesk
Nobel
Spartan
Cable (Klingspor)
Gill Sans
Granby
Grotesque 215
ITC Kabel
Metro
Tempo

SANS SERIF

* These letters show special or 'style' characteristics. (NB. J, Q, & and g will usually vary from one typeface to another).

Neuzeit-Grotesk **255**

abcdefghijklmnopqrstuvwxyz1234567890

Nobel **256**

abcdefghijklmnopqrstuvwxyz1234567890

Spartan **257**

abcdefghijklmnopqrstuvwxyz1234567890

Cable (Klingspor) **258**

abcdefghijklmnopqrstuvwxyz1234567890

Gill Sans **259**

abcdefghijklmnopqrstuvwxyz1234567890

Granby **260**

abcdefghijklmnopqrstuvwxyz1234567890

Grotesque 215 **261**

abcdefghijklmnopqrstuvwxyz1234567890

ITC Kabel **262**

abcdefghijklmnopqrstuvwxyz1234567890

Metro **263**

abcdefghijklmnopqrstuvwxyz1234567890

Tempo **264**

abcdefghijklmnopqrstuvwxyz1234567890

Neuzeit Grotesk
Nobel
Spartan
Cable (Klingspor)
Gill Sans
Granby
Grotesque 215
ITC Kabel
Metro
Tempo

SANS SERIF

NB. On lower case letters generally look at the x height and length of ascenders and descenders.

265 Venus

ABCDEFGHIJKLMNOPQRSTUVWXYZ&

*medium
with capital G
no spur
flatter base*

266 Frutiger

ABCDEFGHIJKLMNOPQRSTUVWXYZ&

267 Univers 55

ABCDEFGHIJKLMNOPQRSTUVWXYZ&

*medium
width
capital G
no spur
no bar
stressed
strokes*

268 Optima

ABCDEFGHIJKLMNOPQRSTUVWXYZ&

269 ITC Souvenir Gothic

ABCDEFGHIJKLMNOPQRSTUVWXYZ&

*medium
width
capital G
no spur
no bar
unstressed
strokes*

270 Syntax

ABCDEFGHIJKLMNOPQRSTUVWXYZ&

*narrow
capital G
no spur
no bar*

271 Antique Olive

ABCDEFGHIJKLMNOPQRSTUVWXYZ&

Venus
Frutiger
Univers 55
Optima
ITC Souvenir Gothic
Syntax
Antique Olive
Clearface Gothic
Akzidenz Grotesk
Berthold Imago

272 Clearface Gothic

ABCDEFGHIJKLMNOPQRSTUVWXYZ&

*wide
capital G
with spur*

273 Akzidenz Grotesk

ABCDEFGHIJKLMNOPQRSTUVWXYZ&

*medium
width
capital G
with spur*

274 Berthold Imago

ABCDEFGHIJKLMNOPQRSTUVWXYZ&

SANS SERIF

* These letters show special or 'style' characteristics. (NB. J, Q, & and g will usually vary from one typeface to another).

Venus **265**

abcdefghijklmnopqrstuvwxyz1234567890

Frutiger **266**

abcdefghijklmnopqrstuvwxyz1234567890

Univers 55 **267**

abcdefghijklmnopqrstuvwxyz1234567890

Optima **268**

abcdefghijklmnopqrstuvwxyz1234567890

ITC Souvenir Gothic **269**

abcdefghijklmnopqrstuvwxyz**1234567890**

Syntax **270**

abcdefghijklmnopqrstuvwxyz1234567890

Antique Olive **271**

abcdefghijklmnopqrstuvwxyz1234567890

Clearface Gothic **272**

abcdefghijklmnopqrstuvwxyz1234567890

Akzidenz Grotesk **273**

abcdefghijklmnopqrstuvwxyz1234567890

Berthold Imago **274**

abcdefghijklmnopqrstuvwxyz1234567890

Venus
Frutiger
Univers 55
Optima
ITC Souvenir Gothic
Syntax
Antique Olive
Clearface Gothic
Akzidenz Grotesk
Berthold Imago

SANS SERIF

GG

NB. On lower case letters generally look at the x height and length of ascenders and descenders.

275 Folio

ABCDEFGHIJKLMNOPQRSTUVWXYZ&

276 Franklin Gothic (ATF)

ABCDEFGHIJKLMNOPQRSTUVWXYZ&

277 ITC Franklin Gothic

ABCDEFGHIJKLMNOPQRSTUVWXYZ&

278 Haas Unica

ABCDEFGHIJKLMNOPQRSTUVWXYZ&

279 Helvetica

ABCDEFGHIJKLMNOPQRSTUVWXYZ&

280 Mercator

ABCDEFGHIJKLMNOPQRSTUVWXYZ&

281 Standard

ABCDEFGHIJKLMNOPQRSTUVWXYZ&

Folio
Franklin Gothic (ATF)
ITC Franklin Gothic
Haas Unica
Helvetica
Mercator
Standard
Transport
Video
Bell Centennial

282 Transport

ABCDEFGHIJKLMNOPQRSTUVWXYZ&

283 Video

ABCDEFGHIJKLMNOPQRSTUVWXYZ&

SANS SERIF

*narrow
capital G
with spur*

284 Bell Centennial

ABCDEFGHIJKLMNOPQRSTUVWXYZ&

* These letters show special or 'style' characteristics. (NB. J, Q, & and g will usually vary from one typeface to another).

Folio **275**

* * * * *

abcdefghijklmnopqrstuvwxyz1234567890

Franklin Gothic (ATF) **276**

* * * * * *

abcdefghijklmnopqrstuvwxyz1234567890

ITC Franklin Gothic **277**

* * * * *

abcdefghijklmnopqrstuvwxyz1234567890

Haas Unica **278**

* * * *

abcdefghijklmnopqrstuvwxyz1234567890

Helvetica **279**

* * *

abcdefghijklmnopqrstuvwxyz1234567890

Mercator **280**

* * * * *

abcdefghijklmnopqrstuvwxyz1234567890

Standard **281**

* * * *

abcdefghijklmnopqrstuvwxyz1234567890

Transport **282**

* * * *

abcdefghijklmnopqrstuvwxyz1234567890

Video **283**

* * * *

abcdefghijklmnopqrstuvwxyz1234567890

Bell Centennial **284**

* * ** *

abcdefghijklmnopqrstuvwxyz1234567890

Folio
Franklin Gothic (ATF)
ITC Franklin Gothic
Haas Unica
Helvetica
Mercator
Standard
Transport
Video
Bell Centennial

SANS SERIF

NB. On lower case letters generally look at the x height and length of ascenders and descenders.

91

285 Bell Gothic

ABCDEFGHIJKLMNOPQRSTUVWXYZ&

286 Lightline Gothic

ABCDEFGHIJKLMNOPQRSTUVWXYZ&

287 News Gothic

ABCDEFGHIJKLMNOPQRSTUVWXYZ&

288 Record Gothic

ABCDEFGHIJKLMNOPQRSTUVWXYZ&

289 Trade Gothic

ABCDEFGHIJKLMNOPQRSTUVWXYZ&

square-shaped

290 Bank Gothic

ABCDEFGHIJKLMNOPQRSTUVWXYZ&

291 Eurostile

ABCDEFGHIJKLMNOPQRSTUVWXYZ&

293 Heldustry

ABCDEFGHIJKLMNOPQRSTUVWXYZ&

sloped

295 ITC Eras

ABCDEFGHIJKLMNOPQRSTUVWXYZ&

rounded

297 ITC Benguiat Gothic

ABCDEFGHIJKLMNOPQRSTUVWXYZ&

Bell Gothic
Lightline Gothic
News Gothic
Record Gothic
Trade Gothic
Bank Gothic
Eurostile
Heldustry
ITC Eras
ITC Benguiat Gothic

SANS SERIF

* These letters show special or 'style' characteristics. (NB. J, Q, & and g will usually vary from one typeface to another).

Bell Gothic **285**

* * * * * *
abcdefghijklmnopqrstuvwxyz1234567890

Lightline Gothic **286**

* * * *
abcdefghijklmnopqrstuvwxyz1234567890

News Gothic **287**

* * * *
abcdefghijklmnopqrstuvwxyz1234567890

Record Gothic **288**

* * * *
abcdefghijklmnopqrstuvwxyz1234567890

Trade Gothic **289**

* * * *
abcdefghijklmnopqrstuvwxyz1234567890

small capitals
Bank Gothic **290**

* * *
ABCDEFGHIJKLMNOPQRSTUVWXYZ1234567890

Eurostile **291**

* * *
abcdefghijklmnopqrstuvwxyz1234567890

Heldustry **293**

* * * *
abcdefghijklmnopqrstuvwxyz1234567890

ITC Eras **295**

* * * * * *
abcdefghijklmnopqrstuvwxyz1234567890

ITC Benguiat Gothic **297**

* * *
abcdefghijklmnopqrstuvwxyz1234567890

Bell Gothic
Lightline Gothic
News Gothic
Record Gothic
Trade Gothic
Bank Gothic
Eurostile
Heldustry
ITC Eras
ITC Benguiat Gothic

SANS SERIF

NB. On lower case letters generally look at the x height and length of ascenders and descenders.

298 Berliner Grotesk

ABCDEFGHIJKLMNOPQRSTUVWXYZ&

299 Churchward 70

ABCDEFGHIJKLMNOPQRSTUVWXYZ&

300 ITC Ronda

ABCDEFGHIJKLMNOPQRSTUVWXYZ&

electronic or machine read

302 IC – Alphabet

ABCDEFGHIJKLMNOPQRSTUVWXYZ

303 OCR-A

ABCDEFGHIJKLMNOPQRSTUVWXYZ

304 OCR-B

ABCDEFGHIJKLMNOPQRSTUVWXYZ&

new entries

304A Abadi (Monotype)

ABCDEFGHIJKLMNOPQRSTUVWXYZ&

304B Arial (Monotype)

ABCDEFGHIJKLMNOPQRSTUVWXYZ&

304C Avenir 55 (Linotype)

ABCDEFGHIJKLMNOPQRSTUVWXYZ&

304D Wolters Map Face (Monotype)

ABCDEFGHIJKLMNOPQRSTUVWXYZ&

* These letters show special or 'style' characteristics. (NB. J, Q, & and g will usually vary from one typeface to another).

Berliner Grotesk
Churchward 70
ITC Ronda
IC – Alphabet
OCR-A
OCR-B
Abadi (Monotype)
Arial (Monotype)
Avenir 55 (Linotype)
Wolters Map Face
(Monotype)

SANS SERIF

Berliner Grotesk **298**

* * * *
abcdefghijklmnopqrstuvwxyz1234567890

Churchward 70 **299**

* * *
abcdefghijklmnopqrstuvwxyz1234567890

ITC Ronda **300**

* * * *
abcdefghijklmnopqrstuvwxyz1234567890

IC – Alphabet **302**

*
1234567890 *no lower case*

OCR-A **303**

* *
1234567890 *no lower case*

OCR-B **304**

* * * * * *
a b c d e f g h i j k l m n o p q r s t u v w x y z 1234567890

Abadi (Monotype) **304A**

* * * * *
abcdefghijklmnopqrstuvwxyz1234567890

Arial (Monotype) **304B**

*
abcdefghijklmnopqrstuvwxyz1234567890

Avenir 55 (Linotype) **304C**

* * *
abcdefghijklmnopqrstuvwxyz1234567890

Wolters Map Face (Monotype) **304D**

* * * * *
abcdefghijklmnopqrstuvwxyz1234567890

Berliner Grotesk
Churchward 70
ITC Ronda
IC – Alphabet
OCR-A
OCR-B
Abadi (Monotype)
Arial (Monotype)
Avenir 55 (Linotype)
Wolters Map Face
(Monotype)

SANS SERIF

G G

NB. On lower case letters generally look at the x height and length of ascenders and descenders.

TEXT TYPEFACE 'EARMARK' TABLES

THESE TABLES OFFER a method of identifying *Text* typefaces (Specimen Nos 1-304) by means of 'earmarks' or special characteristic features on individual letters. They represent an alternative but companion identification process to the *Text* typeface classification system beginning on page 12.

The tables are divided into two parts – 'Common' and 'Special Earmarks', but there is, however, a small overlap between the two parts.

'Common Earmark' Tables

These show typical, commonplace letter features and give examples of typefaces with each feature. 'Common' letters are identifiable either by their general appearance or by 'marked' features or captions. (see illustration below).

119 Century Schoolbook
137 Impressum
145 Primus Antiqua
poor contrast

153 Bauer Bodoni
156 Didot
161 Walbaum (Linotype)

'Special Earmark' Tables

These show more distinctive and unusual identifying features.

'Special earmarks' are indicated on letters by arrows, lines or captions and *Text* typefaces with each feature are listed by number below each. (see illustration below). Each letter has been 'analysed' in parts or by features generally starting from the top and working downwards to the bottom. It should be noted that the general 'style' of typefaces with the same 'earmark' can vary slightly.

27, 60, 63

35, **38**-41, 61-2, 74, 76, 99, 123-4, 132, 147

Figures are divided throughout into two kinds – 'lining' and 'non-lining'. An example of each is given below:

lining

1234567890

non-lining

1234567890

e.g. Baskerville

In both sets of tables, letters are arranged in a continuous sequence from a to z in both capital and lower case forms (plus ampersand and figures). The 'earmarks' of each letter are then divided (by rules) into groups representing *Text* typeface categories used in the book as follows:

Category Nos. 1-4 (Roman Serif)
(Specimen Nos. 1-150)

No. 5 (Modern Serif)
(Specimen Nos. 151-187)

No. 6 (Slab Serif)
(Specimen Nos. 188-217)

No. 7 (Wedge Serif)
(Specimen Nos. 218-240)

No. 8 (Sans Serif)
(Specimen Nos. 245-304)

NB. There are no 'common earmarks' for the Wedge Serif category since it generally comprises of more 'unusual' typefaces.

Looking for 'earmarks'

1. Consult the recommended selection order for 'earmarks' on this page and choose a letter as early in the order as possible.

2. Look in the 'Common Earmark' Tables to see whether or not the specimen letter you have chosen has a 'common earmark'. If it has, then select alternative specimen letters until you find one which has features which do not appear in these tables as 'common features will not generally assist in rapid typeface identification.

3. Find this letter in the following 'Special Earmark' Tables.

4. Look through the listings of illustrated specimen letters which are divided by rules into typeface categories (as listed previously) and match your specimen against the 'earmarks' shown.

5. When you have successfully matched your specimen to one or more of the 'earmarks' then look up in turn the typeface specimens whose numbers are given below each until you identify your particular typeface specimen.

6. If specific typeface identification is not easily obtainable with the specimen letter you have chosen then select alternative letters until a positive 'photofit' picture of the typeface is achieved.

Recommended order for selecting 'earmarks':

Capital letters and ampersand:
Q, &, J, G, W, A, K, C, R, M, E, P, S, T, F, B, N, O, U, X, Y, D, H, Z, L, V, I.

Lower case letters:
g, a, j, y, k, t, f, r, q, w, e, b, s, c, d, p, m, u, x, o, v, h, n, i, l, z.

Figures:
3, 7, 5, 2, 1, 4, 9, 6, 8, 0

'Common Earmarks'

The 'common earmarks' (or typical identifying features) are indicated either by the general appearance of letters or by 'marked' features. The general 'style' of typefaces with the same 'earmark' may vary. Example typefaces with their specimen numbers are listed against each letter.

Throughout these tables 'earmarks' are divided into Text typeface categories by fine horizontal rules as described in the introduction on page 97.

A
19 Centaur
52 Times Roman (Linotype)
79 Baskerville (Linotype)

A *flat top*
56 Bookman
70 Old Style No. 7
86 Times Europa

A *wide flat top*
57 ITC Bookman
71 Olympian
138 Melior

A
35 Bembo
39 Plantin
76 Aster

A
59 Caslon Old Face No. 2
73 Ehrhardt
94 Garamond (Stempel)

A *poor contrast*
119 Century Schoolbook
137 Impressum
145 Primus Antiqua

A
153 Bauer Bodoni
156 Didot
161 Walbaum (Linotype)

A
196 Memphis
197 Rockwell
199 Stymie (ATF)

A
254 Futura
258 Cable (Klingspor)
264 Tempo

A
259 Gill Sans
267 Univers 55
279 Helvetica

B *equal size bowls*
24 ITC Clearface
67 Imprint
90 Fournier

B *bottom heavy*
19 Centaur
79 Baskerville (Linotype)
88 Sabon

B *poor contrast*
115 Excelsior
119 Century Schoolbook
121 Ionic 5

B
153 Bauer Bodoni
156 Didot
161 Walbaum (Linotype)

B
194 ITC Lubalin Graph
197 Rockwell
198 Serifa 55

B
261 Grotesque 215
265 Univers 55
279 Helvetica

C
5 Windsor
56 Bookman
69 Old Style No. 2

C
49 Goudy Catalogue
52 Times Roman (Linotype)
67 Imprint

C
35 Bembo
39 Plantin
92 Garamond (Stempel)

C
20 Horley Old Style
61 Caslon 540
79 Baskerville (Linotype)

C *poor contrast*
119 Century Schoolbook
121 Ionic 5
145 Primus Antiqua

C
171 Augustea
179 Modern No. 20
186 Scotch 2 (Linotype)

C
196 Memphis
197 Rockwell
198 Serifa 55

C
254 Futura
257 Spartan
259 Gills Sans

C *poor contrast*
256 Nobel
261 Grotesque 215
273 Akzidenz Grotesque

C
267 Univers 55
275 Folio
279 Helvetica

D
39 Plantin
52 Times Roman (Linotype)
69 Old Style No. 2

D *concave*
49 Goudy Catalogue
91 Garamond (Monotype)
100 Concorde

D *poor contrast*
114 Century Expanded
119 Century Schoolbook
121 Ionic 5

D
153 Bauer Bodoni
156 Didot
163 Bodoni (Haas)

D
196 Memphis
197 Rockwell
198 Serifa 55

D
267 Univers 55
275 Folio
279 Helvetica

E
5 Windsor
61 Caslon 540
69 Old Style No. 2

E
35 Bembo
39 Plantin
52 Times Roman (Linotype)

E
153 Bauer Bodoni
161 Walbaum (Linotype)
174 Caledonia

E
193 Glypha 55
198 Serifa 55
199 Stymie (ATF)

E *bracketed slab*
207 Consort
209 Clarendon (Linotype)
212 Egizio

E *narrow*
253 Erbar
254 Futura
257 Spartan

E *wider*
267 Univers
279 Helvetica
281 Standard

F
5 Windsor
61 Caslon 540
69 Old Style No. 2

F
35 Bembo
39 Plantin
52 Times Roman (Linotype)

F
153 Bauer Bodoni
161 Walbaum (Linotype)
174 Caledonia

F
193 Glypha 55
198 Serifa 55
199 Stymie (ATF)

F *bracketed slab*
207 Consort
209 Clarendon (Linotype)
212 Egizio

F *narrow*
253 Erbar
254 Futura
257 Spartan

F *wider*
267 Univers 55
279 Helvetica
281 Standard

G
49 Goudy Catalogue
70 Old Style No. 7
80 Baskerville No. 2

G
15 Cloister
97 Spectrum
105 Romulus

'Common Earmarks'

The 'common earmarks' (or typical identifying features) are indicated either by the general appearance of letters or by 'marked' features. The general 'style' of typefaces with the same 'earmark' may vary. Example typefaces with their specimen numbers are listed against each letter.

Column 1 — G, H

G
- 52 Times Roman (Linotype)
- 67 Imprint
- 90 Garamond (Stempel)

G *poor contrast*
- 119 Century Schoolbook
- 121 Ionic 5
- 142 Textype

G
- 175 ITC Century
- 177 De Vinne
- 186 Scotch 2 (Linotype)

G *bracketed slab*
- 196 Memphis
- 198 Serifa 55
- 199 Stymie (ATF)

G *bracketed slab*
- 207 Consort
- 209 Clarendon (Linotype)
- 212 Egizio

G *circular (or nearly so) no spur*
- 253 Erbar
- 254 Futura
- 257 Spartan

G *with spur*
- 275 Folio
- 279 Helvetica
- 281 Standard

H
- 39 Plantin
- 60 Caslon 128
- 79 Baskerville (Linotype)

H
- 153 Bauer Bodoni
- 158 Fairfield
- 161 Walbaum (Linotype)

H
- 197 Rockwell
- 198 Serifa 55
- 199 Stymie (ATF)

H
- 207 Consort
- 209 Clarendon (Linotype)
- 212 Egizio

H
- 267 Univers 55
- 279 Helvetica
- 281 Standard

Column 2 — I, J

I
- 35 Bembo
- 39 Plantin
- 92 Garamond (Stempel)

I *poor contrast*
- 118 Aurora
- 119 Century Schoolbook
- 121 Ionic 5

I
- 152 Basilia
- 153 Bauer Bodoni
- 168 Walbaum (Monotype)

I
- 196 Memphis
- 197 Rockwell
- 199 Stymie (ATF)

I *bracketed slab*
- 207 Consort
- 209 Clarendon (Linotype)
- 212 Egizio

I
- 259 Gill Sans
- 267 Univers 55
- 279 Helvetica

J *short tail non-lining*
- 16 Cloister
- 60 Caslon 128
- 67 Imprint

J *medium length tail non-lining*
- 31 Vendôme
- 52 Times Roman (Linotype)
- 99 Caslon 3

J *rounded tail non-lining*
- 25 Lutetia
- 66 Granjon
- 148 Electra

J *poor contrast lining*
- 119 Century Schoolbook
- 121 Ionic 5
- 146 Textype

J
- 168 Walbaum (Linotype)
- 171 Augustea
- 177 De Vinne

J
- 196 Memphis
- 197 Rockwell
- 199 Stymie (ATF)

Column 3 — J, K, L

J *short tail*
- 253 Erbar
- 266 Frutiger
- 282 Standard

J *full rounded tail*
- 267 Univers 55
- 275 Folio
- 279 Helvetica

K *single junction*
- 70 Old Style No. 7
- 76 Aster
- 92 Garamond (Stempel)

K *single junction*
- 35 Bembo
- 38 Plantin
- 88 Sabon

K *double junction*
- 115 Excelsior
- 119 Century Schoolbook
- 121 Ionic 5

K
- 153 Bauer Bodoni
- 163 Bodoni (Haas)
- 165 ITC Fenice

K
- 196 Memphis
- 198 Serifa 55
- 199 Stymie (ATF)

K
- 261 Grotesque 215
- 279 Helvetica
- 281 Standard

L
- 35 Bembo
- 38 Plantin
- 61 Caslon 540

L
- 79 Baskerville (Linotype)
- 123 Cheltenham
- 138 Melior

L *poor contrast*
- 115 Excelsior
- 119 Century Schoolbook
- 121 Ionic 5

L
- 171 Augustea
- 174 Caledonia
- 177 De Vinne

Column 4 — L, M, N

L
- 197 Rockwell
- 198 Serifa 55
- 199 Stymie (ATF)

L *narrow*
- 254 Futura
- 257 Spartan
- 264 Tempo

L *wider*
- 267 Univers 55
- 279 Helvetica
- 281 Standard

M
- 61 Caslon 540
- 67 Imprint
- 79 Baskerville (Linotype)

M
- 35 Bembo
- 39 Plantin
- 73 Ehrhardt

M
- 153 Bauer Bodoni
- 158 Fairfield
- 168 Walbaum (Linotype)

M
- 193 Glypha 55
- 196 Memphis
- 197 Rockwell

M
- 209 Clarendon (Linotype)
- 212 Egizio
- 213 Consort

M
- 275 Folio
- 279 Helvetica
- 281 Standard

N
- 61 Caslon 540
- 92 Garamond (Stempel)
- 105 Romulus

N *poor contrast*
- 56 Bookman
- 71 Olympian
- 138 Melior

N
- 153 Bauer Bodoni
- 156 Didot
- 158 Fairfield

'Common Earmarks'

The 'common earmarks' (or typical identifying features) are indicated either by the general appearance of letters or by 'marked' features. The general 'style' of typefaces with the same 'earmark' may vary. Example typefaces with their specimen numbers are listed against each letter.

N
193 Glypha 55
196 Memphis
197 Rockwell

N *bracketed slab*
209 Clarendon (Linotype)
212 Egizio
213 Fortune

N
275 Folio
279 Helvetica
281 Standard

O
19 Centaur
35 Bembo
39 Plantin

O
52 Times Roman (Linotype)
58 Bulmer
79 Baskerville (Linotype)

O
153 Bauer Bodoni
156 Didot
168 Walbaum (Monotype)

O
189 Beton
196 Memphis
199 Stymie (ATF)

O *circular*
254 Futura
258 Cable (Klingspor)
259 Gill Sans

O
267 Univers 55
279 Helvetica
281 Standard

P
35 Bembo
38 Plantin
70 Old Style No. 7

P
49 Goudy Catalogue
84 Palatino
92 Garamond (Stempel)

P *poor contrast*
115 Excelsior
119 Century Schoolbook
137 Impressum

P
153 Bauer Bodoni
156 Didot
158 Fairfield

P
196 Memphis
197 Rockwell
198 Serifa 55

P
259 Gill Sans
260 Granby
261 Grotesque 215

Q
35 Bembo
52 Times Roman (Linotype)
116 Perpetua

Q *poor contrast*
115 Excelsior
119 Century Schoolbook
121 Ionic 5

Q
152 Basilia
153 Bauer Bodoni
174 Caledonia

Q
189 Beton
193 Glypha 55
198 Serifa 55

Q
209 Clarendon (Linotype)
212 Egizio
213 Consort

Q
278 Haas Unica
279 Helvetica
283 Video

R
35 Bembo
37 Goudy Old Style
87 Quadriga Antiqua

R
39 Plantin
70 Old Style No. 7
94 Garamond (Berthold)

R
19 Centaur
31 Vendôme
75 Aldus

R *poor contrast*
115 Excelsior
119 Century Schoolbook
145 Primus Antiqua

R
153 Bauer Bodoni
156 Didot
168 Walbaum (Monotype)

R
188 A & S Gallantin
196 Memphis
198 Serifa 55

R
254 Futura
257 Spartan
258 Cable (Klingspor)

R
273 Akzidenz Grotesque
281 Standard
287 News Gothic

R
267 Univers 55
275 Folio
279 Helvetica

S
52 Times Roman (Linotype)
73 Ehrhardt
80 Baskerville No. 2

S
70 Old Style No. 7
77 Baskerville (Berthold)
99 Caslon 3

S
39 Plantin
95 ITC Garamond
130 Columbia

S *poor contrast*
115 Excelsior
119 Century Schoolbook
121 Ionic 5

S
153 Bauer Bodoni
156 Didot
174 Caledonia

S
196 Memphis
197 Rockwell
198 Stymie (ATF)

S *narrow*
254 Futura
257 Spartan
262 ITC Kabel

S *wider*
267 Univers 55
279 Helvetica
281 Standard

T
35 Bembo
69 Old Style No. 2
107 Van Dijck

T
52 Times Roman (Linotype)
76 Aster
80 Baskerville No. 2

T *poor contrast*
118 Aurora
119 Century Schoolbook
121 Ionic 5

T
153 Bauer Bodoni
158 Fairfield
161 Walbaum (Linotype)

T
196 Memphis
197 Rockwell
198 Serifa 55

T
154 Futura
267 Univers 55
279 Helvetica

U
39 Plantin
44 Trump Mediaeval
92 Garamond (Stempel)

U *good contrast*
67 Imprint
79 Baskerville (Linotype)
116 Perpetua

U *poor contrast*
118 Aurora
119 Century Schoolbook
121 Ionic 5

U
153 Bauer Bodoni
156 Didot
168 Walbaum (Monotype)

U
196 Memphis
197 Rockwell
198 Serifa 55

U
254 Futura
257 Spartan
264 Tempo

U
267 Univers 55
275 Folio
279 Helvetica

V
52 Times Roman (Linotype)
61 Caslon 540
69 Old Style No. 2

V *poor contrast*
118 Aurora
119 Century Schoolbook
121 Ionic 5

V *line serifs*
153 Bauer Bodoni
156 Didot
168 Walbaum (Monotype)

V *bracketed serifs*
171 Augustea
177 De Vinne
186 Scotch 2 (Linotype)

V
196 Memphis
197 Rockwell
198 Serifa 55

V
254 Futura
258 Cable (Klingspor)
259 Gill Sans

V
261 Grotesque 215
267 Univers 55
279 Helvetica

W *crossed centre strokes*
39 Plantin
88 Sabon
92 Garamond (Stempel)

W *stepped centre strokes*
52 Times Roman (Linotype)
61 Caslon 540
107 Van Dijck

W *centre strokes meet at cap height*
67 Imprint
69 Old Style No. 2
74 Galliard

W *no centre serif*
75 Aldus
79 Baskerville (Linotype)
84 Palatino

W
171 Augustea
174 Caledonia
185 Scotch 2 (Linotype)

W
196 Memphis
197 Rockwell
202 Egyptian 173

W
254 Futura
263 Metro
264 Tempo

W
267 Univers 55
277 ITC Franklin Gothic
279 Helvetica

X
35 Bembo
39 Plantin
92 Garamond (Stempel)

X *poor contrast*
115 Excelsior
119 Century Schoolbook
121 Ionic 5

X
158 Fairfield
171 Augustea
174 Caledonia

X
196 Memphis
197 Rockwell
199 Stymie (ATF)

X *narrow*
253 Erbar
254 Futura
264 Tempo

X *wider*
267 Univers 55
279 Helvetica
281 Standard

Y
67 Imprint
92 Garamond (Stempel)
116 Perpetua

Y
153 Bauer Bodoni
158 Fairfield
161 Walbaum (Linotype)

Y
196 Memphis
192 Rockwell
198 Serifa 55

Y *high junction*
253 Erbar
254 Futura
264 Tempo

Y *lower junction*
275 Folio
279 Helvetica
281 Standard

Z
60 Caslon 128
70 Old Style No. 7
88 Sabon

Z
52 Times Roman (Linotype)
84 Palatino
105 Romulus

Z
161 Walbaum (Linotype)
171 Augustea
174 Caledonia

Z
196 Memphis
197 Rockwell
198 Serifa 55

Z
254 Futura
257 Spartan
264 Tempo

Z
267 Univers 55
279 Helvetica
287 News Gothic

&
35 Bembo
39 Plantin
80 Baskerville No. 2

&
97 Spectrum
105 Romulus
138 Melior

&
52 Times Roman (Linotype)
76 Aster
107 Van Dijck

&
161 Walbaum (Linotype)
166 Modern (Linotype)
178 Madison

&
193 Glypha 55
197 Rockwell
198 Serifa 55

&
259 Gill Sans
260 Granby
267 Univers 55

&
255 Neuzeit-Grotesk
263 Metro
268 Optima

&
261 Grotesque 215
277 ITC Franklin Gothic
287 News Gothic

a
20 Horley Old Style
70 Old Style No. 7
97 Spectrum

a
52 Times Roman (Linotype)
100 Concorde
131 French Round Face

a
35 Bembo
39 Plantin
75 Aldus

a *poor contrast*
114 Century Expanded
119 Century Schoolbook
121 Ionic 5

a
153 Bauer Bodoni
156 Didot
186 Scotch 2 (Linotype)

'Common Earmarks'

The 'common earmarks' (or typical identifying features) are indicated either by the general appearance of letters or by 'marked' features. The general 'style' of typefaces with the same 'earmark' may vary. Example typefaces with their specimen numbers are listed against each letter.

a
196 Memphis
197 Rockwell
198 Serifa 55

a *double storey*
267 Univers 55
279 Helvetica
281 Standard

a *single storey*
254 Futura
255 Neuzeit-Grotesk
257 Spartan

b
39 Plantin
52 Times Roman (Linotype)
73 Ehrhardt

b
69 Old Style No 2
77 Baskerville (Berthold)
92 Garamond (Stempel)

b *poor contrast*
117 Primer
119 Century Schoolbook
121 Ionic 5

b
153 Bauer Bodoni
156 Didot
158 Fairfield

b
196 Memphis
197 Rockwell
198 Serifa 55

b *low join to stem*
253 Erbar
254 Futura
257 Spartan

b *higher join to stem*
267 Univers 55
278 Haas Unica
279 Helvetica

c
39 Plantin
52 Times Roman (Linotype)
60 Caslon 128

c
35 Bembo
79 Baskerville (Linotype)
90 Fournier

c *poor contrast*
114 Century Expanded
119 Century Schoolbook
146 Textype

c
153 Bauer Bodoni
156 Didot
161 Walbaum (Linotype)

c
194 ITC Lubalin Graph
196 Memphis
197 Rockwell

c
254 Futura
257 Spartan
259 Gill Sans

c
261 Grotesque 215
267 Univers 55
281 Standard

d
35 Bembo
52 Times Roman (Linotype)
61 Caslon 540

d
116 Perpetua
117 Primer
119 Century Schoolbook

d
153 Bauer Bodoni
168 Walbaum (Monotype)
174 Caledonia

d
196 Memphis
197 Rockwell
198 Serifa 55

d *low join to stem*
254 Futura
256 Nobel
257 Spartan

d *higher join to stem*
267 Univers 55
273 Akzidenz Grotesk
279 Helvetica

e
6 Kennerley
16 Jenson
19 Centaur

e
35 Bembo
39 Plantin
52 Times Roman (Linotype)

e *poor contrast*
71 Olympian
119 Century Schoolbook
136 Franklin Antiqua

e
153 Bauer Bodoni
156 Didot
161 Walbaum (Linotype)

e
194 ITC Lubalin Graph
196 Memphis
197 Rockwell

e
261 Grotesque 215
267 Univers 55
279 Helvetica

f *short hook*
39 Plantin
70 Old Style No 7
109 Janson

f *medium length hook*
69 Old Style No 2
123 Cheltenham
130 Columbia

f *long hook*
19 Centaur
35 Bembo
94 Garamond (Berthold)

f *poor contrast*
114 Century Expanded
119 Century Schoolbook
137 Impressum

f
153 Bauer Bodoni
161 Walbaum (Linotype)
186 Scotch 2 (Linotype)

f
194 ITC Lubalin Graph
196 Memphis
198 Serifa 55

f *low bar*
254 Futura
256 Nobel
257 Spartan

f *higher bar*
267 Univers 55
279 Helvetica
281 Standard

g
44 Trump Mediaeval
71 Olympian
105 Romulus

g
35 Bembo
39 Plantin
93 Garamond 3 (Linotype)

g *poor contrast*
119 Century Schoolbook
121 Ionic 5
137 Impressum

g
153 Bauer Bodoni
156 Didot
174 Caledonia

g
194 ITC Lubalin Graph
196 Memphis
198 Serifa 55

g
267 Univers 55
279 Helvetica
281 Standard

h
39 Plantin
52 Times Roman (Linotype)
67 Imprint

h
19 Centaur
51 Minister
75 Aldus

h *poor contrast*
116 Perpetua
117 Primer
119 Century Schoolbook

h
153 Bauer Bodoni
168 Walbaum (Monotype)
174 Caledonia

h
196 Memphis
197 Rockwell
198 Serifa 55

h
low junction to stem
254 Futura
257 Spartan
258 Cable (Klingspor)

h
higher junction to stem
277 ITC Franklin Gothic
278 Haas Unica
279 Helvetica

i
37 Goudy Old Style
52 Times Roman (Linotype)
69 Old Style No. 2

i
poor contrast
115 Excelsior
119 Century Schoolbook
137 Impressum

i
153 Bauer Bodoni
156 Didot
158 Fairfield

i
193 Glypha 55
198 Serifa
202 Egyptian 202

i
254 Futura
259 Gill Sans
264 Tempo

i
267 Univers 55
279 Helvetica
281 Standard

j
pointed flat short curve
39 Plantin
138 Melior
148 Electra

j
rounded curve with pear
73 Ehrhardt
84 Palatino
105 Romulus

j
wedge ended curve
35 Bembo
52 Times Roman (Linotype)
70 Old Style No 7

j
'ball' terminal
115 Excelsior
119 Century Schoolbook
121 Ionic 5

j
152 Basilia
162 Bodoni 135 (Monotype)
186 Scotch 2 (Linotype)

j
196 Memphis
197 Rockwell
198 Serifa 55

j
rounded curve
253 Erbar
255 Neuzeit-Grotesk
262 ITC Kabel

j
flatter curve
267 Univers 55
279 Helvetica
281 Standard

k
single junction
35 Bembo
52 Times Roman (Linotype)
93 Garamond 3 (Linotype)

k
single junction
39 Plantin
79 Baskerville (Linotype)
116 Perpetua

k
double junction
6 Kennerley
65 Fontana
92 Garamond (Stempel)

k
double junction
71 Olympian
85 Poppl-Pontifex
132 Goudy Modern

k
158 Fairfield
161 Walbaum (Linotype)
168 Walbaum (Monotype)

k
196 Memphis
197 Rockwell
198 Serifa 55

k
single junction
253 Erbar
254 Futura
258 Cable (Klingspor)

k
267 Univers 55
278 Haas Unica
283 Video

k
double junction
273 Akzidenz Grotesk
279 Helvetica
287 News Gothic

l
concave
35 Bembo
52 Times Roman (Linotype)
93 Garamond 3 (Linotype)

l
19 Centaur
51 Minister
75 Aldus

l
116 Perpetua
117 Primer
119 Century Schoolbook

l
153 Bauer Bodoni
156 Didot
158 Fairfield

l
194 ITC Lubalin Graph
196 Memphis
197 Rockwell

l
254 Futura
267 Univers 55
279 Helvetica

m
52 Times Roman (Linotype)
61 Caslon 540
79 Baskerville (Linotype)

m
concave
49 Goudy Catalogue
68 Monticello
91 Garamond 156 (Monotype)

m
19 Centaur
35 Bembo
72 Ronaldson

m
poor contrast
115 Excelsior
119 Century Schoolbook
121 Ionic 5

m
153 Bauer Bodoni
156 Didot
158 Fairfield

m
196 Memphis
197 Rockwell
198 Serifa 55

m
267 Univers 55
279 Helvetica
281 Standard

n
52 Times Roman (Linotype)
61 Caslon 540
79 Baskerville (Linotype)

n
concave
49 Goudy Catalogue
68 Monticello
91 Garamond 156 (Monotype)

n
115 Excelsior
119 Century Schoolbook
121 Ionic 5

n
poor contrast
19 Centaur
35 Bembo
72 Ronaldson

n
153 Bauer Bodoni
156 Didot
158 Fairfield

n
196 Memphis
197 Rockwell
198 Serifa 55

n
267 Univers 55
279 Helvetica
281 Standard

o
19 Centaur
35 Bembo
52 Times Roman (Linotype)

o
69 Old Style No 2
79 Baskerville (Linotype)
88 Sabon

o
poor contrast
115 Excelsior
119 Century Schoolbook
146 Textype

'Common Earmarks'
The 'common earmarks' (or typical identifying features) are indicated either by the general appearance of letters or by 'marked' features. The general 'style' of typefaces with the same 'earmark' may vary. Example typefaces with their specimen numbers are listed against each letter.

'Common Earmarks'

The 'common earmarks' (or typical identifying features) are indicated either by the general appearance of letters or by 'marked' features. The general 'style' of typefaces with the same 'earmark' may vary. Example typefaces with their specimen numbers are listed against each letter.

o
153 Bauer Bodoni
156 Didot
158 Fairfield

o
196 Memphis
197 Rockwell
198 Serifa 55

o *circular (or nearly so)*
254 Futura
257 Spartan
258 Cable (Klingspor)

o
267 Univers 55
279 Helvetica
281 Standard

p
35 Bembo
39 Plantin
61 Caslon 540

p
54 Fry's Baskerville
79 Baskerville (Linotype)
105 Romulus

p *poor contrast*
118 Aurora
119 Century Schoolbook
137 Impressum

p
153 Bauer Bodoni
156 Didot
158 Fairfield

p
196 Memphis
197 Rockwell
198 Serifa 55

p *long descender*
254 Futura
257 Spartan
273 Akzidenz

p *shorter descender*
267 Univers 55
277 ITC Franklin Gothic
279 Helvetica

q
35 Bembo
39 Plantin
61 Caslon 540

q
114 Century Expanded
119 Century Schoolbook
121 Ionic 5

q
153 Bauer Bodoni
156 Didot
158 Fairfield

q
194 ITC Lubalin Graph
197 Rockwell
199 Stymie (ATF)

q *long descender*
254 Futura
257 Spartan
273 Akzidenz Grotesk

q *shorter descender*
267 Univers 55
279 Helvetica
277 ITC Franklin Gothic

r
56 Bookman
88 Sabon
92 Garamond (Stempel)

r
52 Times Roman (Linotype)
92 Spectrum
105 Romulus

r *poor contrast*
115 Excelsior
119 Century Schoolbook
121 Ionic 5

r
153 Bauer Bodoni
161 Walbaum (Linotype)
177 De Vinne

r
196 Memphis
197 Rockwell
198 Serifa 55

r
254 Futura
257 Spartan
259 Gill Sans

r
258 Cable (Klingspor)
261 Grotesque 215
267 Univers 55

s
52 Times Roman (Linotype)
73 Ehrhardt
80 Baskerville No 2

s
39 Plantin
95 ITC Garamond
130 Columbia

s
153 Bauer Bodoni
171 Augustea
172 Bell

s
196 Memphis
197 Rockwell
198 Serifa 55

s *bracketed slab*
207 Consort
209 Clarendon (Linotype)
212 Egizio

s
254 Futura
257 Spartan
281 Standard

s
267 Univers 55
279 Helvetica
281 Standard

t
39 Plantin
52 Times Roman (Linotype)
92 Garamond (Stempel)

t *definite concave head*
35 Bembo
70 Old Style No 7
98 Weiss

t
24 ITC Clearface
84 Palatino
138 Melior

t *poor contrast*
115 Excelsior
119 Century Schoolbook
121 Ionic 5

t
171 Augustea
174 Caledonia
186 Scotch 2 (Linotype)

t
267 Univers 55
277 ITC Franklin Gothic
278 Haas Unica

u
39 Plantin
49 Goudy Catalogue
69 Old Style No 2

u
52 Times Roman (Linotype)
61 Caslon 540
93 Garamond 3 (Linotype)

u *poor contrast*
111 Joanna
119 Century Schoolbook
133 Apollo

u
153 Bauer Bodoni
156 Didot
158 Fairfield

u
188 A & S Gallatin
196 Memphis
197 Rockwell

u
259 Gill Sans
267 Univers 55
279 Helvetica

v
35 Bembo
52 Times Roman (Linotype)
79 Baskerville (Linotype)

v *poor contrast*
115 Excelsior
119 Century Schoolbook
121 Ionic 5

v
153 Bauer Bodoni
158 Fairfield
174 Caledonia

v
194 ITC Lubalin Graph
196 Memphis
197 Rockwell

v
261 Grotesque 215
267 Univers 55
279 Helvetica

'Common Earmarks'
The 'common earmarks' (or typical identifying features) are indicated either by the general appearance of letters or by 'marked' features. The general 'style' of typefaces with the same 'earmark' may vary. Example typefaces with their specimen numbers are listed against each letter.

W — centre strokes meet at centre
35 Bembo
39 Plantin
61 Caslon 540

W — stepped centre strokes
52 Times Roman (Linotype)
73 Ehrhardt
91 Garamond 156 (Monotype)

W — no centre serif
15 Cloister
77 Baskerville (Berthold)
123 Cheltenham

W
188 A & S Gallatin
196 Memphis
197 Rockwell

W
254 Futura
259 Gill Sans
264 Tempo

W
261 Grotesque 215
267 Univers 55
279 Helvetica

X
35 Bembo
78 Baskerville 169 (Monotype)
93 Garamond 3 (Linotype)

X
153 Bauer Bodoni
161 Walbaum (Linotype)
174 Caledonia

X
196 Memphis
197 Rockwell
198 Serifa 55

X — narrow
273 Akzidenz Grotesk
281 Standard
287 News Gothic

X — wider
259 Gill Sans
267 Univers 55
279 Helvetica

y — rounded tail with pear
35 Bembo
52 Times Roman (Linotype)
94 Garamond (Berthold)

y — short tail
25 Lutetia
59 Caslon Old Face No. 2
79 Baskerville (Linotype)

y — rounded tail with ball
114 Century Expanded
119 Century Schoolbook
149 Iridium

y
153 Bauer Bodoni
161 Walbaum (Linotype)
171 Augustea

y
261 Grotesque 215
273 Akzidenz Grotesque
279 Helvetica

z
19 Centaur
69 Old Style No 2
72 Ronaldson

z
52 Times Roman (Linotype)
79 Baskerville (Linotype)
90 Fournier

z
153 Bauer Bodoni
171 Augustea
174 Caledonia

z
193 Glypha 55
196 Memphis
197 Rockwell

z
254 Futura
257 Spartan
259 Gill Sans

z
216 Grotesque 215
267 Univers 55
279 Helvetica

1
52 Times Roman (Linotype)
56 Bookman
73 Ehrhardt

1
35 Bembo
75 Aldus
117 Primer

1 — non-lining
40 Poliphilus
78 Baskerville 169 (Monotype)
91 Garamond 156 (Monotype)

1
153 Bauer Bodoni
161 Walbaum (Linotype)
181 Paganini

1
194 ITC Lubalin Graph
196 Memphis
197 Rockwell

1
253 Erbar
267 Univers 55
277 Franklin Gothic

1 — concave
273 Akzidenz Grotesk
279 Helvetica
281 Standard

2
35 Bembo
52 Times Roman (Linotype)
39 Plantin

2
24 ITC Clearface
119 Century Schoolbook
121 Ionic 5

2 — non-lining
19 Centaur
59 Caslon 128
107 Van Dijck

2
153 Bauer Bodoni
175 ITC Century
176 Century Nova

2
196 Memphis
197 Rockwell
198 Serifa 55

2
254 Futura
259 Gill Sans
264 Tempo

2
267 Univers 55
273 Akzidenz Grotesk
281 Standard

3
39 Plantin
52 Times Roman (Linotype)
67 Imprint

3
24 ITC Clearface
119 Century Schoolbook
146 Textype

3 — non-lining
69 Old Style No 2
91 Garamond 156 (Monotype)
132 Goudy Modern

3
152 Basilia
153 Bauer Bodoni
156 Didot

3
196 Memphis
197 Rockwell
198 Serifa 55

3
258 Cable (Klingspor)
279 ITC Franklin Gothic
287 News Gothic

3
254 Futura
267 Univers 55
279 Helvetica

4
35 Bembo
39 Plantin
52 Times Roman (Linotype)

4
56 Bookman
64 Concorde Nova
86 Times Europa

4
115 Excelsior
119 Century Schoolbook
121 Ionic 5

4 — non-lining
40 Poliphilus
60 Caslon 128
65 Fontana

4
194 ITC Lubalin Graph
197 Rockwell
199 Stymie (ATF)

'Common Earmarks'

The 'common earmarks' (or typical identifying features) are indicated either by the general appearance of letters or by 'marked' features. The general 'style' of typefaces with the same 'earmark' may vary. Example typefaces with their specimen numbers are listed against each letter.

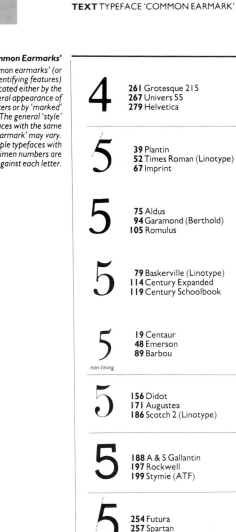

4
261 Grotesque 215
267 Univers 55
279 Helvetica

5
39 Plantin
52 Times Roman (Linotype)
67 Imprint

5
75 Aldus
94 Garamond (Berthold)
105 Romulus

5
79 Baskerville (Linotype)
114 Century Expanded
119 Century Schoolbook

5
19 Centaur
48 Emerson
89 Barbou
non-lining

5
156 Didot
171 Augustea
186 Scotch 2 (Linotype)

5
188 A & S Gallatin
197 Rockwell
199 Stymie (ATF)

5
254 Futura
257 Spartan
260 Granby

5
267 Univers 55
279 Helvetica
281 Standard

6
35 Bembo
39 Plantin
52 Times Roman (Linotype)

6
57 ITC Bookman
119 Century Schoolbook
121 Ionic 5
poor contrast

6
25 Lutetia
65 Fontana
107 Van Dijck
non-lining

6
171 Augustea
174 Caledonia
186 Scotch 2 (Linotype)

6
196 Memphis
197 Rockwell
198 Serifa 55

6
254 Futura
258 Cable (Klingspor)
259 Gill Sans

6
267 Univers 55
279 Helvetica
281 Standard

7
full serif
35 Bembo
39 Plantin
52 Times Roman (Linotype)

7
half serif
61 Caslon 540
67 Imprint
79 Baskerville (Linotype)

7
half serif
118 Aurora
119 Century Schoolbook
145 Primus Antiqua

7
4 Pastonchi
91 Garamond 156 (Monotype)
97 Spectrum
non-lining

7
171 Augustea
175 ITC Century
177 De Vinne

7
188 A & S Gallatin
197 Rockwell
199 Stymie (ATF)

7
curve
207 Consort
209 Clarendon (Linotype)
212 Egizio

7
255 Neuzeit-Grotesk
257 Spartan
260 Granby

7
275 Folio
277 ITC Franklin Gothic
279 Helvetica

8
diagonal crossover
16 Jenson
35 Bembo
39 Plantin

8
bowls touching (no crossover)
80 Baskerville No 2
119 Century Schoolbook
138 Melior

8
non-lining
25 Lutetia
40 Poliphilus
60 Caslon 128

8
174 Caledonia
177 De Vinne
186 Scotch 2 (Linotype)

8
196 Memphis
197 Rockwell
198 Serifa 55

8
narrow
254 Futura
257 Spartan
259 Gill Sans

8
wider
267 Univers 55
279 Helvetica
281 Standard

9
35 Bembo
39 Plantin
52 Times Roman (Linotype)

9
57 ITC Bookman
119 Century Schoolbook
121 Ionic 5

9
non-lining
25 Lutetia
65 Fontana
107 Van Dijck

9
171 Augustea
174 Caledonia
186 Scotch 2 (Linotype)

9
196 Memphis
197 Rockwell
198 Serifa 55

9
254 Futura
258 Cable (Klingspor)
259 Gill Sans

9
267 Univers 55
279 Helvetica
281 Standard

0
35 Bembo
52 Times Roman (Linotype)
77 Baskerville (Berthold)

0
56 Bookman
119 Century Schoolbook
121 Ionic 5
poor contrast

0
69 Old Style No 2
72 Ronaldson
78 Baskerville 169 (Monotype)
non-lining

0
153 Bauer Bodoni
161 Walbaum (Linotype)
174 Caledonia

0
193 Glypha 55
197 Rockwell
188 A & S Gallatin

0
narrow
254 Futura
257 Spartan
262 ITC Kabel

0
wider
277 ITC Franklin Gothic
279 Helvetica
281 Standard

'Special Earmarks'
The 'special earmarks'
(or distinctive identifying
features) are indicated on
each letter. The general
'style' of typefaces with the
same 'earmark' may vary.
The figures refer to
specimen numbers.

For foot serif 'earmarks' of A refer to those of H as they are generally the same. Other 'earmarks' are as follows:

(general)

99, **112**, 123-4, 127 — wide

29, 43, **64**, 93 — narrow

1, 12, **30**, 42 — bowing

(top)

27, 60, 63

35, **38**-41, 61-2, 74, 76, 99, 123-4, 132, 147

36, 46, 126-7, 129

32, 44, 56-7, **71**, 73, 85, 101-2, 106, 121, 125, 128, 136, 138, 141, 145-6

28, 82

51

33

23-4, 27, 59, 66, **72**, 92, 94, 150

110

143

107 — sheared

8, 128

A16 — 1-3, 9, 12, 29, 42, 140, 142

(bar)

6, 14, 20, 47, **65**, 81, 95, 97, 128 — high

12, 29, 36, 78, 98-9, 123-4, **126**-7, 129, 142 — low

74

142

164, **184** — wide

160, 176 — narrow

155

182 — high bar

170, **176**-7, 183 — low bar

189, **194**-5

A27 — half serifs

190, 192

201, 207 — long serifs

220, **225**, 227-8, 236, 238

230

231

223-4, 229, 232, 234-**5** — no serif

226

218-9, **233**, 257 — high bar

239-40 — slightly rounded

221

240 — 'nick' on bar

246, 249, 290, 292 — wide

284-**9** — narrow

269 — bowing

272

296, **299**

256, **258**, 262, 295 — high bar

246, 249, 253, 284-5, 290, 292, 294, 298, 300-1, 303 — low bar

297

296

270

(general)

7, 56-7, 131 — wide

4, 8, **47** — narrow

(top)

B11 — concave

2, 3, 12, **14**, 17, 48-9, 102

B12

26, 40, 42, 108

B13 — squashed

125, 136, 138, 140, 150

113 — concave back

(bar)

B4 — low bar

36, 73, 89

3, **5**, 14, 42 — high bar

2

12-3, 22, **104**

9, **28**, 30, 128

29

73, 147

(serifs)

27, **46**, 56-7, 59, 72, 86, 92, 115, 146 — long

5, 7, 13, 22, 28-30, **82**, 98, 123-4, 126-7, 129 — short

134 — no bottom serif

164, **184** — wide

155, **176** — narrow

NB. *Bold figures indicate the specimen illustrated above.*

107

'Special Earmarks'
The 'special earmarks' (or distinctive identifying features) are indicated on each letter. The general 'style' of typefaces with the same 'earmark' may vary. The figures refer to specimen numbers.

NB. *Bold figures indicate the specimen illustrated above.*

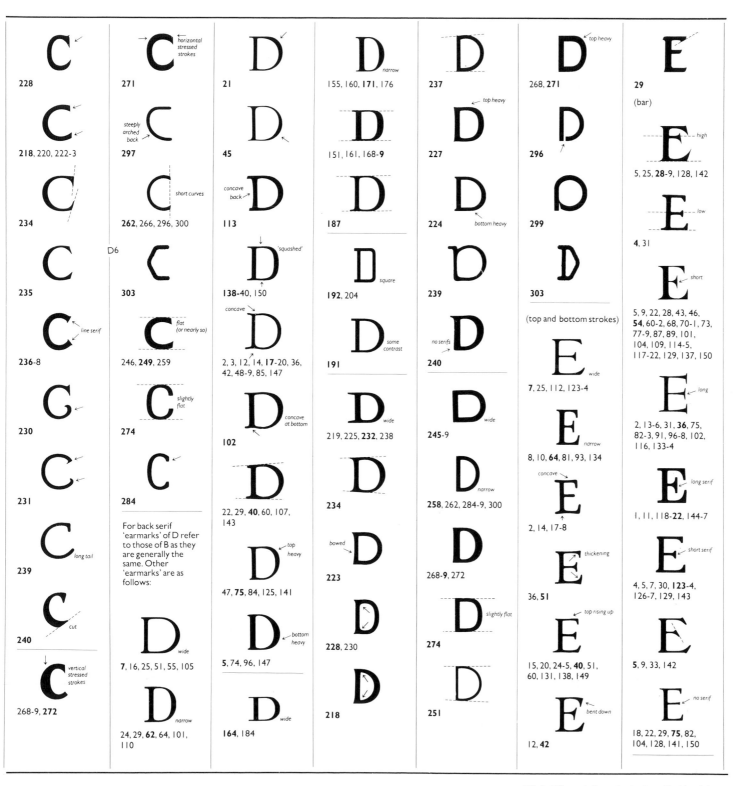

228

271 horizontal stressed strokes

218, 220, 222-3

297 steeply arched back

234 short curves

262, 266, 296, 300

235

D6

303

236-8 line serif

246, **249**, 259 flat (or nearly so)

230

274 slightly flat

231

284

239 long tail

For back serif 'earmarks' of D refer to those of B as they are generally the same. Other 'earmarks' are as follows:

240 cut

268-9, **272** vertical stressed strokes

21

D wide

7, 16, 25, 51, 55, 105

45 concave back

113

D narrow

24, 29, **62**, 64, 101, 110

155, 160, **171**, 176

151, 161, 168-**9**

187

138-40, 150 'squashed'

2, 3, 12, 14, **17**-20, 36, 42, 48-9, 85, 147 concave

102 concave at bottom

22, 29, **40**, 60, 107, 143

47, **75**, 84, 125, 141 top heavy

5, 74, 96, 147 bottom heavy

164, 184 wide

237

227

224

192, 204 square

191 some contrast

219, 225, **232**, 238 wide

234

223 bowed

228, 230

218

268-9, 272

274

251

top heavy

top heavy

bottom heavy

239

240 no serifs

245-9 wide

D narrow

258, 262, 284-9, 300

D slightly flat

268, **271** top heavy

296

299

303

(top and bottom strokes)

7, 25, 112, 123-4 wide

8, 10, **64**, 81, 93, 134 narrow

2, 14, 17-8 concave

36, **51** thickening

15, 20, 24-5, **40**, 51, 60, 131, 138, 149 top rising up

12, **42** bent down

29 (bar)

E high

5, 25, **28**-9, 128, 142 low

4, 31

E short

5, 9, 22, 28, 43, 46, **54**, 60-2, 68, 70-1, 73, 77-9, 87, 89, 101, 104, 109, 114-5, 117-22, 129, 137, 150

E long

2, 13-6, 31, **36**, 75, 82-3, 91, 96-8, 102, 116, 133-4

E long serif

1, 11, 118-**22**, 144-7

E short serif

4, 5, 7, 30, **123**-4, 126-7, 129, 143

5, 9, 33, 142

E no serif

18, 22, 29, **75**, 82, 104, 128, 141, 150

'Special Earmarks'
The 'special earmarks' (or distinctive identifying features) are indicated on each letter. The general 'style' of typefaces with the same 'earmark' may vary. The figures refer to specimen numbers.

NB. *Bold figures indicate the specimen illustrated above.*

'Special Earmarks'
The 'special earmarks' (or distinctive identifying features) are indicated on each letter. The general 'style' of typefaces with the same 'earmark' may vary. The figures refer to specimen numbers.

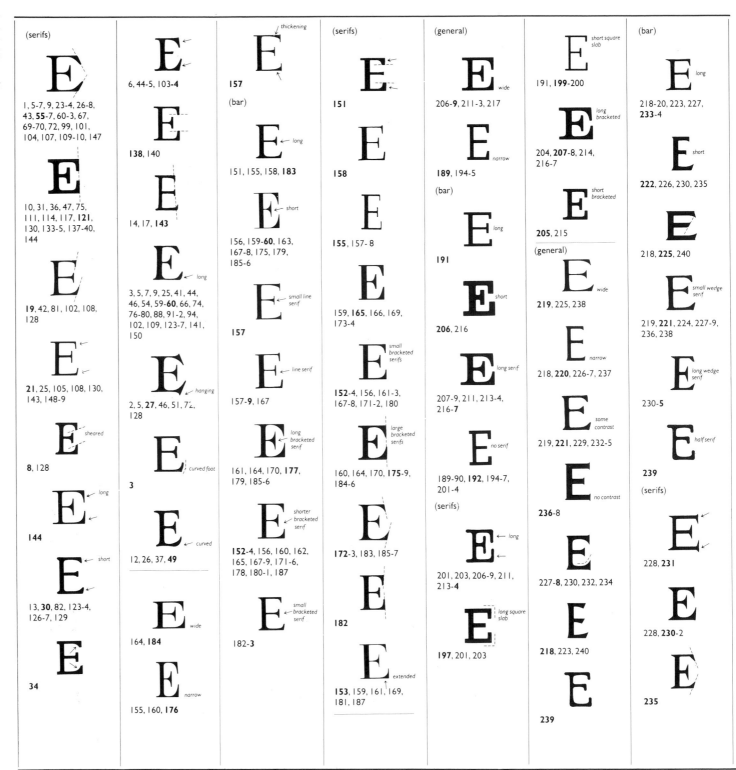

(serifs)

1, 5-7, 9, 23-4, 26-8, 43, **55**-7, 60-3, 67, 69-70, 72, 99, 101, 104, 107, 109-10, 147

10, 31, 36, 47, 75, 111, 114, 117, **121**, 130, 133-5, 137-40, 144

19, 42, 81, 102, 108, 128

21, 25, 105, 108, 130, 143, 148-9

sheared
8, 128

long
144

short
13, **30**, 82, 123-4, 126-7, 129

34

6, 44-5, 103-**4**

138, 140

14, 17, **143**

3, 5, 7, 9, 25, 41, 44, 46, 54, 59-**60**, 66, 74, 76-80, 88, 91-2, 94, 102, 109, 123-7, 141, 150

hanging
2, 5, **27**, 46, 51, 72, 128

curved foot
3

curved
12, 26, 37, **49**

wide
164, **184**

narrow
155, 160, **176**

thickening
157

(bar)

long
151, 155, 158, **183**

short
156, 159-**60**, 163, 167-8, 175, 179, 185-6

small line serif
157

line serif
157-**9**, 167

long bracketed serif
161, 164, 170, **177**, 179, 185-6

shorter bracketed serif
152-4, 156, 160, 162, 165, 167-9, 171-6, 178, 180-1, 187

small bracketed serif
182-**3**

(serifs)

151

158

155, **157**- 8

small bracketed serifs
159, **165**, 166, 169, 173-4

large bracketed serifs
152-4, 156, 161-3, 167-8, 171-2, 180

160, 164, 170, **175**-9, 184-6

172-3, 183, 185-7

182

extended
153, 159, 161, 169, 181, 187

(general)

wide
206-**9**, 211-3, 217

narrow
189, 194-5

(bar)

long
155, 157- 8

191

short
206, 216

long serif
207-9, 211, 213-4, 216-**7**

no serif
189-90, **192**, 194-7, 201-4

(serifs)

long
201, 203, 206-9, 211, 213-4

197, 201, 203

short square slab
191, **199**-200

long bracketed
204, **207**-8, 214, 216-7

short bracketed
205, 215

(general)

wide
219, 225, 238

narrow
218, **220**, 226-7, 237

some contrast
219, **221**, 229, 232-5

no contrast
236-8

227-**8**, 230, 232, 234

long square slab
218, 223, 240

239

(bar)

long
218-20, 223, 227, **233**-4

short
222, 226, 230, 235

218, **225**, 240

small wedge serif
219, **221**, 224, 227-9, 236, 238

long wedge serif
230-5

half serif
239

(serifs)

228, **231**

228, **230**-2

235

218, 222

219-21, 226-**7**, 229, 232-5, 240

226

223, 231, **236**-9

231

(general)

245 8, 290, **292**

vertical stressed strokes

268-9, **272**

horizontal stressed strokes

271

296

299

(bar)

short

247-8, 272, **276**, 286-90, 302-3

251

high

252, 254, **265**, 297-8

low

251, **256**

(top and bottom strokes)

258, **261**-2, 269

rounded

297-**8**, ,301, 303

'Earmarks' for F are generally the same as for E with the following exceptions: (for foot serif 'earmarks' refer to those of I)

lower

75, 136

shorter

189, 197. 203

shorter

226, **231**

longer

303

shorter

245, 247-8, 258, **262**, 280, 290, 293, 304

296, **299**

For top serif 'earmarks' of G refer to those of C as they are generally the same. Other 'earmarks' are as follows:

(general/top)

high arch

23-4, 43, 62 69, 72, 101, 129

28, **40**, 44, 81, 135

arched back

14, 16, 19, **31**, 97, 105, 109, 113

slightly square

138, 140

(bar)

high

1, 3, 9, 13, 15-6, 25, 27, 38-9, 42, **48**, 53, 56, 64, 68, 71, 73, 101, 110, 121, 128, 132, 142

low

14, 17-8, 23-4, 26, 31, 40, 44, 46, 51, 54, 58, 72, 75, 79-81 97-8, 109, 123-4, 126-7, 136, 138, 148

long serif

8, 18, 46, 55, 71, 87, **91**-3, 96, 113, 118-9, 121, 125, 144-5, 150

short serif

1, 4-5, 7, **13**, 24, 28 40, 45, 47, 98

spur

9, **20**, 43, 56-7, 110, 117, 131, 142, 150

15, 18-9, 27, 36-7, 75, 84, 86, 128, **141**

12, 29-31, **123**-4, 126-7, 129, 140, 142

142

concave

14, **17**, 19-20, 81

2, 4, **75**, 84

93, 107

(base)

up

74

spur

32-43, 40, 111

longer spur

114-5, **118**-21, 137, 144-6

2, 6, 27, 36, 54-5, 58, 62, 65, **68**-70, 72, 77-70, 130

117

with 'nib'

5, 28, 40, 44, 83, 98, 123-4, 126, 135-6, 138

12

no 'nib'

14-17, 97, 102, 104-5, 113, 125, 133

141

34, 111

(top)

flat

169

(bar)

high

171-2, 178, 187

low

153-4, 159, 162-3, 174, 185

small gap

177-9

long serif

151, 162-3, 170, 172, **177**-9, 181, 185-7

short serif

176

half serif

155, **182**

(base)

short

153-4, 156, 159, 162-3

152, **156**, 159, 173, 180, 185

'Special Earmarks'
The 'special earmarks' (or distinctive identifying features) are indicated on each letter. The general 'style' of typefaces with the same 'earmark' may vary. The figures refer to specimen numbers.

NB. *Bold figures indicate the specimen illustrated above.*

'Special Earmarks'
The 'special earmarks' (or distinctive identifying features) are indicated on each letter. The general 'style' of typefaces with the same 'earmark' may vary. The figures refer to specimen numbers.

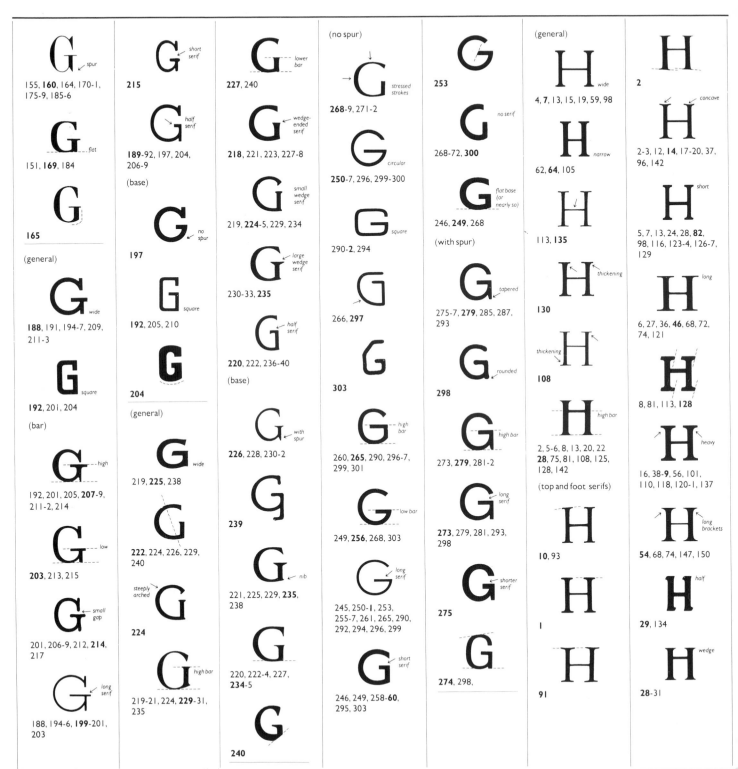

G *spur*
155, **160**, 164, 170-1, 175-9, 185-6

G *flat*
151, **169**, 184

G
165

(general)

G *wide*
188, 191, 194-7, 209, 211-3

G *square*
192, 201, 204

(bar)

G *high*
192, 201, 205, **207**-9, 211-2, 214

G *low*
203, 213, 215

G *small gap*
201, 206-9, 212, **214**, 217

G *long serif*
188, 194-6, **199**-201, 203

G *short serif*
215

G *half serif*
189-92, 197, 204, 206-9

(base)

G *no spur*
197

G *square*
192, 205, 210

G
204

(general)

G *wide*
219, **225**, 238

G
222, 224, 226, 229, 240

G *steeply arched*
224

G *high bar*
219-21, 224, **229**-31, 235

G *lower bar*
227, 240

G *wedge-ended serif*
218, 221, 223, 227-8

G *small wedge serif*
219, **224**-5, 229, 234

G *large wedge serif*
230-33, **235**

G *half serif*
220, 222, 236-40

(base)

G *with spur*
226, 228, 230-2

G
239

G *nib*
221, 225, 229, **235**, 238

G *short serif*
220, 222-4, 227, **234**-5

G
240

(no spur)

G *stressed strokes*
268-9, 271-2

G *circular*
268-72, **300**

G *square*
250-7, 296, 299-300

G
290-2, 294

G
266, **297**

G *high bar*
260, **265**, 290, 296-7, 299, 301

G *low bar*
249, **256**, 268, 303

G *long serif*
245, 250-1, 253, 255-7, 261, 265, 290, 292, 294, 296, 299

G *short serif*
246, 249, 258-**60**, 295, 303

G
253

G *no serif*
268-72, **300**

G *flat base (or nearly so)*
246, **249**, 268

(with spur)

G *tapered*
275-7, **279**, 285, 287, 293

G *rounded*
298

G *high bar*
273, **279**, 281-2

G *long serif*
273, 279, 281, 293, 298

G *shorter serif*
275

G
274, 298,

(general)

H *wide*
4, **7**, 13, 15, 19, 59, 98

H *narrow*
62, **64**, 105

H
113, **135**

H *thickening*
130

H *thickening*
108

H *high bar*
2, 5-6, 8, 13, 20, 22 **28**, 75, 81, 108, 125, 128, 142

(top and foot serifs)

H
10, 93

H
1

H
91

H
2

H *concave*
2-3, 12, **14**, 17-20, 37, 96, 142

H *short*
5, 7, 13, 24, 28, **82**, 98, 116, 123-4, 126-7, 129

H *long*
6, 27, 36, **46**, 68, 72, 74, 121

H
8, 81, 113, **128**

H *heavy*
16, 38-**9**, 56, 101, 110, 118, 120-1, 137

H *long brackets*
54, 68, 74, 147, 150

H *half*
29, 134

H *wedge*
28-31

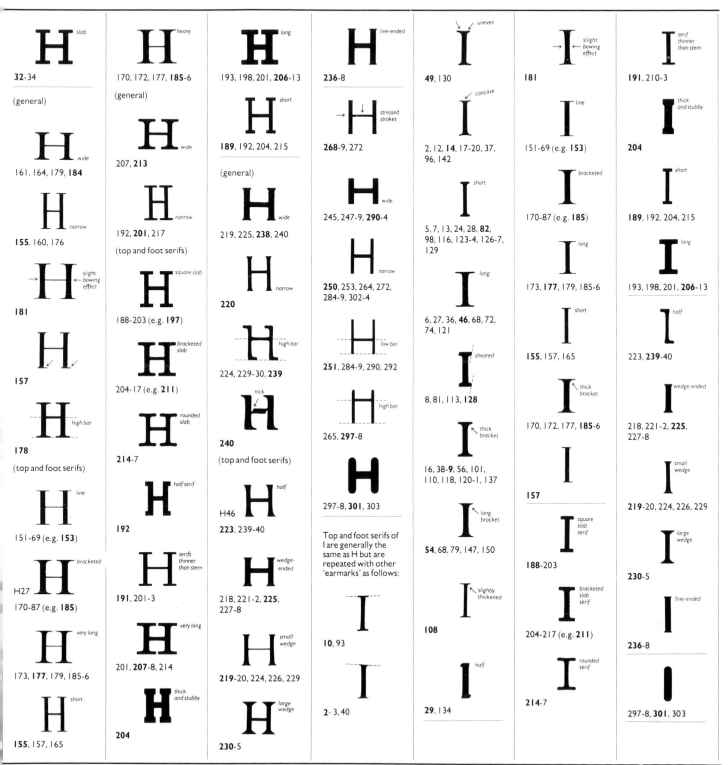

Column 1 (H)

slab
32-34
(general)

wide
161, 164, 179, 184

narrow
155, 160, 176

slight bowing effect
181

157

high bar
178
(top and foot serifs)

line
151-69 (e.g. 153)

bracketed
H27
170-87 (e.g. 185)

very long
173, 177, 179, 185-6

short
155, 157, 165

Column 2 (H)

heavy
170, 172, 177, 185-6
(general)

wide
207, 213

narrow
192, 201, 217
(top and foot serifs)

square slab
188-203 (e.g. 197)

bracketed slab
204-17 (e.g. 211)

rounded slab
214-7

half serif
192

serifs thinner than stem
191, 201-3

very long
201, 207-8, 214

thick and stubby
204

Column 3 (H)

long
193, 198, 201, 206-13

short
189, 192, 204, 215
(general)

wide
219, 225, 238, 240

narrow
220

high bar
224, 229-30, 239

nick
240
(top and foot serifs)

half
H46
223, 239-40

wedge-ended
218, 221-2, 225, 227-8

small wedge
219-20, 224, 226, 229

large wedge
230-5

Column 4 (H)

line-ended
236-8

stressed strokes
268-9, 272

wide
245, 247-9, 290-4

narrow
250, 253, 264, 272, 284-9, 302-4

low bar
251, 284-9, 290, 292

high bar
265, 297-8

297-8, 301, 303

Top and foot serifs of I are generally the same as H but are repeated with other 'earmarks' as follows:

10, 93

2- 3, 40

Column 5 (I)

uneven
49, 130

concave
2, 12, 14, 17-20, 37, 96, 142

short
5, 7, 13, 24, 28, 82, 98, 116, 123-4, 126-7, 129

long
6, 27, 36, 46, 68, 72, 74, 121

sheared
8, 81, 113, 128

thick bracket
16, 38-9, 56, 101, 110, 118, 120-1, 137

long bracket
54, 68, 79, 147, 150

slightly thickened
108

half
29, 134

Column 6 (I)

slight bowing effect
181

line
151-69 (e.g. 153)

bracketed
170-87 (e.g. 185)

long
173, 177, 179, 185-6

short
155, 157, 165

thick bracket
170, 172, 177, 185-6

157

square slab serif
188-203

bracketed slab serif
204-217 (e.g. 211)

rounded serif
214-7

Column 7 (I)

serif thinner than stem
191, 210-3

thick and stubby
204

short
189, 192. 204, 215

long
193, 198, 201, 206-13

half
223, 239-40

wedge-ended
218, 221-2, 225, 227-8

small wedge
219-20, 224, 226, 229

large wedge
230-5

fine-ended
236-8

297-8, 301, 303

'Special Earmarks'

The 'special earmarks' (or distinctive identifying features) are indicated on each letter. The general 'style' of typefaces with the same 'earmark' may vary. The figures refer to specimen numbers.

NB. *Bold figures indicate the specimen illustrated above.*

'Special Earmarks'

The 'special earmarks' (or distinctive identifying features) are indicated on each letter. The general 'style' of typefaces with the same 'earmark' may vary. The figures refer to specimen numbers.

For top serif 'earmarks' of J refer to those of H or I as they are generally the same. Other 'earmarks' are as follows:

(non-lining)

(short tail)

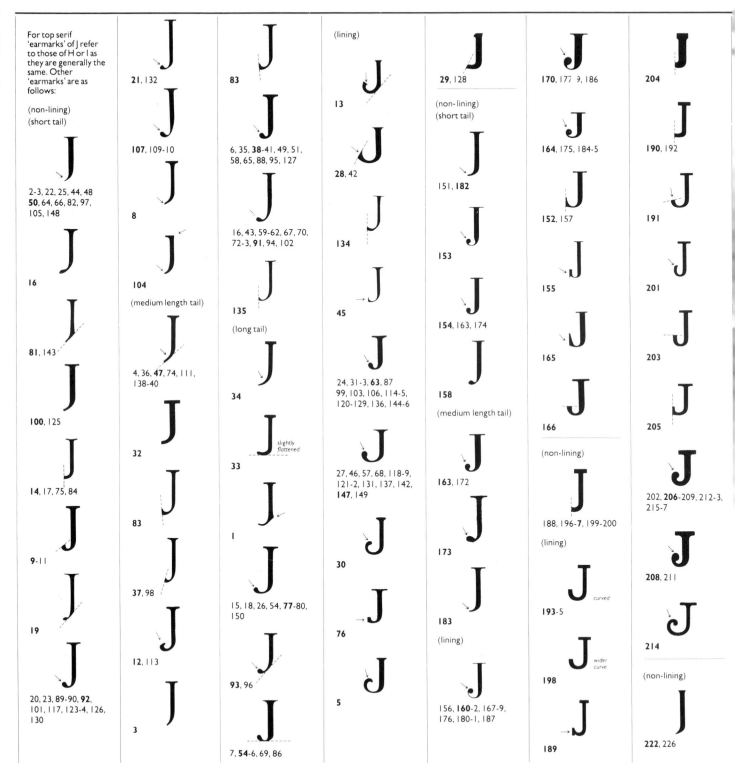

2-3, 22, 25, 44, 48 **50**, 64, 66, 82, 97, 105, 148

16

81, 143

100, 125

14, 17, 75, 84

9-11

19

20, 23, 89-90, **92**, 101, 117, 123-4, 126, 130

21, 132

107, 109-10

8

(medium length tail)

4, 36, **47**, 74, 111, 138-40

32

83

37, 98

12, 113

3

83

6, 35, **38**-41, 49, 51, 58, 65, 88, 95, 127

16, 43, 59-62, 67, 70, 72-3, **91**, 94, 102

135

(long tail)

34

slightly flattened

33

1

15, 18, 26, 54, **77**-80, 150

93, 96

7, **54**-6, 69, 86

(lining)

13

28, 42

134

45

24, 31-3, **63**, 87 99, 103, 106, 114-5, 120-129, 136, 144-6

27, 46, 57, 68, 118-9, 121-2, 131, 137, 142, **147**, 149

30

76

5

29, 128

(non-lining)
(short tail)

151, **182**

152, 157

153

154, 163, 174

158

(medium length tail)

163, 172

173

183

(lining)

156, **160**-2, 167-9, 176, 180-1, 187

170, 177-9, 186

164, 175, 184-5

155

165

166

(non-lining)

188, 196-**7**, 199-200

(lining)

193-5   *curved*

198   *wider curve*

189

204

190, 192

191

201

203

205

202, **206**-209, 212-3, 215-7

208, 211

214

(non-lining)

222, 226

NB. *Bold figures indicate the specimen illustrated above.*

220

229, **235**

221

218, **232**, 240

(lining)

219, **224**, 227, 236, 238

223, **225**, 228, 233

234

237

230

240

(non-lining)

246, **249**

259, 267

(lining)

275

260-1, 265

245, 247-8

250-1, 284, 286, 303
279-80, 283, 284,
286, 303

252, **254**, 257-8, 262,
285, 287-9, 299

253, **256**, ,264, 266,
270, 272-4, 276-8,
281-2, 296, 300

269

271

square
290-4, 303

rounded
297, **301**

255

302

298

For top and foot serif
'earmarks' of K refer
those of H as they are
generally the same.
Other 'earmarks' are
as follows:

(single junction)

14, 17, 50, 74, 91,
100, 104-5, 130

just touching
23, **38**, 58, 84, 86, 88,
106, 116, 133, 148

horizontal bar
18, 35, 44, 64, **67**, 87,
90, 107, 109, 136,
149-50

full serif
4, 16, 25, 31-2, 34, 40,
47, **52**-3, 59-60, 73,
76, 83, 86-7, 90, 93
95-8, 101, 105-7, 109,
111, 123-4, 126-7,
129-30, 149

half serif
6, 37-9, 41, 61, 75, 81,
88, 104, 108, 116,
125, 135, 138-9, 141,
148, 150

half serif
10, **84**

half serifs
19

sheared
29

blob
half serif
3, 12

tapering
2-3, 14-5, 17-8, 33,
74

bowing
11, 91

bowing
8, 19, **68**, 102

bowing
13, **35**, 113, 123-4

36, 134

(double junction)

full serif
5, 9, 30, 51, **54**-6,
62-3, 65-6, 69-70,
77-80, 89, 92, 114-5,
117-22, 131, 137,
144-7

half serif
7, 12, 20-1, 26, 46,
48-9, 71-2, 82, 85, **94**,
99, 112, 132, 140

hybrid serif
45, 143

blob
half serif
142

tapering
110

half serifs
128

43

46

narrow top
77, 92

full serif
5, 23-4, 57, 103

26

bowing
28

30

(single junction)

183

just touching
162-3, 181-2,

horizontal bar
156, 158, 161, 167-8,
187

155

full serif
152-4, 159, **174**,
181-4

narrow
167-8, 187

(double junction)

full serif
160, 164, **166**, 170-1,
173, 175-80, 185-6

half serif
151, 165, 169,

curved foot
157

172

'Special Earmarks'
*The 'special earmarks'
(or distinctive identifying
features) are indicated on
each letter. The general
'style' of typefaces with the
same 'earmark' may vary.
The figures refer to
specimen numbers.*

NB. Bold figures indicate the specimen illustrated above.

'Special Earmarks'
The 'special earmarks' (or distinctive identifying features) are indicated on each letter. The general 'style' of typefaces with the same 'earmark' may vary. The figures refer to specimen numbers.

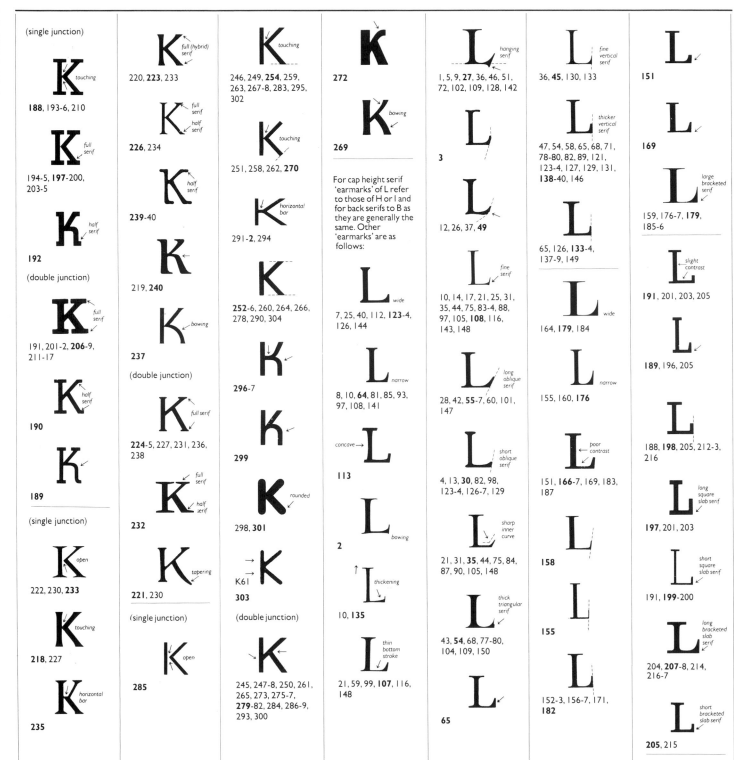

(single junction)

K touching
188, 193-6, 210

K full serif
194-5, **197**-200, 203-5

K half serif
192

(double junction)

K full serif
191, 201-2, **206**-9, 211-17

K half serif
190

K
189

(single junction)

K open
222, 230, **233**

K touching
218, 227

K horizontal bar
235

K full (hybrid) serif
220, **223**, 233

K full serif / half serif
226, 234

K half serif
239-40

K
219, **240**

K bowing
237

(double junction)

K full serif
224-5, 227, 231, 236, 238

K full serif / half serif
232

K tapering
221, 230

(single junction)

K open
285

K touching
246, 249, **254**, 259, 263, 267-8, 283, 295, 302

K touching
251, 258, 262, **270**

K horizontal bar
291-**2**, 294

K
252-6, 260, 264, 266, 278, 290, 304

K
296-7

K
299

K rounded
298, **301**

K K61
303

(double junction)

K
245, 247-8, 250, 261, 265, 273, 275-7, **279**-82, 284, 286-9, 293, 300

K
272

K bowing
269

For cap height serif 'earmarks' of L refer to those of H or I and for back serifs to B as they are generally the same. Other 'earmarks' are as follows:

L wide
7, 25, 40, 112, **123**-4, 126, 144

L narrow
8, 10, **64**, 81, 85, 93, 97, 108, 141

L concave →
113

L
2

L bowing
10, **135**

L thin bottom stroke
21, 59, 99, **107**, 116, 148

L hanging serif
1, 5, 9, **27**, 36, 46, 51, 72, 102, 109, 128, 142

L
3

L
12, 26, 37, **49**

L fine serif
10, 14, 17, 21, 25, 31, 35, 44, 75, 83-4, 88, 97, 105, **108**, 116, 143, 148

L long oblique serif
28, 42, **55**-7, 60, 101, 147

L short oblique serif
4, 13, **30**, 82, 98, 123-4, 126-7, 129

L sharp inner curve
21, 31, **35**, 44, 75, 84, 87, 90, 105, 148

L thick triangular serif
43, **54**, 68, 77-80, 104, 109, 150

L
65

L fine vertical serif
36, **45**, 130, 133

L thicker vertical serif
47, 54, 58, 65, 68, 71, 78-80, 82, 89, 121, 123-4, 127, 129, 131, **138**-40, 146

L
65, 126, **133**-4, 137-9, 149

L wide
164, **179**, 184

L narrow
155, 160, **176**

L poor contrast
151, **166**-7, 169, 183, 187

L
158

L
155

L
152-3, 156-7, 171, **182**

L
151

L
169

L large bracketed serif
159, 176-7, **179**, 185-6

L slight contrast
191, 201, 203, 205

L
189, 196, 205

L
188, **198**, 205, 212-3, 216

L long square slab serif
197, 201, 203

L short square slab serif
191, **199**-200

L long bracketed slab serif
204, **207**-8, 214, 216-7

L short bracketed slab serif
205, 215

NB. Bold figures indicate the specimen illustrated above.

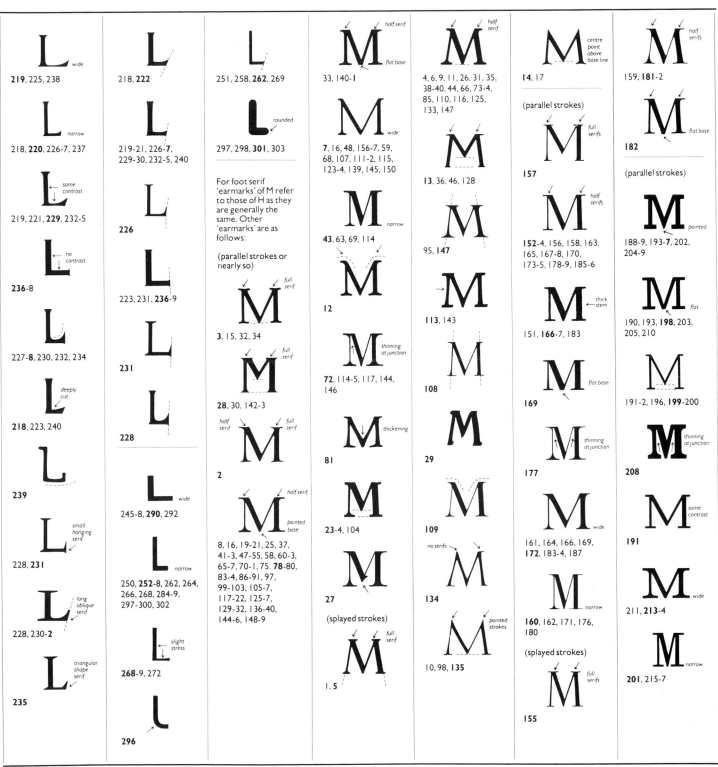

'Special Earmarks'
The 'special earmarks'
(or distinctive identifying
features) are indicated on
each letter. The general
'style' of typefaces with the
same 'earmark' may vary.
The figures refer to
specimen numbers.

L wide
219, 225, 238

L narrow
218, **220**, 226-7, 237

L some contrast
219, 221, **229**, 232-5

L no contrast
236-8

L
227-**8**, 230, 232, 234

L deeply cut
218, 223, 240

L
239

L small hanging serif
228, **231**

L long oblique serif
228, 230-**2**

L triangular shape serif
235

L
218, **222**

L
219-21, 226-**7**, 229-30, 232-5, 240

L
226

L
223, 231, **236**-9

L
231

L
228

L wide
245-8, **290**, 292

L narrow
250, **252**-8, 262, 264, 266, 268, 284-9, 297-300, 302

L slight stress
268-9, 272

L
296

L
251, 258, **262**, 269

L rounded
297, 298, **301**, 303

For foot serif 'earmarks' of M refer to those of H as they are generally the same. Other 'earmarks' are as follows:

(parallel strokes or nearly so)

M full serif
3, 15, 32, 34

M full serif
28, 30, 142-3

M half serif / full serif
2

M half serif / pointed base
8, 16, 19-21, 25, 37, 41-3, 47-55, 58, 60-3, 65-7, 70-1, 75. **78**-80, 83-4, 86-91, 97, 99-103, 105-7, 117-22, 125-7, 129-32, 136-40, 144-6, 148-9

M half serif / flat base
33, 140-**1**

M wide
7, 16, 48, 156-7, 59, 68, 107, 111-2, 115, 123-4, 139, 145, 150

M narrow
43, 63, 69, 114

M
12

M thinning at junction
72, 114-5, 117, 144, 146

M thickening
81

M
23-4, 104

M
27

(splayed strokes)

M full serif
1, **5**

M half serif
4, 6, 9, 11, 26, 31, 35, 38-40, 44, 66, 73-4, 85, 110, 116, 125, 133, 147

M full serifs
13, 36, 46, 128

M
95, **147**

M
113, 143

M
108

M
29

M
109

M
134

M pointed strokes
10, 98, **135**

M centre point above base line
14, 17

(parallel strokes)

M full serifs
157

M half serifs
152-4, 156, 158, 163, 165, 167-8, 170, 173-5, 178-9, 185-6

M thick stem
151, **166**-7, 183

M flat base
169

M thinning at junction
177

M wide
161, 164, 166, 169, **172**, 183-4, 187

M narrow
160, 162, 171, 176, 180

(splayed strokes)

M full serifs
155

M half serifs
159, **181**-2

M flat base
182

(parallel strokes)

M pointed
188-9, 193-**7**, 202, 204-9

M flat
190, 193, **198**, 203, 205, 210

M
191-2, 196, **199**-200

M thinning at junction
208

M some contrast
191

M wide
211, **213**-4

M narrow
201, 215-7

'Special Earmarks'
The 'special earmarks' (or distinctive identifying features) are indicated on each letter. The general 'style' of typefaces with the same 'earmark' may vary. The figures refer to specimen numbers.

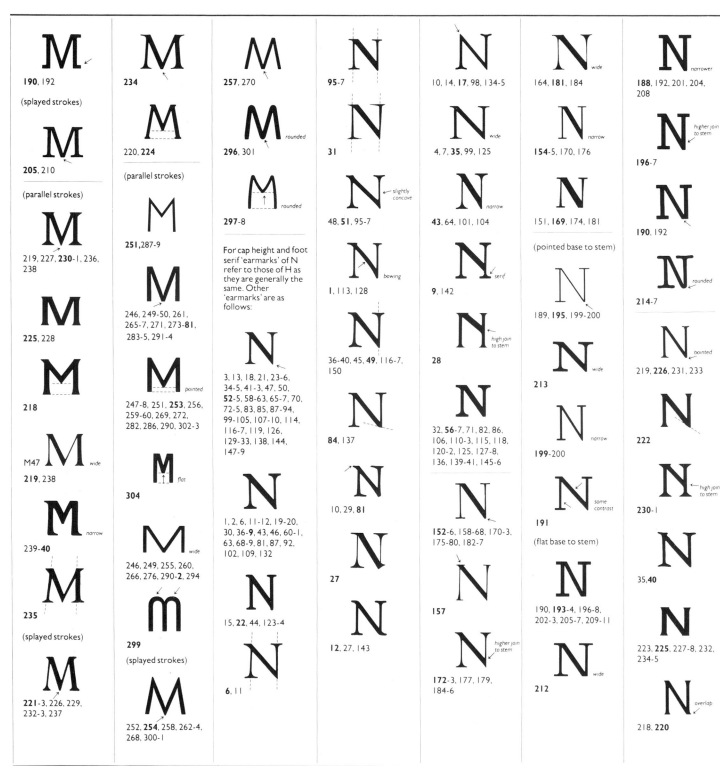

190, 192

(splayed strokes)

205, 210

(parallel strokes)

219, 227, **230**-1, 236, 238

225, 228

218

M47   *wide*
219, 238

narrow
239-**40**

235

(splayed strokes)

221-3, 226, 229, 232-3, 237

234

220, **224**

(parallel strokes)

251, 287-9

246, 249-50, 261, 265-7, 271, 273-**81**, 283-5, 291-4

pointed
247-8, 251, **253**, 256, 259-60, 269, 272, 282, 286, 290, 302-3

flat
304

wide
246, 249, 255, 260, 266, 276, 290-**2**, 294

299

(splayed strokes)

252, **254**, 258, 262-4, 268, 300-1

257, 270

rounded
296, 301

rounded
297-8

For cap height and foot serif 'earmarks' of N refer to those of H as they are generally the same. Other 'earmarks' are as follows:

3, 13, 18, 21, 23-6, 34-5, 41-3, 47, 50, **52**-5, 58-63, 65-7, 70, 72-5, 83, 85, 87-94, 99-105, 107-10, 114, 116-7, 119, 126, 129-33, 138, 144, 147-9

1, 2, 6, 11-12, 19-20, 30, 36-**9**, 43, 46, 60-1, 63, 68-9, 81, 87, 92, 102, 109, 132

15, **22**, 44, 123-4

6, 11

95-7

31

48, **51**, 95-7

bowing
1, 113, 128

36-40, 45, **49**, 116-7, 150

84, 137

10, 29, **81**

27

12, 27, 143

10, 14, **17**, 98, 134-5

wide
4, 7, **35**, 99, 125

slightly concave
43, 64, 101, 104

serif
9, 142

high join to stem
28

32, **56**-7, 71, 82, 86, 106, 110-3, 115, 118, 120-2, 125, 127-8, 136, 139-41, 145-6

152-6, 158-68, 170-3, 175-80, 182-7

higher join to stem
172-3, 177, 179, 184-6

---

wide
164, **181**, 184

narrow
154-5, 170, 176

151, **169**, 174, 181

(pointed base to stem)

189, **195**, 199-200

wide
213

narrow
199-200

some contrast
191

(flat base to stem)

190, **193**-4, 196-8, 202-3, 205-7, 209-11

212

---

narrower
188, 192, 201, 204, 208

higher join to stem
196-7

190, 192

rounded
214-7

pointed
219, **226**, 231, 233

222

high join to stem
230-1

35, **40**

223, **225**, 227-8, 232, 234-5

overlap
218, **220**

NB. *Bold figures indicate the specimen illustrated above.*

'Special Earmarks'

The 'special earmarks' (or distinctive identifying features) are indicated on each letter. The general 'style' of typefaces with the same 'earmark' may vary. The figures refer to specimen numbers.

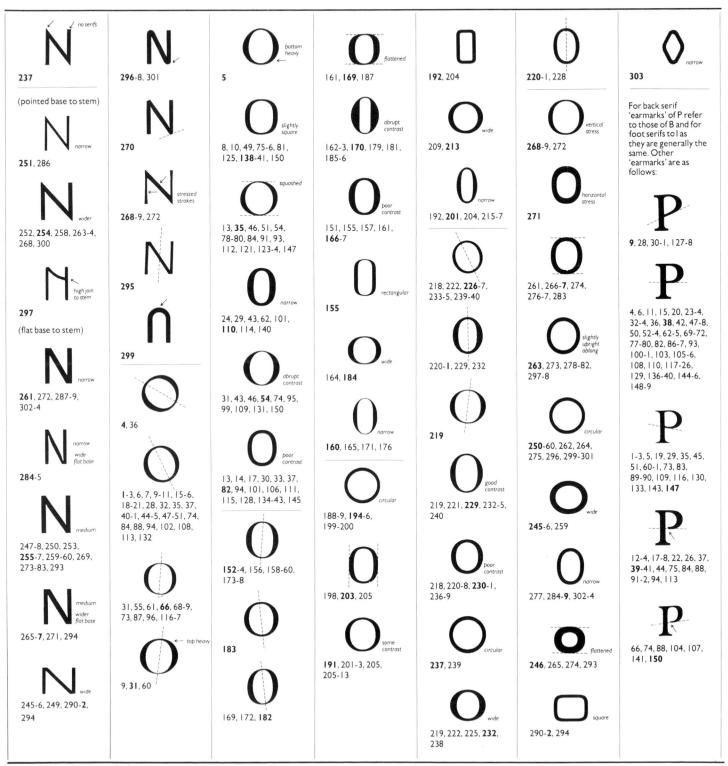

N *no serifs*
237
(pointed base to stem)

N *narrow*
251, 286

N *wider*
252, **254**, 258, 263-4, 268, 300

N *high join to stem*
297
(flat base to stem)

N *narrow*
261, 272, 287-9, 302-4

N *narrow wide flat base*
284-5

N *medium*
247-8, 250, 253, **255**-7, 259-60, 269, 273-83, 293

N *medium wider flat base*
265-**7**, 271, 294

N *wide*
245-6, 249, 290-**2**, 294

N
296-8, 301

N
270

N *stressed strokes*
268-9, 272

N
295

N
299

O
4, 36

O
1-3, 6, 7, 9-11, 15-6, 18-21, 28, 32, 35, 37, 40-1, 44-5, 47-51, 74, 84, 88, 94, 102, 108, 113, 132

O
31, 55, 61, **66**, 68-9, 73, 87, 96, 116-7

O *top heavy*
9, **31**, 60

O *bottom heavy*
5

O *slightly square*
8, 10, 49, 75-6, 81, 125, **138**-41, 150

O *squashed*
13, **35**, 46, 51, 54, 78-80, 84, 91, 93, 112, 121, 123-4, 147

O *narrow*
24, 29, 43, 62, 101, **110**, 114, 140

O *abrupt contrast*
31, 43, 46, **54**, 74, 95, 99, 109, 131, 150

O *poor contrast*
13, 14, 17, 30, 33, 37, **82**, 94, 101, 106, 111, 115, 128, 134-43, 145

O *circular*
152-4, 156, 158-60, 173-8

O
183

O *flattened*
161, **169**, 187

O *abrupt contrast*
162-3, **170**, 179, 181, 185-6

O *poor contrast*
151, 155, 157, 161, **166**-7

O *rectangular*
155

O *wide*
164, **184**

O *narrow*
160, 165, 171, 176

O *circular*
188-9, **194**-6, 199-200

O *some contrast*
191, 201-3, 205, 205-13

O
192, 204

O *wide*
209, **213**

O *narrow*
192, **201**, 204, 215-7

O
218, 222, **226**-7, 233-5, 239-40

O
220-1, 229, 232

O
219

O *good contrast*
219, 221, **229**, 232-5, 240

O *poor contrast*
218, 220-8, **230**-1, 236-9

O *circular*
237, 239

O *wide*
219, 222, 225, **232**, 238

O
220-1, 228

O *vertical stress*
268-9, 272

O *horizontal stress*
271

O
261, 266-**7**, 274, 276-7, 283

O *slightly upright oblong*
263, 273, 278-82, 297-8

O *circular*
250-60, 262, 264, 275, 296, 299-301

O *wide*
245-6, 259

O *narrow*
277, 284-**9**, 302-4

O *flattened*
246, 265, 274, 293

O *square*
290-**2**, 294

O *narrow*
303

For back serif 'earmarks' of P refer to those of B and for foot serifs to I as they are generally the same. Other 'earmarks' are as follows:

P
9, 28, 30-1, 127-8

P
4, 6, 11, 15, 20, 23-4, 32-4, 36, **38**, 42, 47-8, 50, 52-4, 62-5, 69-72, 77-80, 82, 86-7, 93, 100-1, 103, 105-6, 108, 110, 117-26, 129, 136-40, 144-6, 148-9

P
1-3, 5, 19, 29, 35, 45, 51, 60-1, 73, 83, 89-90, 109, 116, 130, 133, 143, **147**

P
12-4, 17-8, 22, 26, 37, **39**-41, 44, 75, 84, 88, 91-2, 94, 113

P
66, 74, 88, 104, 107, 141, **150**

P–Q

'Special Earmarks'
*The 'special earmarks'
(or distinctive identifying
features) are indicated on
each letter. The general
'style' of typefaces with the
same 'earmark' may vary.
The figures refer to
specimen numbers.*

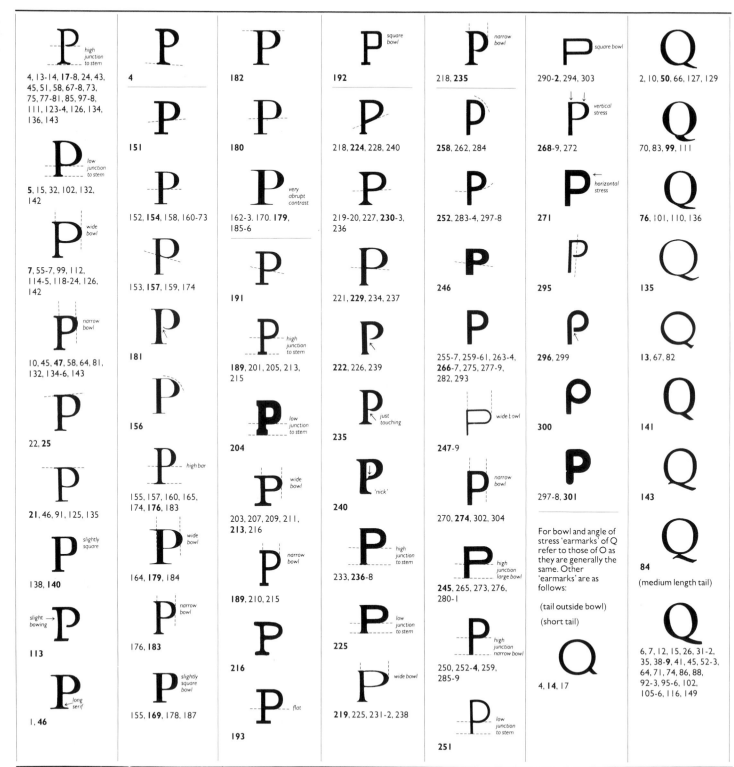

4, 13-14, **17**-8, 24, 43,
45, 51, 58, 67-8, 73,
75, 77-81, 85, 97-8,
111, 123-4, 126, 134,
136, 143

5, 15, 32, 102, 132,
142

7, 55-7, 99, 112,
114-5, 118-24, 126,
142

10, 45, **47**, 58, 64, 81,
132, 134-6, 143

22, **25**

21, 46, 91, 125, 135

138, **140**

113

1, 46

4

151

152, **154**, 158, 160-73

153, **157**, 159, 174

181

156

155, 157, 160, 165,
174, **176**, 183

164, **179**, 184

176, **183**

155, **169**, 178, 187

182

180

162-3, 170, **179**,
185-6

191

189, 201, 205, 213,
215

204

203, 207, 209, 211,
213, 216

189, 210, 215

216

193

192

218, **224**, 228, 240

219-20, 227, **230**-3,
236

221, **229**, 234, 237

222, 226, 239

235

240

233, **236**-8

225

219, 225, 231-2, 238

218, **235**

258, 262, 284

252, 283-4, 297-8

246

255-7, 259-61, 263-4,
266-7, 275, 277-9,
282, 293

247-9

270, **274**, 302, 304

245, 265, 273, 276,
280-1

250, 252-**4**, 259,
285-9

251

290-**2**, 294, 303

268-9, 272

271

295

296, 299

300

297-8, **301**

For bowl and angle of
stress 'earmarks' of Q
refer to those of O as
they are generally the
same. Other
'earmarks' are as
follows:

(tail outside bowl)

(short tail)

4, **14**, 17

2, 10, **50**, 66, 127, 129

70, 83, **99**, 111

76, 101, 110, 136

135

13, 67, 82

141

143

84

(medium length tail)

6, 7, 12, 15, 26, 31-2,
35, 38-**9**, 41, 45, 52-3,
64, 71, 74, 86, 88,
92-3, 95-6, 102,
105-6, 116, 149

NB. Bold figures indicate the specimen illustrated above.

Q

'Special Earmarks'
The 'special earmarks'
(or distinctive identifying
features) are indicated on
each letter. The general
'style' of typefaces with the
same 'earmark' may vary.
The figures refer to
specimen numbers.

42, 47, 90, 103, 109, **123**-4, 126

34, 46, 89, 98, **100**, 112

91

113

11, 29, **37**, 49, 140

27, 150

131

36, 75

43, 69, **72**

22

1, 51

148

8, 81, 130

147

(long tail)

21, 25, 40, **65**, 87, 96, 107

73, **108**, 132

97

94

77-80, 85

(tail extends into bowl)
(short tail)

122

3, 23-4, 142

48

33, 128

5

30

44

104

(medium length tail)

68

114-5, 117-21, 137, 144-6

122

9

28

134

125

138

139

(tail outside bowl)

154, 157

153, 155, 165, 167-8

160

152, 161, **174**-4, 180-1, 187

162-3

159, 166, 173, **183**

156, 187

158

172

169

182

(tail extends into bowl)

151

171

164, 170, **175**-9, 185-6

184

(tail outside bowl)

189, 193, 198, 210

192

201

203-4

197

190

205

206

199-200, 202

(tail extends into bowl)

188, 196

191

194-5

207-**9**, 211-7

(tail outside bowl)

218

226

239

227

220

'Special Earmarks'
The 'special earmarks' (or distinctive identifying features) are indicated on each letter. The general 'style' of typefaces with the same 'earmark' may vary. The figures refer to specimen numbers.

NB. Bold figures indicate the specimen illustrated above.

'Special Earmarks'
*The 'special earmarks'
(or distinctive identifying
features) are indicated on
each letter. The general
'style' of typefaces with the
same 'earmark' may vary.
The figures refer to
specimen numbers.*

(second stem)

half serif
151, 173

straight stem half serif
157

152-155, 158, 161, 172, 174, 180, 182-3, 184, 187

153-4, 156, 159-60, 162-4, 171, 175-6, 181

(bowl)

wide bowl
170, **177**-9, 185-6

194-5

narrow bowl
203

(second stem)

straight
197

curved stem
188, **190**, 192-5, 198, 204

199-200

189, 202-3, **205**, 215-7

201, 206-**209**, 211-214

bowing
216

(bowl)

218

open
222, **226**, 230, 237, 239

'nick'
240

wide
219, 221, 225, **229**, 231-2, 238

narrow
218, **235**

(junctions)

high junction to stem
220

low junction to stem
221, **234**

close to stem
218, **223**

wide apart
219, 225, 238

(second stem)

218, 222-**4**, 226-7

open
219-20, 225, **228**

tapered
221, 229

tapered & curved
236

half serif
224, 226, 231-**3**, 239-40

(junctions)

high
234-5

237

full serif
220, **236**, 238

(bowl)

258, 262

263-4, 269

open
250-1, 295-6

299

wide bowl
250, **271**, 280

narrow bowl
253, 259, 262, 264, 284, 302

(junctions)

high
265, 276, 297, 303

low
251, 298

2nd junction close to stem
252-8, 262, 264, 268, 271-2, 298-301

wide apart
245-8, 261, **267**, 273-5, 278-9, 291-4

(second stem)

245, 247-8, 250, 252-7, 260, 265, 268-9, 272-3, 276-**7** 280-90, 295, 300, 302, 304

251, 258, **270**, 299

301, 304

246, 249, 259, 266-7, 274-5, 278-**9**, 291-4, 296

298

bowing
269, **297**

(general)

vertical stress
268-9, 272

271

296, 299-**300**

(second stem)

For 'earmarks' for
capital S refer to
those of lower case s
as they are generally
the same. Exceptions
are as follows:

(top and bottom serifs)

4

12

13

19

23-**4**, 142

34

horizontal stress

49

90

59-60, 63, **67**, 99

61, 148

123-4, 126, 129

134

143

(top serif only)

29

15, 40

86-7

'Special Earmarks'
The 'special earmarks' (or distinctive identifying features) are indicated on each letter. The general 'style' of typefaces with the same 'earmark' may vary. The figures refer to specimen numbers.

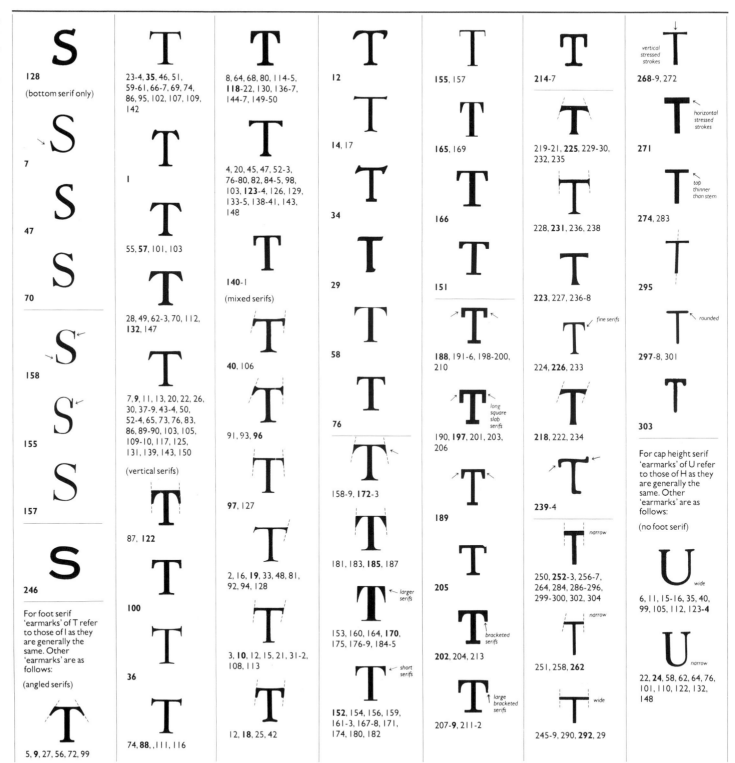

128

(bottom serif only)

7

47

70

158

155

157

246

For foot serif 'earmarks' of T refer to those of I as they are generally the same. Other 'earmarks' are as follows:

(angled serifs)

5, **9**, 27, 56, 72, 99

23-4, **35**, 46, 51, 59-61, 66-7, 69, 74, 86, 95, 102, 107, 109, 142

I

55, **57**, 101, 103

28, 49, 62-3, 70, 112, **132**, 147

7, **9**, 11, 13, 20, 22, 26, 30, 37-9, 43-4, 50, 52-4, 65, 73, 76, 83, 86, 89-90, 103, 105, 109-10, 117, 125, 131, 139, 143, 150

(vertical serifs)

87, **122**

100

36

74, **88**, ,111, 116

8, 64, 68, 80, 114-5, **118**-22, 130, 136-7, 144-7, 149-50

4, 20, 45, 47, 52-3, 76-80, 82, 84-5, 98, 103, **123**-4, 126, 129, 133-5, 138-41, 143, 148

140-1

(mixed serifs)

40, 106

91, 93, **96**

97, 127

2, 16, **19**, 33, 48, 81, 92, 94, 128

3, **10**, 12, 15, 21, 31-2, 108, 113

12

14, 17

34

29

58

76

158-9, **172**-3

181, 183, **185**, 187

153, 160, 164, **170**, 175, 176-9, 184-5

larger serifs

short serifs

large bracketed serifs

152, 154, 156, 159, 161-3, 167-8, 171, 174, 180, 182

155, 157

165, 169

166

151

188, 191-6, 198-200, 210

190, **197**, 201, 203, 206

189

205

202, 204, 213

207-**9**, 211-2

214-7

219-21, **225**, 229-30, 232, 235

228, **231**, 236, 238

223, 227, 236-8

fine serifs

224, **226**, 233

long square slab serifs

218, 222, 234

239-4

narrow

250, **252**-3, 256-7, 264, 284, 286-296, 299-300, 302, 304

narrow

251, 258, **262**

wide

245-9, 290, **292**, 29

---

vertical stressed strokes

268-9, 272

horizontal stressed strokes

271

top thinner than stem

274, 283

295

rounded

297-8, 301

303

For cap height serif 'earmarks' of U refer to those of H as they are generally the same. Other 'earmarks' are as follows:

(no foot serif)

wide

6, 11, 15-16, 35, 40, 99, 105, 112, 123-**4**

narrow

22, **24**, 58, 62, 64, 76, 101, 110, 122, 132, 148

NB. *Bold figures indicate the specimen illustrated above.*

'Special Earmarks'
The 'special earmarks' (or distinctive identifying features) are indicated on each letter. The general 'style' of typefaces with the same 'earmark' may vary. The figures refer to specimen numbers.

long serifs
27, **46**, 56, 65, 71, 74, 101, 114, 121

short serifs
7, 13, 30, 37, 45, 82, 98, 108, 123-4, 126-7, 129-30, 148

good contrast
21, 27, 31, 43, 54, **58**, 60, 95, 99, 131

poor contrast
4, 8, 13-14, 17-18, 22, **26**, 28, 30-4, 44, 56-7, 71, 106, 110, 113, 115, 127-8, 133, 137, 141, 145-6

no contrast
13, 32-4, 82

68, 71, 73

slightly flattened base
11, 19, **40**, 57, 105, 132, 138, 140

thicker stem
111

thickening
2

thickening
113, 134-5, 150

sheared
8, **128**

147

59-**60**, 102, 104, 107-8

14, **17**, 19, 31, 87

5, 9, 28, 46

bowing
28, **30**, 134

(with foot serif)

full
1, 25

half
48, 81, 116

3

high join to stem
10, 98

143

wide
161, 164, **184**

narrow
154, **160**, 165, 170-1, 176, 182

long serifs
177-9

short serifs
155, 157, **180**

poor contrast
151, 183

abrupt contrast
162-3, **170**, 179, 185-6

thickening
157

flattened base
161, 167-8, **182**, 187

158

thicker second stem
183

slight bowing
181

155

wide
213

narrow
192, **194**-5, 201, 203-4, 215, 217

long serifs
201, 206-9, 211, 213-4, 217

shorter serifs
189, **203**-4, 215

some contrast
201, 207, **209**, 211-3

poor contrast
188

very
189, 191, 201-3, **207**-13

half serif
216

192

204

218, 220, 223, 225, **227**-8

219, **221**, 224, 226, 229

wide
219, 225, 238

narrow
220, 226, 228, 237, 239

some contrast
219, 221, 229, 232-**3**, 235

long serifs
230, **232**

thicker second stem
231

223

slightly flattened base
219

240

218

222

224

239

wide
245-8, 290-2, 294

narrow
250, 252-3, 262, 272, 284-9, 296, 299-300, 302, 304

slightly flattened base
245, **265**, 274, 283, 291, 293

290, **292**, 294, 303

269, **297**

thicker stem
276-**7**

vertical stress
268-9, 272

horizontal stress
271

295

298, **301**

258, 298

'Special Earmarks'
The 'special earmarks' (or distinctive identifying features) are indicated on each letter. The general 'style' of typefaces with the same 'earmark' may vary. The figures refer to specimen numbers.

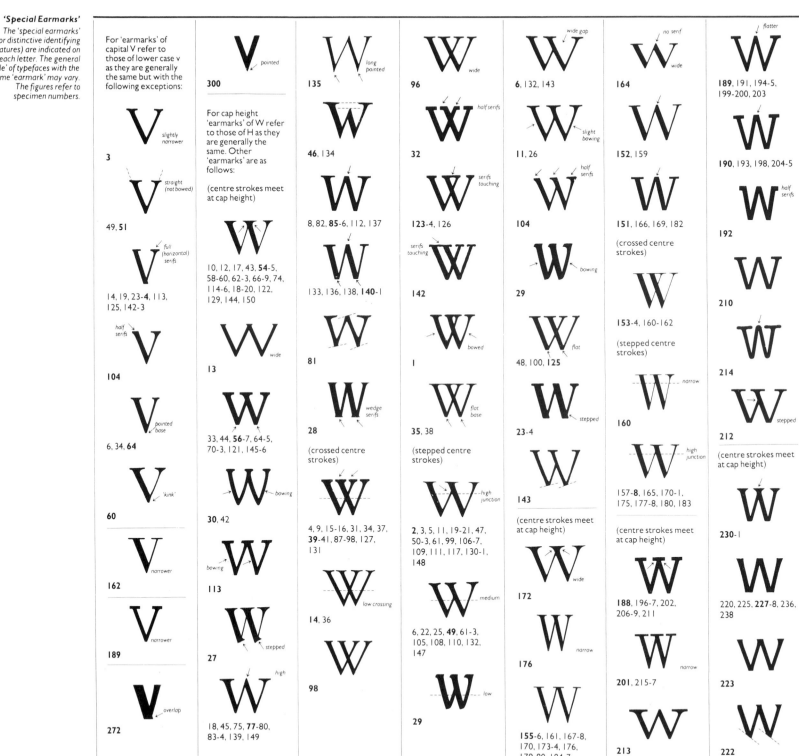

For 'earmarks' of capital V refer to those of lower case v as they are generally the same but with the following exceptions:

3 slightly narrower

49, 51 straight (not bowed)

14, 19, 23-4, 113, 125, 142-3 full (horizontal) serifs

104 half serifs

6, 34, 64 pointed base

60 'kink'

162 narrower

189 narrower

272 overlap

For cap height 'earmarks' of W refer to those of H as they are generally the same. Other 'earmarks' are as follows:

(centre strokes meet at cap height)

10, 12, 17, 43, 54-5, 58-60, 62-3, 66-9, 74, 114-6, 18-20, 122, 129, 144, 150

13 wide

33, 44, 56-7, 64-5, 70-3, 121, 145-6

30, 42 bowing

113 bowing

27 stepped

18, 45, 75, 77-80, 83-4, 139, 149 high

300 pointed

135 long pointed

46, 134

8, 82, 85-6, 112, 137

133, 136, 138, 140-1

81 wide

28 wedge serifs

(crossed centre strokes)

4, 9, 15-16, 31, 34, 37, 39-41, 87-98, 127, 131

14, 36 low crossing

98

96 wide

32 half serifs

123-4, 126 serifs touching

142 serifs touching

1 bowed

35, 38 flat base

(stepped centre strokes)

23-4 high junction

143

(centre strokes meet at cap height)

2, 3, 5, 11, 19-21, 47, 50-3, 61, 99, 106-7, 109, 111, 117, 130-1, 148 wide

6, 22, 25, 49, 61-3, 105, 108, 110, 132, 147 medium

29 low

6, 132, 143 wide gap

11, 26 slight bowing

104 half serifs

29 bowing

48, 100, 125 flat

160 narrow

157-8, 165, 170-1, 175, 177-8, 180, 183 high junction

(centre strokes meet at cap height)

172 wide

176 narrow

155-6, 161, 167-8, 170, 173-4, 176, 179-80, 184-7

164 no serif

152, 159

151, 166, 169, 182

(crossed centre strokes)

153-4, 160-162

(stepped centre strokes)

188, 196-7, 202, 206-9, 211

201, 215-7 narrow

213

189, 191, 194-5, 199-200, 203 flatter

190, 193, 198, 204-5

192 half serifs

210

214

212 stepped

(centre strokes meet at cap height)

230-1

220, 225, 227-8, 236, 238

223

222

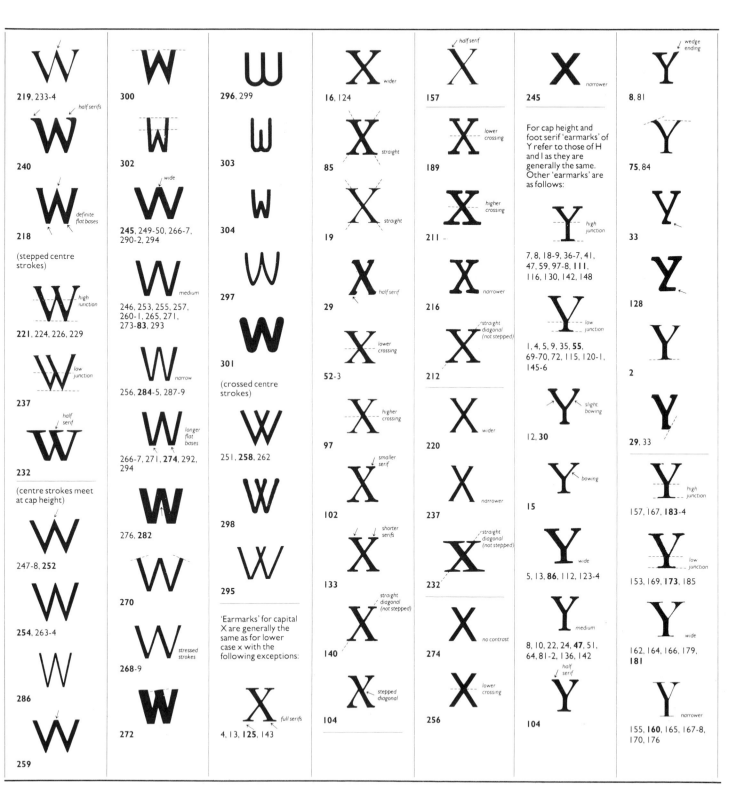

219, 233-4

300

296, 299

16, 124

157

245

8, 81

240

302

303

85

189

75, 84

218

definite flat bases

245, 249-50, 266-7, 290-2, 294

304

19

211 –

For cap height and foot serif 'earmarks' of Y refer to those of H and I as they are generally the same. Other 'earmarks' are as follows:

33

(stepped centre strokes)

246, 253, 255, 257, 260-1, 265, 271, 273-**83**, 293

297

29

216

7, 8, 18-9, 36-7, 41, 47, 59, 97-8, **111**, 116, 130, 142, 148

128

221, 224, 226, 229

256, **284**-5, 287-9

301

52-3

212

1, 4, 5, 9, 35, **55**, 69-70, 72, 115, 120-1, 145-6

2

237

266-7, 271, **274**, 292, 294

(crossed centre strokes)

97

220

12, **30**

29, 33

232

251, **258**, 262

102

237

15

157, 167, **183**-4

(centre strokes meet at cap height)

276, **282**

298

133

232

5, 13, **86**, 112, 123-4

153, 169, **173**, 185

247-8, **252**

270

295

140

274

8, 10, 22, 24, **47**, 51, 64, 81-2, 136, 142

162, 164, 166, 179, **181**

254, 263-4

268-9

'Earmarks' for capital X are generally the same as for lower case x with the following exceptions:

104

256

104

155, **160**, 165, 167-8, 170, 176

286

272

4, 13, **125**, 143

259

'Special Earmarks'
The 'special earmarks' (or distinctive identifying features) are indicated on each letter. The general 'style' of typefaces with the same 'earmark' may vary. The figures refer to specimen numbers.

'Special Earmarks'
The 'special earmarks' (or distinctive identifying features) are indicated on each letter. The general 'style' of typefaces with the same 'earmark' may vary. The figures refer to specimen numbers.

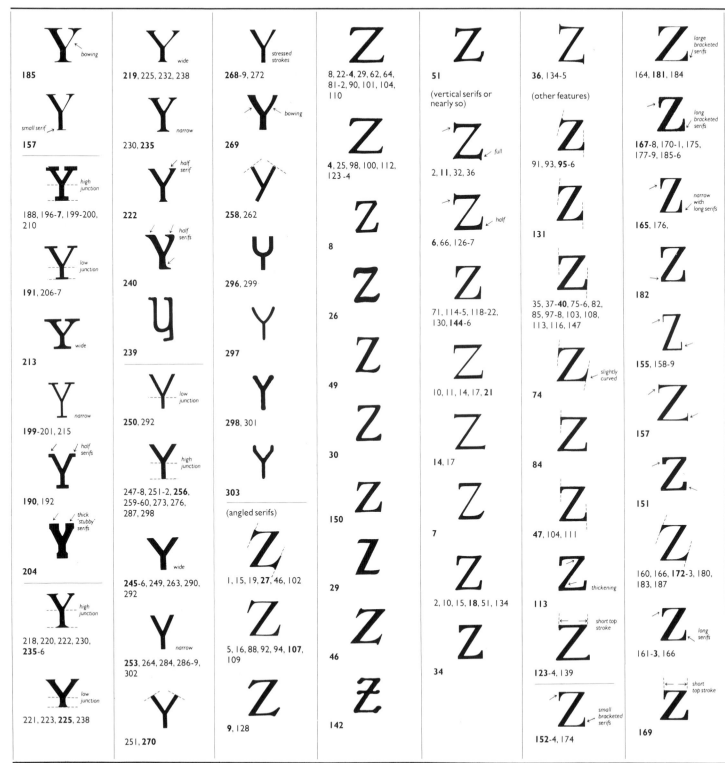

Y bowing
185

Y small serif
157

Y high junction
188, 196-**7**, 199-200, 210

Y low junction
191, 206-7

Y wide
213

Y narrow
199-201, 215

Y half serifs
190, 192

Y thick 'stubby' serifs
204

Y high junction
218, 220, 222, 230, **235-6**

Y low junction
221, 223, **225**, 238

Y wide
219, 225, 232, 238

Y narrow
230, **235**

Y half serif
222

Y half serifs
240

Y
239

Y low junction
250, 292

Y high junction
247-8, 251-2, **256**, 259-60, 273, 276, 287, 298

Y wide
245-6, 249, 263, 290, 292

Y narrow
253, 264, 284, 286-9, 302

Y
251, **270**

Y stressed strokes
268-9, 272

Y bowing
269

Y
258, 262

Y
296, 299

Y
297

Y
298, 301

Y
303

(angled serifs)

Z
1, 15, 19, **27**, 46, 102

Z
5, 16, 88, 92, 94, **107**, 109

Z
9, 128

Z
8, 22-**4**, 29, 62, 64, 81-2, 90, 101, 104, 110

Z
4, 25, 98, 100, 112, 123-4

Z
8

Z
26

Z
49

Z
30

Z
150

Z
29

Z
46

Z
142

Z
51

(vertical serifs or nearly so)

Z full
2, **11**, 32, 36

Z half
6, 66, 126-7

Z
71, 114-5, 118-22, 130, **144**-6

Z
10, 11, 14, 17, **21**

Z
14, 17

Z
7

Z
2, 10, 15, **18**, 51, 134

Z
34

Z
36, 134-5

(other features)

Z
91, 93, **95**-6

Z
131

Z
35, 37-**40**, 75-6, 82, 85, 97-8, 103, 108, 113, 116, 147

Z slightly curved
74

Z
84

Z thickening
47, 104, 111

Z short top stroke
123-4, 139

Z small bracketed serifs
152-4, 174

Z large bracketed serifs
164, **181**, 184

Z long bracketed serifs
167-8, 170-1, 175, 177-9, 185-6

Z narrow with long serifs
165, 176,

Z
182

Z
155, 158-9

Z
157

Z
151

Z
160, 166, **172**-3, 180, 183, 187

Z long serifs
161-3, 166

Z short top stroke
169

'Special Earmarks'
The 'special earmarks'
(or distinctive identifying
features) are indicated on
each letter. The general
'style' of typefaces with the
same 'earmark' may vary.
The figures refer to
specimen numbers.

Z *slightly extended bottom* **187**	Z **230, 233**	*curved* Z **269**, 297	& **50**, 52-3, 76, 101, 107, 112, 114, 119-22, 129, 131	& **125**	& 6, **150**	& 156, 164, 167, 170, **173**, 186
Z **189**, 210	Z *no contrast* **236**-8	Z **296**, 299	& 68	& 5	& 2, **108**	& 161, 166, 170-1, **175**-80, 185, 187
Z 191, **207**-9	Z *full serif* **231**	(closed bowls) & 96	& 58, 62, 69, **79**	& **21**, **23**-4, 49, 51, 132	& 3	& 153, **160**
Z *short serifs* **194**-5	Z *wide top stroke* **232**	& 1, 12, 19-20, 27, 42, 45-6, 57, 71, 89-90, **97**-8, 105, 126, 133, 138, 147, 149	& 56	& 22, **37**, 140	& 4	& 169
Z *longer serifs* **201**, 203, 207-8, 214	Z **239**	& **64**, 100	& 142	& 29, **32**	& 134	& **158**, 172
Z **218**, 220, 225	Z 245, **251**-9, 262-4, 300, 302	& 113	& 10, **74**-5, 116, 139, 147	& 9	& 135	& *open* 157
Z **223**, 227	Z 253	& 127	& 141	& 104, 110	& 13	& **189**, 193, 196, 198
Z 228	Z 248, 270	& 44	& 14, 17-8, ,33, 77	& 8, 81	& 143	& 197
Z *wedge serifs* **219**, 221, 226, 229, 232, 234-5, 240	Z *stressed strokes* **268**	& 1	& 82	**&** 128	& 151-2, **159**, 165, 174, 184-4	& 191
Z 224	Z **298**, 301, 303	& 123-4, 126	& 2	& 36, 130	**&** 154, **162**-3. 165, 181-2	& 190

129

201, **206**-9, 211-3

222

224, 237

261, 265, 276-**8**, 285-9

292, 294

wedge — 49, 74, 112

thick wedge — 18, 76, 140-1

215-6

231-2

226

269

257

wedge — 9, 13, 26, 147

thick wedge — 42, 128

(bowl)

194-5

218

223

299

wedge — 38-9, 41, **75**, 83

188, 192, 199-200, 202

236, 238

273, 280-2, 295

300

pear — 4, **6**, 11, 20, 31, 43, 46, 51, 54, 55-67, 69-70, 72, 89-90, 95-7, 102, 107, 110, 129-30, 132, 139

large — 1, 30, 33, 129, 135

203

228

227

245

(top terminal)

small and angular — 10, 16, 19, 74, 87, 92, 94, 102

214

220, 240

252, 256-7

297

thin point — 1, **2**, 5, 12, 111, 113, 116, 133-4

vertical pear — 7, 37, 52-3, 100, 103, 106, 109, 117, 123-6, 149-50

31, 32, 35, 40, 66, 73, 83, 91-2, 94-6, 105, 109, 111, 148

204

221

255, 263, 268

247-8, 253

thick point — 22, **30**, 34, 36, 40, 48

pear — 23-4

5, 29, 36, 134, 141-2

205, 210

239

271

272

32, 85

thinner pear — 47, 91, 93, 105

15, 27, 30, **56**, ,82, 112, 115, 130, 135, 138, 144-7, 149

235

230

250, 254, 264, 270

296

81

angular — 10, 16, 19, 21, 35, 44-5, 88, 92, 94, 108, 143, 148

smooth — 54, 131, 137, 150

219

225

262

291

29, **82**

large ball — 68, 71, 99, 114-5, 118-22, 131, 136-7, 144-5

22, **104**, 128

wedge — 3, 14, 17, 28, 98, 104, 128, 135

NB. *Bold figures indicate the specimen illustrated above.*

'Special Earmarks'
*The 'special earmarks'
(or distinctive identifying
features) are indicated on
each letter. The general
'style' of typefaces with the
same 'earmark' may vary.
The figures refer to
specimen numbers.*

(back)

5, 13, 104, 123-4, 129

23-4, 29-30

40, **44**, 47, 73, 87, 91-6

wide opening
8, **14**, 17, 23-4, 48, 77-81, 98, 135, 143

(foot serif)

thin
1, 75, 84, 125, 131, 134-5

thicker
81, 113, **133**, 136, 138, 140-3, 150

short and thick
8, 12, 22, 29-30, 56, 71, 82, 104, 112, 126, 128

pointed
28

short
2-3, 10, 15, 37, 45, 47, 66, 76, 98, 102, 108, 142, 148

short and heavy
44

longer
19, 42, 97, 108, 147

14, 17-8, 21, 37, 46, 111, 129

short and rounded
4, 7, 15, 23-4, 26, 32-3, 38-9, 41, 48, 50-2, 60-4, 66-8, 74, 78, 89-90, 100, 106, 115, 118-9, 120, 124, 128, 130, 139, 144, 146

long and rounded
5, **6**, 9, 11, 13, 16, 20, 25, 27, 31, 34-6, 43, 53-4, 65, 69-70, 72, 77-80, 83, 85, 91-2, 99, 101, 103, 107, 109-10, 114, 117, 121, 127, 132, 149

35-6, **40**, 42, 49, 55, 58-9, 73, 76, 83, 87-8, 93-7, 105, 115-6

86, 122

long curled up
70, 78, 114, **137**

(top terminal)
151, 182

157, **165**

155, **166**

ball
160, 162-4, 170-1, 175-81, 184-6

pear
152-4, **156**, 167-9, 172-4

thin pear
158-9, 161, **172**, 187

pointed
183

(bowl)
155, **157**, 159

153, 161-3, 187

smooth
156, 160, 164, 169, 178-81

(foot serif)

angled and flat
151-2, 155, 165, **183**

161, 167-8, 171, 180, 182, 187

158

curled up
160, 164, 170, 173, 175-9, **185**-6

(double storey)
188-9, 191, 197, 203

190, 204, 206-9, 211

192, **198**, 201-2, 205, 210, 215

212-4, 216-7

189, 204-5

188, 191

188-**93**, 197-8, 203-5

201, 206-9, 211-5, 217

(single storey)
194-6

(double storey)
199-200

wide
219, 225

218, 222, 225, 235, 240

227, 231

223-4, 226, 228, 234

pear
229, 232

curl
230

231

pointed
233

smooth
222, **226**, 228, 230

239

(single storey)

237

(double storey)
291-2, 297

curl
284

square

245-6, **249**, 251, 253, 256, 261, 264-5, 270, 282, 285-9

259, 262, 266, 268-9, 271-2, 295

267, 273-81, 283, 291-3, 304

284

251, **253**, 262, 264

smooth
245, **261**, 265, 268, 271, 275, 279, 295

large top
271

small top
270

259, **270**

NB. Bold figures indicate the specimen illustrated above.

a–c

'Special Earmarks'
The 'special earmarks' (or distinctive identifying features) are indicated on each letter. The general 'style' of typefaces with the same 'earmark' may vary. The figures refer to specimen numbers.

245, 261, **265**, ,268, 273, 279-81, 283, 285, 293

246, 249, 251, 278, **282**, 286

253, 256, 260, 262, 264, 266, 269, 271-2, **277**-8, 284, 287-9, 291-2, 295, 297-8, 304

272, **274**-6, 286-9

(single storey)

250, 252, 254-5, 257

301

263

299

296

flat

300

Ascender serif 'earmarks' for b, d, h, k and l are all generally the same. Typefaces with slight variations between these letters are numbers 40, 60, 68, 93, 96, 110, 115, 141, 143, 177, 182, 208, 211-3 and 215. 'Earmarks' are as follows:

(ascender serif)

1, 36

concave

51

hammer

12, 30, **48**, 82

14, **17**, 33-4

short

13, 15, 66

4, 32, **60**, 92, 110

40

29, 113, 128

142

(bowl)

top heavy

1, 8, 14, 18, 41-3, 47, 52-3, **71**, 75, 84, 88, 100, 102, 104, 106, 110, 125, 133

5

bottom heavy

sheared

10, **44**, 75, 141

22, 44, **104**

parallel

28, **105**, 148

14, 17, **82**, 84-5

small bowl

15, 34, **36**, 46, 123

large bowl

28-9, **57**, 71, 104, 110, 112, 118, 121, 141

(foot serif)

1, 4, **28**

3, 22, 128

concave

12, 19, 20, **51**, 110

36, 58, 89-**90**, 131-2, 141, 149

long

23-4, **42**, 51, 114-5, 118-21

140

13

8, **81**, 102, 104, 111, 116, 148

203, 215

17-8, 30, 113, 134-**5**, 142-3

curved in

157

151, 166-8

157, 159

183

181

201, **214**, 217

narrow

201

circular bowl

188-9, 194-200, 212-3, 215

square

192

218, 227-9

wedge serif

219, 221, **226**, 235

large serif

220, 223-5, 230

232, 240

218, **235**, 240

222, 239

bent foot

219-20, 225

235

251, 259, 269, 297

263, 298

258, 262, 296, 299-300

296, 299

small bowl

253, 256, 258, 264

(top terminal)

23, 58, **114**-5, 118-21, 131, 144-6, 149

big pear

7, 18, 23-4, 27, 38-9, 50, 52-4, 57-8, 60-5, 67, 71, 91, **99**-100, 103, 106, 109, 123-4, 127, 129-30, 132, 136, 142, 148, 150

small pear

6, 11, 14-7, 20, 25, 31, **35**, 41, 43, 46, 47, 51, 55-6, 59, 65-6, 68-70, 73-4, 77-80, 87-94, 96-7, 102, 105, 107, 123, 126, 139, 148

pear hanging down

18, 101

NB. *Bold figures indicate the specimen illustrated above.*

Column 1 (c):

1, 22, 28

2, 3, 5, 10, 12-3, **26**, 29, 42, 49, 128, 143

117

4, 16, **19**, 32, 34, 48, 83, 108

81, 147

rounded wedge
86, **125**

33, **37**, 45, 82, 95, 98, 134-5

hook
75, 84-5, 104, 112-3, 133, 138, 140-1

square pear
44, **76**, 138, 140-1

Column 2 (c):

identical serifs
28, **138**, 140-2

44 (general)

narrow
8, 18, 23-4, 29, **64**, 75, 93, 104, 134

2, 4, 6, 21, **43**, 45, 70, 72, 83

23, 26, 31, 35, 41, 87 **93**, 102, 113

ball
153-4, 160, 162-4, 170-1, 175-81, 184-6

pear
152, 156, 167-9, 174, 187

thin pear
158-9, 161, 172-3

serif
157, 183

Column 3 (c):

spiked serif
165-6

square
151, 182

155

narrow
155, 165, **176**

188, 191, **196**-7, 199

190, 193-4, 198

half serif
189

narrow opening
201-3

205, 210

ball
206-9, 211-7

Column 4 (c):

218, 220, 222-3, 225-8

219, 233-4

narrow
221, **229**

flat top
235

hook
224, 231, 240

curl
230-1

250, 265, 267, 273-5, 278-280, 283, 291-3, 304

246, 249, 252, **254**, 257-60, 263-4, 266, 269, 271, 295-6

245, 247-8, 251, 253, **255**-6, 261-2, 270, 276-7, 282, 285-9, 299-300

Column 5 (c/d):

281

slight contrast
268

top heavy
slight contrast
271

bottom heavy
272

small serifs
284

297

298

For ascender serif and bowl 'earmarks' of d refer to those of b as they are generally the same. Other 'earmarks' are as follows:

(foot serif)

flat
1, 28, 111, 116

Column 6 (d):

4, 8-10, 12, 22, 27, 33, 56-7, **62**, 64, 75, 78, 80-2, 84, 87, 89-90, 104, 110, 112-5, 118-149

6, 7, 11, 14-9, 21, 26, 31-2, 34-5, **37**-44, 47, 49, 52-5, 58-61, 63, 65-72, 74, 76, 83, 85-6, 88, 91-7, 99-103, 105-7, 146, 148

2, 3, 5, 13, **20**, 23-5, 45-6, 48, 50-1, 73, 77, 79, 98, 108-9, 117, 150

30

rounded
36

angular
42

157, 159

171-2, 182-3

Column 7 (d):

wide bowl
169

208-213

218-30

231-5, 240

tapered
246

269

272

top heavy
271

251, 259, 297

299-**300**

NB. *Bold figures indicate the specimen illustrated above.*

e–f

'Special Earmarks'
The 'special earmarks'
(or distinctive identifying
features) are indicated on
each letter. The general
'style' of typefaces with the
same 'earmark' may vary.
The figures refer to
specimen numbers.

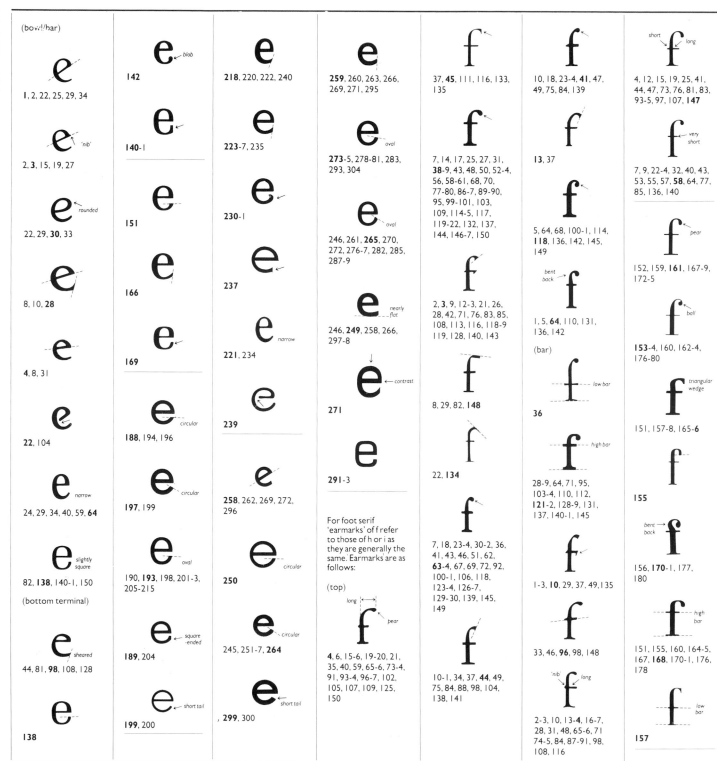

(bowl/bar)

1, 2, 22, 25, 29, 34

2, **3**, 15, 19, 27 'nib'

22, 29, **30**, 33 rounded

8, 10, **28**

4, 8, 31

22, 104

24, 29, 34, 40, 59, **64** narrow

82, **138**, 140-1, 150 slightly square

(bottom terminal)

44, 81, **98**, 108, 128 sheared

138

---

142 blob

140-1

151

166

169

188, 194, 196 circular

197, 199 circular

190, **193**, 198, 201-3, 205-215 oval

189, 204 square-ended

199, 200 short tail

218, 220, 222, 240

223-7, 235

230-1

237

221, 234 narrow

239 circular

258, 262, 269, 272, 296

250 circular

245, 251-7, **264** circular

, **299**, 300 short tail

259, 260, 263, 266, 269, 271, 295

273-5, 278-81, 283, 293, 304 oval

246, 261, **265**, 270, 272, 276-7, 282, 285, 287-9 oval

246, **249**, 258, 266, 297-8 nearly flat

271 contrast

291-3

For foot serif
'earmarks' of f refer
to those of h or i as
they are generally the
same. Earmarks are as
follows:

(top)

long ← → f pear

4, 6, 15-6, 19-20, 21, 35, 40, 59, 65-6, 73-4, 91, 93-4, 96-7, 102, 105, 107, 109, 125, 150

37, **45**, 111, 116, 133, 135

7, 14, 17, 25, 27, 31, **38**-9, 43, 48, 50, 52-4, 56, 58-61, 68, 70, 77-80, 86-7, 89-90, 95, 99-101, 103, 109, 114-5, 117, 119-22, 132, 137, 144, 146-7, 150

2, **3**, 9, 12-3, 21, 26, 28, 42, 71, 76, 83, 85, 108, 113, 116, 118-9, 119, 128, 140, 143

8, 29, 82, **148**

22, **134**

7, 18, 23-4, 30-2, 36, 41, 43, 46, 51, 62, **63**-4, 67, 69, 72, 92, 100-1, 106, 118, 123-4, 126-7, 129-30, 139, 145, 149

10-1, 34, 37, **44**, 49, 75, 84, 88, 98, 104, 138, 141

10, 18, 23-4, **41**, 47, 49, 75, 84, 139

13, 37

5, 64, 68, 100-1, 114, **118**, 136, 142, 145, 149

1, 5, **64**, 110, 131, 136, 142 bent back

(bar)

36 low bar

28-9, 64, 71, 95, 103-4, 110, 112, **121**-2, 128-9, 131, 137, 140-1, 145 high bar

1-3, **10**, 29, 37, 49, 135

33, 46, **96**, 98, 148

2-3, **10**, 13-**4**, 16-7, 28, 31, 48, 65-6, 71, 74-5, 84, 87-91, 98, 108, 116 'nib' long

---

short f long

4, 12, 15, 19, 25, 41, 44, 47, 73, 76, 81, 83, 93-5, 97, 107, **147**

7, 9, 22-4, 32, 40, 43, 53, 55, 57, **58**, 64, 77, 85, 136, 140 very short

152, 159, **161**, 167-9, 172-5 pear

153-4, 160, 162-4, 176-80 ball

151, 157-8, 165-**6** triangular wedge

155

156, **170**-1, 177, 180 bent back

151, 155, 160, 164-5, 167, **168**, 170-1, 176, 178 high bar

157 low bar

188-9, 192, 194-6, 200

229

bent back

258, 296, 299

8, **16**-7, 19, 21, 25, 35-6, 39-41, 52-3, 64, 66, 73-4, 76, 81, 83, 88, 93-6, 109, 132, 148

curled down

1, 20-2, 33, 42-3, **76**, 115, 117, 127, 136, 144-7

link protruding

153-4, **161**-3, 165, 167-8, 186-7

(single storey)

188-9, **190**, 193-6, 198

190, 192-3, 198, 204

239-40

thinning

263, 269

37, 49

157, 164

squared

191, **197**

191, **197**, 199, 201-3, 214

220, 225, **228**, 230, 234-5, 240

short top
short bar

253, 256, 264

6, 15, 26, 37-8, 44-5, 48, **59**, 60-1, 63, 65, 67, 70-1, 75, 84, 89-92, 95, 98-100, 103, 105, 108, 110, 114-5, 117-22, 128, 136-42, 144-7, 149

9, 26, 36, 65, 125, 132, 150

158

short tail

199, 200

ball

206-7, **208**-9, 211-3, 215-7

250, 255-6, 258, 300

(single storey)

g

2, 3, 28-30, **104**, 112

pear

152, 165, 182, 183

serif

204, **205**

square wedge

205, 210

246, 249, 254, 257, 259, 262, **266**-7, 269-70, 272-89, 291-3, 295-9, 304

(double storey)

open

1, 4, 22, 27, 46, 58, **77**, 78-80, 82, 131, 135

5, 10-1, 14, 17-8, 32, 34, 43, 47, 49-51, 55-7, **62**, 69, 72, 85, 97, 101, 106, 111, 114, 116, 130, 148

5, 7, 11-12, 23-4, 27, 46, 50, 54-63, 67-70, 72-3, 77-**80** 89, 99, 101, 103, 109, 114, 118-121, 129-131, 137, 142, 149

155

diamond

(double storey)

203, 210

wedge

218, 223-4, 228. 233. 237

245, 252, **260**, 271

top heavy

32, **36**, 63, 142

90, 110, 123-4, 126

169, **174**

201-2

ball curled down

steeply rounded

220, 226, 226

251

bottom heavy

14, **61**, 85, 128, 132, 136, 147, 150

diamond

10, 81

154, 159, **161**-3, 167-8, 171-2, 175, 178, 186-7

206, 208, 211, 213, 215-7

9, 12-3, 33, 42, 134

(single storey)

sharp curve

219, 225, 227, 234

261, 265, 267, 272-89, 296-9, 309

squashed bowl

18, 20, 68, 123-4, 126-7, 129, **150**

23, 32, 49, 60, 63, 110, 115, 140, 142

151

153, 156, 160, 164, 170, 175-7, 179-81, 184, **185**

207, 209, 211, 213

hook

wedge

12-3, **123**-4, 126-7, 129

(double storey)

pear

230, **231**, 240

268

no spur

134

open

160, 181

173

ball curled up

pear

221, 229, **232**, 235

wedge curled up

7, 87, **107**

6, 9, 26, 32

166, **176**, 183

212

'Special Earmarks'
The 'special earmarks' (or distinctive identifying features) are indicated on each letter. The general 'style' of typefaces with the same 'earmark' may vary. The figures refer to specimen numbers.

NB. Bold figures indicate the specimen illustrated above.

'Special Earmarks'
*The 'special earmarks'
(or distinctive identifying
features) are indicated on
each letter. The general
'style' of typefaces with the
same 'earmark' may vary.
The figures refer to
specimen numbers.*

(single storey)

223, 225, 228, 237

224

239

(double storey)

open
222, 226, 230

221, 229, 234

218, 233, 235

diamond
240

curved wedge
219

230

ball
221, **229**, 231-2

(double storey)

259, 270

slight contrast
268

276-7, 286, **287**, 288-9

258, 262

298

(single storey)

251, 260, 263-4, 269, 272, 295, 297

circular bowl
250, 252, 254

245, **253**, 255, 257, 260, 282

246, **249**

oblong bowl
267, 273-5, 278, **279**-80, 283, 304

256, 282

246, 266, **271**, 284-5

261, 265

291-3

296, 299, 300

301

For ascender serif 'earmarks' of h refer to those of b as they are generally the same. Other 'earmarks' are as follows:

(stems)

small x height
4, 15, 21, 25, 36, 40, 105, 116, 123, 126, 132, **147**

1, 27, 47, **72**, 101, 110

5, 9

16, 19, 40, 113, 133-5, 142

(foot serifs)

2

flat *triangular*
4

full
8, 81, 113

half
29

concave
3, **14**, 17-8, 36, 102

long
6, **11**, 27, 36, 44, 53, 72, 91, 111, 119, 137-8, 149

short
5, 13, 30, 82, **98**, 123-4, 126, 129

heavy brackets
16, 38-**9**, 56, 101, 110, 118, 120-1, 137

long brackets
54, 68, 74, 147, 150

wedge
28-31

slab
32-4

curled up
12, 42

half
75, **84**, 104, 134-5, 140-3

no serif
134

no serif
143

small x height
154, 156-9, 162-3, 181

line serifs
151-69 (e.g. **153**)

bracketed serifs
155, 157, 165

small serifs
170-87 (e.g. **185**)

long serifs
173, **177**, 179, 185-6

thick bracketed serifs
170, 172, 177, 185-6

half serifs
155, **175**

216

194-5

188, 196-7

square slab
188-203 (e.g **197**)

bracketed slab
204-17 (e.g. **211**)

rounded slab
214-7

serifs thinner than stem
191, 201-3

small gap
201, 207-8, 214

thick stubby serifs
204

short serifs
189, 192, 204, 215

half serif
189, **190**, 192, 197, 204

NB. *Bold figures indicate the specimen illustrated above.*

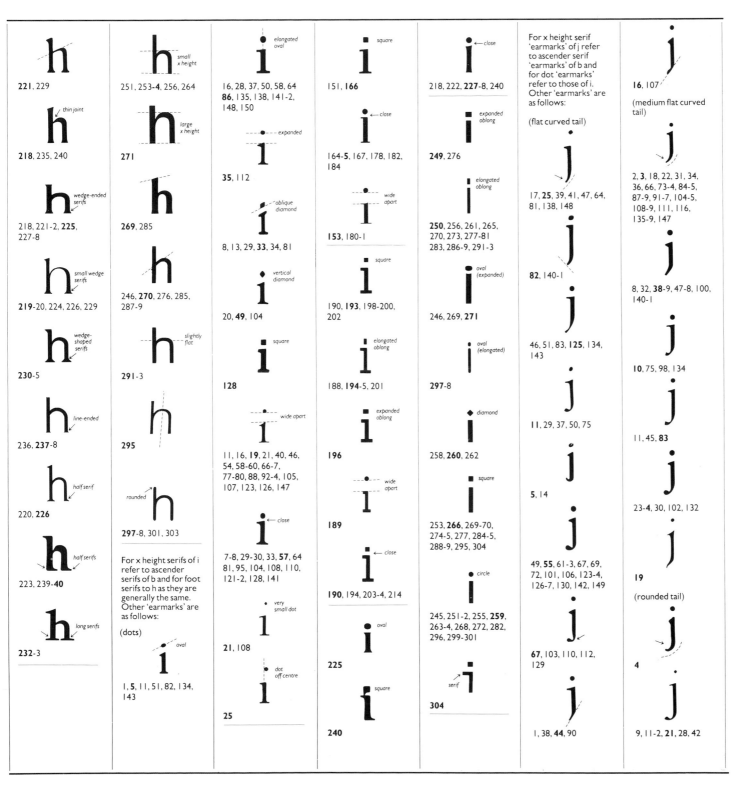

221, 229

thin joint
218, 235, 240

wedge-ended serifs
218, 221-2, **225**, 227-8

small wedge serifs
219-20, 224, 226, 229

wedge-shaped serifs
230-5

line-ended
236, **237-8**

half serif
220, **226**

half serifs
223, 239-**40**

long serifs
232-3

---

small x height
251, 253-**4**, 256, 264

large x height
271

269, 285

246, **270**, 276, 285, 287-9

slightly flat
291-3

rounded
295

297-8, 301, 303

For x height serifs of i refer to ascender serifs of b and for foot serifs to h as they are generally the same. Other 'earmarks' are as follows:

(dots)

oval
1, **5**, 11, 51, 82, 134, 143

---

elongated oval
16, 28, 37, 50, 58, 64 **86**, 135, 138, 141-2, 148, 150

expanded
35, 112

oblique diamond
8, 13, 29, **33**, 34, 81

vertical diamond
20, **49**, 104

square
128

wide apart
11, 16, **19**, 21, 40, 46, 54, 58-60, 66-7, 77-80, 88, 92-4, 105, 107, 123, 126, 147

close
7-8, 29-30, 33, **57**, 64 81, 95, 104, 108, 110, 121-2, 128, 141

very small dot
21, 108

dot off centre
25

---

square
151, **166**

close
164-**5**, 167, 178, 182, 184

wide apart
153, 180-1

square
190, **193**, 198-200, 202

elongated oblong
188, **194**-5, 201

expanded oblong
196

close
189

close
190, 194, 203-4, 214

oval
225

square
240

---

close
218, 222, **227**-8, 240

expanded oblong
249, 276

elongated oblong
250, 256, 261, 265, 270, 273, 277-81 283, 286-9, 291-3

oval (expanded)
82, 140-1

oval (elongated)
246, 269, **271**

diamond
297-8

square
258, **260**, 262

circle
253, **266**, 269-70, 274-5, 277, 284-5, 288-9, 295, 304

serif
245, 251-2, 255, **259**, 263-4, 268, 272, 282, 296, 299-301

304

For x height serif 'earmarks' of j refer to ascender serif 'earmarks' of b and for dot 'earmarks' refer to those of i. Other 'earmarks' are as follows:

(flat curved tail)

17, **25**, 39, 41, 47, 64, 81, 138, 148

82, 140-1

46, 51, 83, **125**, 134, 143

11, 29, 37, 50, 75

5, 14

253, **266**, 269-70, 274-5, 277, 284-5, 288-9, 295, 304

49, **55**, 61-3, 67, 69, 72, 101, 106, 123-4, 126-7, 130, 142, 149

67, 103, 110, 112, 129

1, 38, **44**, 90

16, 107

(medium flat curved tail)

2, **3**, 18, 22, 31, 34, 36, 66, 73-4, 84-5, 87-9, 91-7, 104-5, 108-9, 111, 116, 135-9, 147

8, 32, **38**-9, 47-8, 100, 140-1

10, 75, 98, 134

11, 45, **83**

23-4, 30, 102, 132

19

(rounded tail)

4

9, 11-2, **21**, 28, 42

'Special Earmarks'
The 'special earmarks' (or distinctive identifying features) are indicated on each letter. The general 'style' of typefaces with the same 'earmark' may vary. The figures refer to specimen numbers.

NB. *Bold figures indicate the specimen illustrated above.*

'Special Earmarks'
The 'special earmarks' (or distinctive identifying features) are indicated on each letter. The general 'style' of typefaces with the same 'earmark' may vary. The figures refer to specimen numbers.

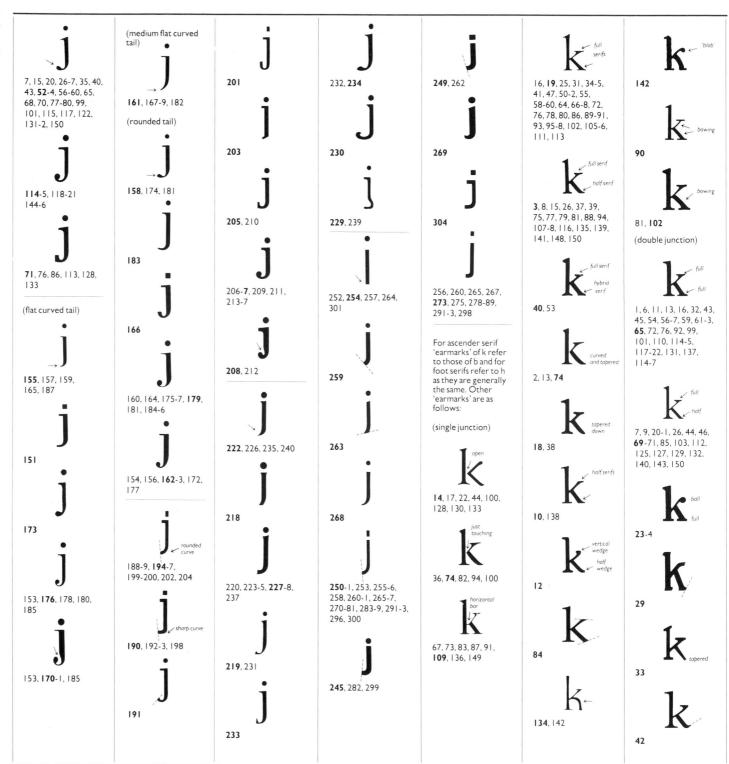

7, 15, 20, 26-7, 35, 40, 43, **52**-4, 56-60, 65, 68, 70, 77-80, 99, 101, 115, 117, 122, 131-2, 150

114-5, 118-21 144-6

71, 76, 86, 113, 128, 133

(flat curved tail)

155, 157, 159, 165, 187

151

173

153, 176, 178, 180, 185

153, 170-1, 185

(medium flat curved tail)

161, 167-9, 182

(rounded tail)

158, 174, 181

183

166

160, 164, 175-7, 179, 181, 184-6

154, 156, 162-3, 172, 177

rounded curve
188-9, 194-7, 199-200, 202, 204

sharp curve
190, 192-3, 198

191

201

203

205, 210

206-7, 209, 211, 213-7

208, 212

218

220, 223-5, 227-8, 237

219, 231

233

232, 234

230

229, 239

252, 254, 257, 264, 301

245, 282, 299

249, 262

269

304

256, 260, 265, 267, 273, 275, 278-89, 291-3, 298

259

263

268

250-1, 253, 255-6, 258, 260-1, 265-7, 270-81, 283-9, 291-3, 296, 300

For ascender serif 'earmarks' of k refer to those of b and for foot serifs refer to h as they are generally the same. Other 'earmarks' are as follows:

(single junction)

open
14, 17, 22, 44, 100, 128, 130, 133

just touching
36, 74, 82, 94, 100

horizontal bar
67, 73, 83, 87, 91, 109, 136, 149

full serifs
16, 19, 25, 31, 34-5, 41, 47, 50-2, 55, 58-60, 64, 66-8, 72, 76, 78, 80, 86, 89-91, 93, 95-8, 102, 105-6, 111, 113

full serif
half serif
3, 8, 15, 26, 37, 39, 75, 77, 79, 81, 88, 94, 107-8, 116, 135, 139, 141, 148, 150

full serif
hybrid serif
40, 53

curved and tapered
2, 13, 74

tapered down
18, 38

half serifs
10, 138

vertical wedge
half wedge
12

84

134, 142

'blob'
142

bowing
90

bowing
81, 102

(double junction)

full
full
1, 6, 11, 13, 16, 32, 43, 45, 54, 56-7, 59, 61-3, 65, 72, 76, 92, 99, 101, 110, 114-5, 117-22, 131, 137, 114-7

full
half
7, 9, 20-1, 26, 44, 46, 69-71, 85, 103, 112, 125, 127, 129, 132, 140, 143, 150

ball
full
23-4

29

tapered
33

42

NB. Bold figures indicate the specimen illustrated above.

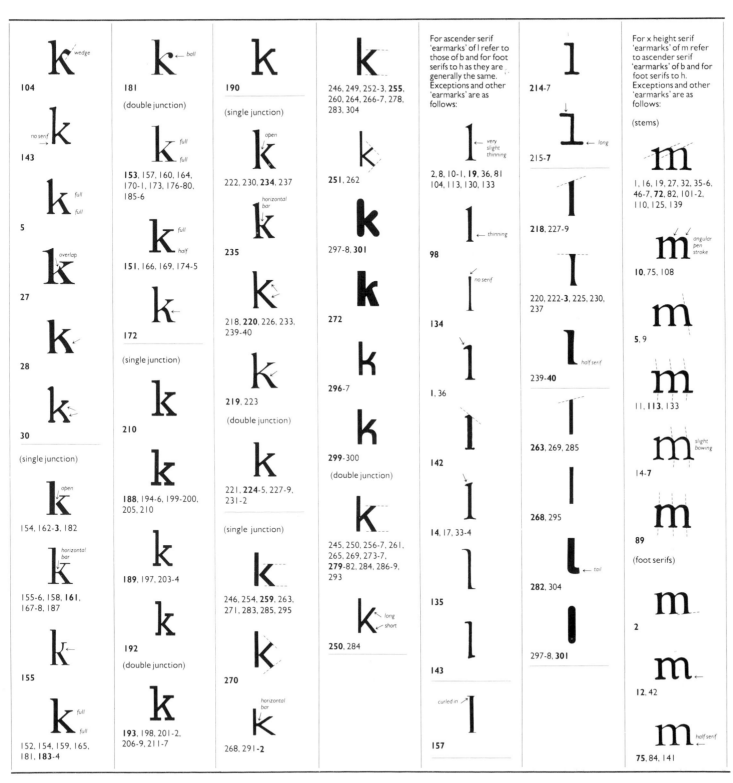

'Special Earmarks'
The 'special earmarks' (or distinctive identifying features) are indicated on each letter. The general 'style' of typefaces with the same 'earmark' may vary. The figures refer to specimen numbers.

k *wedge*

104

k *no serif*

143

k *full* *full*

5

k *overlap*

27

k

28

k

30

(single junction)

k *open*

154, 162-**3**, 182

k *horizontal bar*

155-6, 158, **161**, 167-8, 187

k

155

k *full* *full*

152, 154, 159, 165, 181, **183-4**

k *ball*

181

(double junction)

k *full* *full*

153, 157, 160, 164, 170-1, 173, 176-80, 185-6

k *full* *half*

151, 166, 169, 174-5

k

172

(single junction)

k

210

k

188, 194-6, 199-200, 205, 210

k

189, 197, 203-4

k

192

(double junction)

k

193, 198, 201-2, 206-9, 211-7

k

190

(single junction)

k *open*

222, 230, **234**, 237

k *horizontal bar*

235

k

218, **220**, 226, 233, 239-40

k

219, 223

(double junction)

k

221, **224**-5, 227-9, 231-2

(single junction)

k

246, 254, **259**, 263, 271, 283, 285, 295

k

270

horizontal bar

k

268, 291-**2**

k

246, 249, 252-3, **255**, 260, 264, 266-7, 278, 283, 304

k

251, 262

k

297-8, **301**

k

272

k

296-7

k

299-300

(double junction)

k

245, 250, 256-7, 261, 265, 269, 273-7, **279**-82, 284, 286-9, 293

k *long* *short*

250, 284

For ascender serif 'earmarks' of l refer to those of b and for foot serifs to h as they are generally the same. Exceptions and other 'earmarks' are as follows:

l *very slight thinning*

2, 8, 10-1, **19**, 36, 81, 104, 113, 130, 133

l *thinning*

98

l *no serif*

134

l

1, 36

l

142

l

14, 17, 33-4

l

135

l

143

l *curled in*

157

l

214-7

l

215-7

l *long*

218, 227-9

l

220, 222-**3**, 225, 230, 237

l *half serif*

239-**40**

l

263, 269, 285

l

268, 295

l *tail*

282, 304

l

297-8, **301**

For x height serif 'earmarks' of m refer to ascender serif 'earmarks' of b and for foot serifs to h. Exceptions and other 'earmarks' are as follows:

(stems)

m

1, 16, 19, 27, 32, 35-6, 46-7, **72**, 82, 101-2, 110, 125, 139

m *angular pen stroke*

10, 75, 108

m

5, 9

m

11, **113**, 133

m *slight bowing*

14-**7**

m

89

(foot serifs)

m

2

m

12, 42

m *half serif*

75, 84, 141

NB. *Bold figures indicate the specimen illustrated above.*

'Special Earmarks'
*The 'special earmarks'
(or distinctive identifying
features) are indicated on
each letter. The general
'style' of typefaces with the
same 'earmark' may vary.
The figures refer to
specimen numbers.*

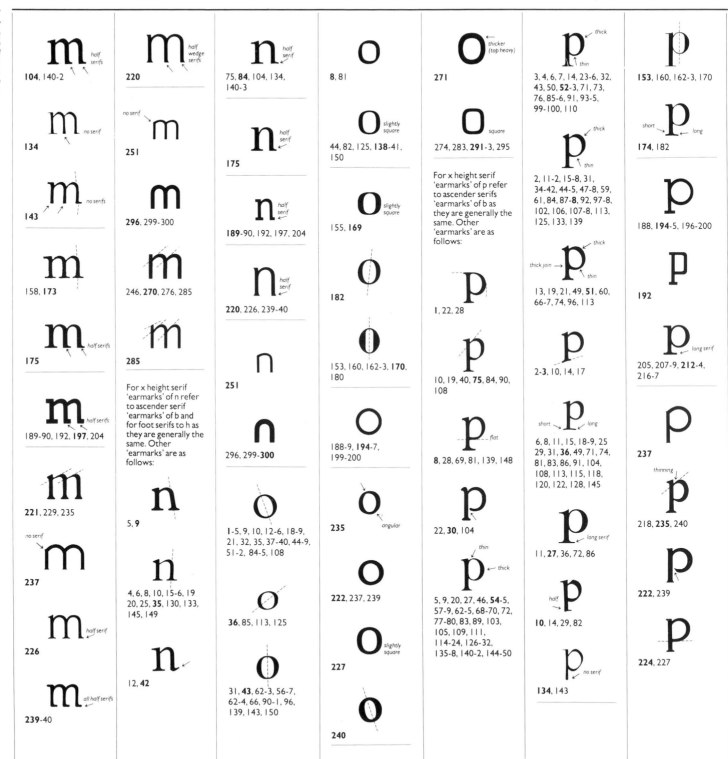

m *half serifs* — **104**, 140-2

m *no serif* — **134**

m *no serifs* — **143**

m — 158, **173**

m *half serifs* — **175**

m *half serifs* — 189-90, 192, **197**, 204

m — **221**, 229, 235

m *no serif* — **237**

m *half serif* — **226**

m *all half serifs* — **239**-40

m *half wedge serifs* — **220**

m *no serif* — **251**

m — **296**, 299-300

m — 246, **270**, 276, 285

m — **285**

For x height serif 'earmarks' of n refer to ascender serif 'earmarks' of b and for foot serifs to h as they are generally the same. Other 'earmarks' are as follows:

n — 5, **9**

n — 4, 6, 8, 10, 15-6, 19, 20, 25, **35**, 130, 133, 145, 149

n — 12, **42**

n *half serif* — 75, **84**, 104, 134, 140-3

n *half serif* — **175**

n *half serif* — 189-90, 192, 197, 204

n *half serif* — **220**, 226, 239-40

n — **251**

n — 296, 299-**300**

o — 8, 81

o *slightly square* — 44, 82, 125, **138**-41, 150

o *slightly square* — 155, **169**

o — **182**

o — 153, 160, 162-3, **170**, 180

o — 188-9, **194**-7, 199-200

o — 1-5, 9, 10, 12-6, 18-9, 21, 32, 35, 37-40, 44-9, 51-2, 84-5, 108

o *angular* — **235**

o — **222**, 237, 239

o — **36**, 85, 113, 125

o — **227**

o *slightly square* — **240**

O *thicker (top heavy)* — **271**

o *square* — 274, 283, **291**-3, 295

For x height serif 'earmarks' of p refer to ascender serifs 'earmarks' of b as they are generally the same. Other 'earmarks' are as follows:

p — **1**, 22, 28

p — 10, 19, 40, **75**, 84, 90, 108

p *flat* — **8**, 28, 69, 81, 139, 148

p — 22, **30**, 104

p *thin* *thick* — 5, 9, 20, 27, 46, **54**-5, 57-9, 62-5, 68-70, 72, 77-80, 83, 89, 103, 105, 109, 111, 114-24, 126-32, 135-8, 140-2, 144-50

p *thick* *thin* — 3, 4, 6, 7, 14, 23-6, 32, 43, 50, **52**-3, 71, 73, 76, 85-6, 91, 93-5, 99-100, 110

p *thick* *thin* — 2, 11-2, 15-8, 31, 34-42, 44-5, 47-8, 59, 61, 84, 87-**8**, 92, 97-8, 102, 106, 107-8, 113, 125, 133, 139

p *thick join* *thick* *thin* — 13, 19, 21, 49, **51**, 60, 66-7, 74, 96, 113

p — 2-**3**, 10, 14, 17

p *short* *long* — 6, 8, 11, 15, 18-9, 25, 29, 31, **36**, 49, 71, 74, 81, 83, 86, 91, 104, 108, 113, 115, 118, 120, 122, 128, 145

p *long serif* — 11, **27**, 36, 72, 86

p *half* — 10, 14, 29, 82

p *no serif* — **134**, 143

p — **153**, 160, 162-3, 170

p *short* *long* — **174**, 182

p — 188, **194**-5, 196-200

p — 192

p *long serif* — 205, 207-9, **212**-4, 216-7

p — 237

p *thinning* — 218, **235**, 240

p — **222**, 239

p — **224**, 227

NB. *Bold figures indicate the specimen illustrated above.*

'Special Earmarks'
*The 'special earmarks'
(or distinctive identifying
features) are indicated on
each letter. The general
'style' of typefaces with the
same 'earmark' may vary.
The figures refer to
specimen numbers.*

Column 1 (p)

p — long serif
232

p — short / long
234

p
231

p — circular bowl
251, 253, **255**, 257-8, 262

p — no serif
251, **259**, 295, 297

p
296, 299-**300**

p
269, 296

For bowl and foot
serif 'earmarks' of q
refer to those of p as
they are generally the
same. Exceptions and
other 'earmarks' are
as follows:

q — no serif
8, 104, 111, 113, **116**, 133-4, 139, 148

q — half serif
3, **4**, 12-3, 23-4, 27, 36, 42, 51, 107

Column 2 (q)

q — flat 'nib'
1, 28

q
125, **150**

q
22, 44, **104**

q — thick join
34

q — small 'nib'
6, 15-6, 25, 33, 40, 44, 61, 63, 66, 69, 74, 76, 83, 85, 87, 123-4, 128, 139

q
14, 17, 89, 98, 112, **131**, 136, 141-2, 147, 149

q
57, 132, **140**, 147

q
2, 3, 10, **14**, 17, 29, 81, 117, 143

q — half serif
29, **40**, 82, 123, 126

Column 3 (q)

q — no serif
134

q
65

q — no serif
183

q — 'nib'
182

q — extended stroke
151, 166-**8**, 187

q
153, 160, **162**-3, 170

q
169

q
191

q — 'nib'
203-4, 214-7

Column 4 (q / r)

q — no 'nib'
233

q — full serif
231

q — half serif
234, 239-40

q
285

For foot serif
'earmarks' of r refer
to those of h as they
are generally the
same. Other
'earmarks' are as
follows:

(angled stem)

r
23-4, 78-80, 122-4

r
30, **77**

r
71
(concave x height
serif)

r
8, **28**, 40

r
108
(heavy triangular
x height serif)

r — squashed pear
102

Column 5 (r)

r — pear
6, 17, 22, 43, **53**, 55-6, 59, 61-4, 66-7, 69, 72, 74, 88, 92-3, 95-6, 99, 110

r — hanging pear
4, 7, 9, **65**, 69, 103, 109

r — club
9, 15, 26, **38**-41, 47-9, 51, 60, 70, 73, 87, 89, 94, 106-7

r — flag
16, 20, **25**, 34-5, 37, 50, 83

r
5, **32**

r
13, 33, **45**, 85

r
71
(concave x height
serif)

r
27, **68**, 91, 110
(thin triangular
x height serif)

r — pear
18, 27, **31**, 36, 44, 46, 52, 54, 57, 62-4, 72, 90, 97, 101, 105, 126-7, 129-30, 132, 139, 148

Column 6 (r)

r — hanging pear
58, 80, 103, 106, 125, 131, 136-7, 145-6, 149-50

r — curled in
114-5, 117-21, 142, 144

r
111, 138

r
10-11, 86, 100, 106, 141, 147

r
2, **19**-20, 76, 83, 104

r
3, 12, 21, 42, 128

r
8, 81

r
14, 82, 84-5, 113, 128, 133-5, 140

r
75, 98

Column 7 (r)

r
112, 141

r
116, 143

r — ball
152-4, **159**-63, 167, 169, 171-2, 178, 180-1, 184, 186-7

r — hanging pear
156, **168**, 170, 185

r — ball
164, 175-**77**, 179

r — club
173-4, 183

r — flag
158

r — wedge
151, 157, 182

r — wedge
155, 166

r — spiked
165

NB. *Bold figures indicate the specimen illustrated above.*

'Special Earmarks'

The 'special earmarks' (or distinctive identifying features) are indicated on each letter. The general style of typefaces with the same 'earmark' may vary. The figures refer to specimen numbers.

NB. Bold figures indicate the specimen illustrated above.

142

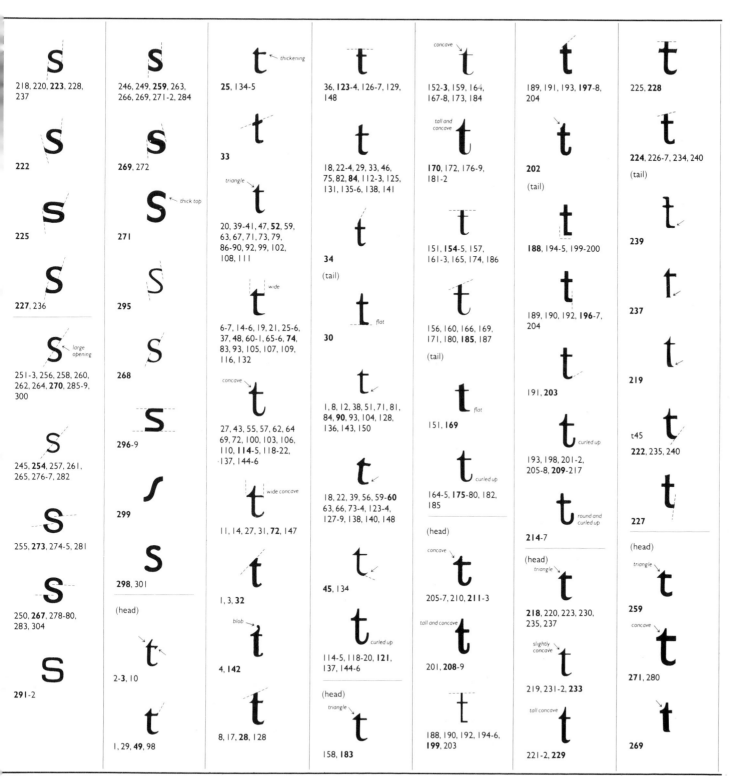

'Special Earmarks'
The 'special earmarks'
(or distinctive identifying
features) are indicated on
each letter. The general
style of typefaces with the
same 'earmark' may vary.
The figures refer to
specimen numbers.

218, 220, **223**, 228, 237

222

225

227, 236

251-3, 256, 258, 260, 262, 264, **270**, 285-9, 300

245, **254**, 257, 261, 265, 276-7, 282

255, **273**, 274-5, 281

250, **267**, 278-80, 283, 304

291-2

246, 249, **259**, 263, 266, 269, 271-2, 284

269, 272

271

295

268

296-9

299

298, 301

(head)

2-**3**, 10

thickening
25, 134-5

33

triangle

20, 39-41, 47, **52**, 59, 63, 67, 71, 73, 79, 86-90, 92, 99, 102, 108, 111

wide
6-7, 14-6, 19, 21, 25-6, 37, 48, 60-1, 65-6, **74**, 83, 93, 105, 107, 109, 116, 132

concave
27, 43, 55, 57, 62, 64, 69, 72, 100, 103, 106, 110, **114**-5, 118-22, 137, 144-6

wide concave
11, 14, 27, 31, **72**, 147

1, 3, **32**

blob
4, 142

triangle
8, 17, **28**, 128

1, 29, **49**, 98

36, **123**-4, 126-7, 129, 148

18, 22-4, 29, 33, 46, 75, 82, **84**, 112-3, 125, 131, 135-6, 138, 141

34
(tail)

flat
30

1, 8, 12, 38, 51, 71, 81, 84, **90**, 93, 104, 128, 136, 143, 150

18, 22, 39, 56, 59-**60**, 63, 66, 73-4, 123-4, 127-9, 138, 140, 148

45, 134

curled up
114-5, 118-20, **121**, 137, 144-6

(head)

triangle
158, **183**

concave
152-**3**, 159, 164, 167-8, 173, 184

tall and concave
170, 172, 176-9, 181-2

151, **154**-5, 157, 161-3, 165, 174, 186

156, 160, 166, 169, 171, 180, **185**, 187
(tail)

flat
151, **169**

curled up
164-5, **175**-80, 182, 185

(head)

concave
205-7, 210, **211**-3

tall and concave
201, **208**-9

tall concave
188, 190, 192, 194-6, **199**, 203

189, 191, 193, **197**-8, 204

202
(tail)

188, 194-5, 199-200

189, 190, 192, **196**-7, 204

191, **203**

curled up
193, 198, 201-2, 205-8, **209**-217

round and curled up
214-7

(head)

triangle
218, 220, 223, 230, 235, 237

slightly concave
219, 231-2, **233**

221-2, **229**

225, **228**

(tail)
224, 226-7, 234, 240

239

237

219

t45
222, 235, 240

227

(head)

triangle
259

concave
271, 280

269

'Special Earmarks'
The 'special earmarks' (or distinctive identifying features) are indicated on each letter. The general 'style' of typefaces with the same 'earmark' may vary. The figures refer to specimen numbers.

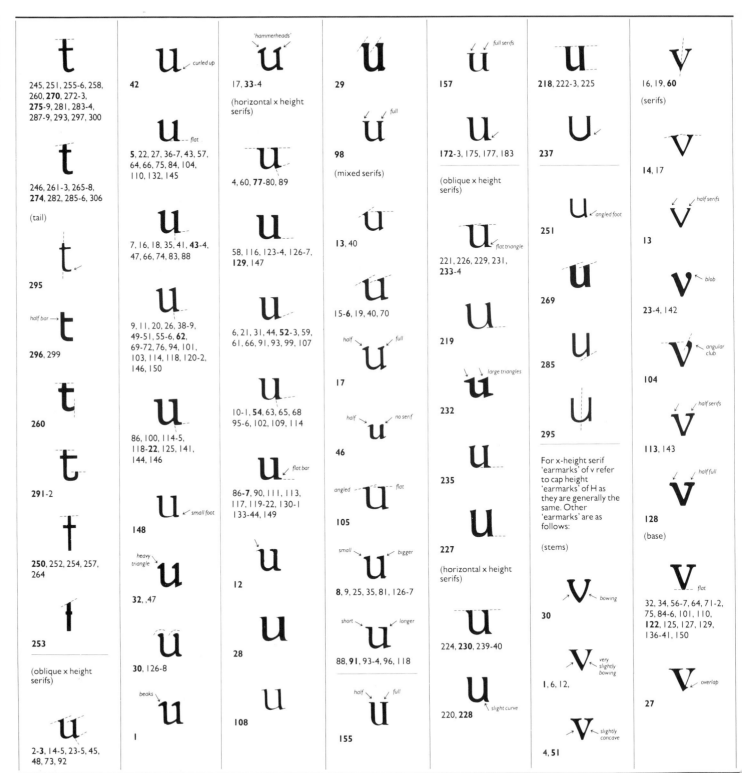

t
245, 251, 255-6, 258, 260, **270**, 272-3, **275**-9, 281, 283-4, 287-9, 293, 297, 300

42 — u *curled up*

u *flat*
5, 22, 27, 36-7, 43, 57, 64, 66, 75, 84, 104, 110, 132, 145

u
7, 16, 18, 35, 41, **43**-4, 47, 66, 74, 83, 88

u
9, 11, 20, 26, 38-9, 49-51, 55-6, **62**, 69-72, 76, 94, 101, 103, 114, 118, 120-2, 146, 150

u
86, 100, 114-5, 118-**22**, 125, 141, 144, 146

148 — u *small foot*

heavy triangle → u
32, ,47

beaks → u
1

u
2-**3**, 14-5, 23-5, 45, 48, 73, 92

t
246, 261-3, 265-8, **274**, 282, 285-6, 306
(tail)

t
295

half bar → **t**
296, 299

t
260

t
291-2

t
250, 252, 254, 257, 264

t
253
(oblique x height serifs)

'*hammerheads*' → **u**
17, **33**-4
(horizontal x height serifs)

u
4, 60, **77**-80, 89

u
58, 116, 123-4, 126-7, **129**, 147

u
6, 21, 31, 44, **52**-3, 59, 61, 66, 91, 93, 99, 107

u
10-1, **54**, 63, 65, 68 95-6, 102, 109, 114

u *flat bar*
86-**7**, 90, 111, 113, 117, 119-22, 130-1 133-44, 149

u
12

u
28

u
108

u
29

u
98
(mixed serifs)

u
13, 40

u
15-**6**, 19, 40, 70

u
17

half → **u** ← *no serif*
46

angled --- **u** --- *flat*
105

small → **u** ← *bigger*
8, 9, 25, 35, 81, 126-7

short → **u** ← *longer*
88, **91**, 93-4, 96, 118

half → **u** ← *full*
155

full serifs → **u**
157
172-3, 175, 177, 183
(oblique x height serifs)

full → **u**
221, 226, 229, 231, **233**-4

u *flat triangle*
219

half → **u** ← *full*
232

large triangles → **u**
235

u
227
(horizontal x height serifs)

u
224, **230**, 239-40

u *slight curve*
220, **228**

u
218, 222-3, 225

u
237

u *angled foot*
251

u
269

u
285

u
295

For x-height serif 'earmarks' of v refer to cap height 'earmarks' of H as they are generally the same. Other 'earmarks' are as follows:

(stems)

V *bowing*
30

V *very slightly bowing*
1, 6, 12,

V *slightly concave*
4, 51

V
16, 19, **60**
(serifs)

V
14, 17

half serifs → **V**
13

V ← *blob*
23-4, 142

V ← *angular club*
104

half serifs → **V**
113, 143

half full → **V**
128
(base)

V *flat*
32, 34, 56-7, 64, 71-2, 75, 84-6, 101, 110, **122**, 125, 127, 129, 136-41, 150

V *overlap*
27

28 — wedge serif

269, 272, 297 — bowing

8, 29, 81-**3** — rounded

76 — For x height serif 'earmarks' of w refer to cap height serifs of H as they are generally the same. Other 'earmarks' are as follows:

(crossed centre strokes)

151, 166, **169**, 181-2

9, 89

(centre strokes meet at x height or stepped)

192 — half serifs

222 — flat base

32-3, 38-9, 57, 70-2, 106, 111, 115, 118, 120, **122**, 145, 150

239-40 — half serifs

8, 81

251-2, **254**, 256, 259, 263-4

14-16, 19, **31**, 60, 135 — bowing

258, **262**

30 — bowing

half serifs

29, 113, 128, 143

270

5, 22, 34, 38-9, 42-3, 56-7, 64, 101, **106**, 110, 120-1 — wedge serifs

27 — 'odd serifs'

76 (no centre serif)

175 — rounded bases

4, 15, 18, 44-6, 54, 77-80, 98, 108, 123-4, 126-7, 134-5

flat bases

75, **84-6**, 112, 125, 129, 133, 136-41

82-3

134

blob

23-4, 142

10

28 — wedge serifs

(centre strokes meet at x height or stepped)

pointed base

155-8, 160-1, 167-**8**, 170, 172-4, 177-9, 183-7

flat base

175 (no centre serif)

stepped / pointed

153, 160, 170-1, 180-1

stepped / flat

165, 170, 174, 176, 186

(no centre serif)

pointed

154, **159**, 162-4

flat

151-2, **166**, 169, 182

(centre strokes meet at x height or stepped)

188, **196-7**, 201-2, 208-9, 211, 213

206-7, 212 — lower join

(no centre serif)

flat

189-91, **193**, 198, 203-5, 210

194-5 — lower join

199-200, 213 — pointed

192

214-7 — flat

(centre strokes meet at x height or stepped)

231, **233** — pointed

228, **229**-30 — flat

221 — blunt

223, 225

224, **226** — stepped

232 — half serif

219, 237 — pointed

234

218, **220**, 227 — flat

218, 227-8 — wedge serifs

239-40 — half serifs

251-2, 254, 256, **259**, 263-4 — pointed

258, 262 — pointed

270 — flat

268, 272, 276 — some contrast

269, **297** — wedge / bowing

296, 299

298

304

295

4, 29, **84**, 141 — all half serifs

125, 128, 143 — half / full

'Special Earmarks'
The 'special earmarks' (or distinctive identifying features) are indicated on each letter. The general 'style' of typefaces with the same 'earmark' may vary. The figures refer to specimen numbers.

NB. Bold figures indicate the specimen illustrated above.

'Special Earmarks'

The 'special earmarks' (or distinctive identifying features) are indicated on each letter. The general 'style' of typefaces with the same 'earmark' may vary. The figures refer to specimen numbers.

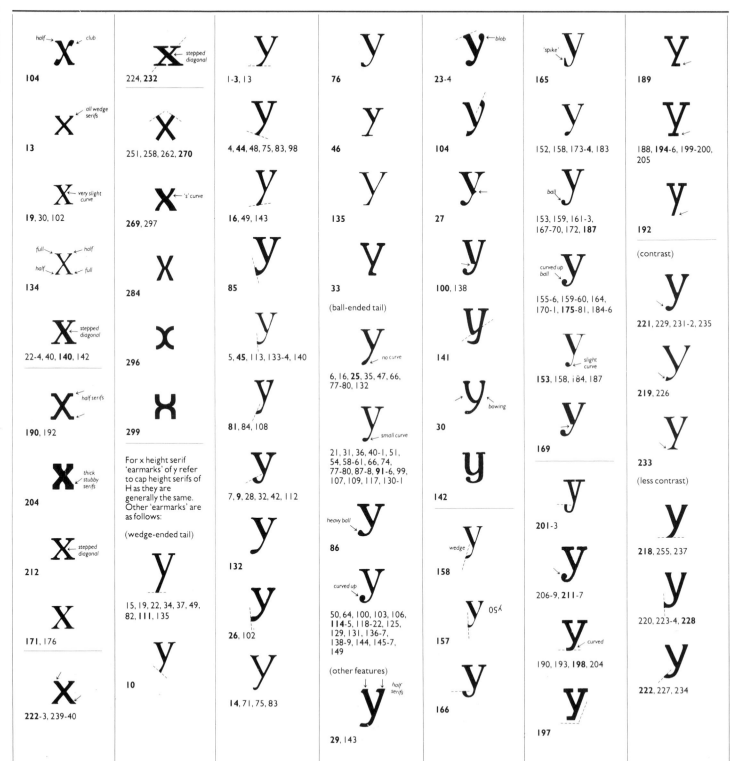

104 — half / club

13 — all wedge serifs

19, 30, 102 — very slight curve

134 — full / half / half / full

22-4, 40, **140**, 142 — stepped diagonal

190, 192 — half serifs

204 — thick stubby serifs

212 — stepped diagonal

171, 176

222-3, 239-40

224, **232** — stepped diagonal

251, 258, 262, **270**

269, 297 — 's' curve

284

296

299

For x height serif 'earmarks' of y refer to cap height serifs of H as they are generally the same. Other 'earmarks' are as follows:

(wedge-ended tail)

15, 19, 22, 34, 37, 49, 82, **111**, 135

10

1-3, 13

4, **44**, 48, 75, 83, 98

16, 49, 143

85

5, **45**, 113, 133-4, 140

81, 84, 108

132

26, 102

14, 71, 75, 83

76

46

135

33

(ball-ended tail)

6, 16, **25**, 35, 47, 66, 77-80, 132 — no curve

21, 31, 36, 40-1, 51, 54, 58-61, 66, 74, 77-80, 87-8, **91**-6, 99, 107, 109, 117, 130-1 — small curve

7, **9**, 28, 32, 42, 112

86 — heavy ball

50, 64, 100, 103, 106, **114**-5, 118-22, 125, 129, 131, 136-7, 138-9, 144, 145-7, 149 — curved up

(other features)

29, 143 — half serifs

23-4 — blob

104

27

100, 138

141

30 — bowing

142

158 — wedge

157 — y50

166

165 — 'spike'

152, 158, 173-4, 183

153, 159, 161-3, 167-70, 172, **187** — ball

155-6, 159-60, 164, 170-1, **175**-81, 184-6 — curved up ball

153, 158, 184, 187 — slight curve

169

201-3

206-9, **211**-7 — curved

190, 193, **198**, 204

197

189

188, **194**-6, 199-200, 205

192

(contrast)

221, 229, 231-2, 235

219, 226

233

(less contrast)

218, 255, 237

220, 223-4, **228**

222, 227, 234

NB. *Bold figures indicate the specimen illustrated above.*

'Special Earmarks'
The 'special earmarks' (or distinctive identifying features) are indicated on each letter. The general 'style' of typefaces with the same 'earmark' may vary. The figures refer to specimen numbers.

Column 1 — y

239-**40**

246, 249-50, 252-5, 257, **259**, 263-4, 267, 271

251, 256, 260-1, 265-6, **273**-89, 291-3, 295, 298, 304

245

258, **262**

270

269, 272

296

297

299-300

Column 2 — y (wide)

292, **304**

(horizontal strokes thicker than diagonal stem)

3, 26, 37, 46, 48-9

2, 7, 10-1, 44, 82

21, 25

full serifs — **6**

full serifs — **32**, 34

14, 17, 98, 134

(diagonal stem thicker than horizontal strokes)

half serifs / half serifs — 15, 38-9, 54, 58, **74**, 86, 97, 105-6, 113, 125-6, 132, 136, 144, 150

full serifs — **1**, **20**, 27

Column 3 — z

full serif / half serif — **35**, 41, 60, 91-6, 107, 109

36, 108

47, **127**

38-9, **88**

(other features)

curved / full serifs — **4**

full serifs — **30**

concave — **51**, 143

33

111-2, 148

142

Column 4 — Z

poor contrast — **29**

172-3, 185-6

158, 166

202-5, **207**-17

219, 221, 226, 232-5, 240

poor contrast — **218**, 220, 222, 225, 227

223, 228, **237**

224

239

245, 251-2, **254**-9, 262-4, 300

Column 5 — z

253

248, 270

296, 299-301

269, 297

Figures:

These can be either 'lining' (i.e. 1234567890) or 'non-lining' (i.e. 1234567890).

(lining)

long point — 24, 28, 42, 62, 83, **125**, 144, 146

129

134

138, 141

Column 6 — 1

concave — 86, 101, **110**, 127, 137, 145

8

29, **128**

21

45, 58, 108, **133**, 148-9

43, 68, **74**

104

18, 33, 55

1

34

Column 7 — 1

no foot serif — 82, **123**-4, 126

(non-lining)

concave — **14**

19

102

46

48

143

slightly rounded — **81**

32

(all lining)

173

I–2

'Special Earmarks'
The 'special earmarks'
(or distinctive
identifying features)
are indicated on
each letter. The general
'style' of typefaces with the
same 'earmark' may vary.
The figures refer to
specimen numbers.

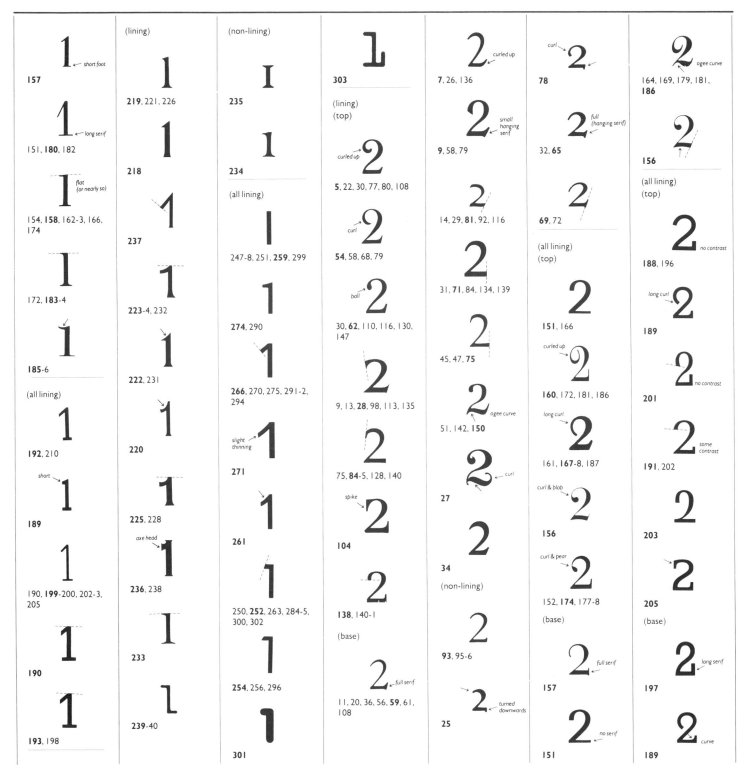

157 — short foot

151, **180**, 182 — long serif

154, **158**, 162-3, 166, 174 — flat (or nearly so)

172, **183-4**

185-6

(all lining)
192, 210

189 — short

190, **199-200**, 202-3, 205 — axe head

190

193, 198

(lining)
219, 221, 226

218

237

223-4, 232

222, 231

220

225, 228

236, 238

233

239-40

(non-lining)
235

234 (lining) (top)

(all lining)
247-8, 251, **259**, 299

274, 290

266, 270, 275, 291-2, 294

271 — slight thinning

261

250, **252**, 263, 284-5, 300, 302

254, 256, 296

301

303

(lining) (top)
5, 22, 30, 77, 80, 108 — curled up

54, 58, 68, 79 — curl

30, **62**, 110, 116, 130, 147 — ball

9, 13, **28**, 98, 113, 135

75, **84-5**, 128, 140 — spike

104

138, 140-1

(base)
93, 95-6

11, 20, 36, 56, **59**, 61, 108 — full serif

25 — turned downwards

7, 26, 136 — curled up

9, 58, 79 — small hanging serif

14, 29, **81**, 92, 116 — curl

31, **71**, 84, 134, 139

45, 47, **75**

51, 142, **150** — ogee curve

27 — curl

34

(non-lining)

78 — curl

32, **65** — full (hanging serif)

69, 72

(all lining) (top)
151, 166

160, 172, 181, 186 — curled up

161, **167-8**, 187 — long curl

156 — curl & blob

152, **174**, 177-8 — curl & pear

(base)
157 — full serif

151 — no serif

164, 169, 179, 181, **186** — ogee curve

156

(all lining) (top)
188, 196 — no contrast

189 — long curl

201 — no contrast

191, 202 — some contrast

203

205

(base)
197 — long serif

189 — curve

NB. Bold figures indicate the specimen illustrated above.

'Special Earmarks'
The 'special earmarks' (or distinctive identifying features) are indicated on each letter. The general 'style' of typefaces with the same 'earmark' may vary. The figures refer to specimen numbers.

203

191, **213**

201-2, **205**

206

203

214 — blob, ogee curve

(lining) (top)

218, 236-8

222, 240

239

230-1

226 (base)

228, 236, 238

230-1, **233**, 239

238

227, 237 (non-lining)

232 — full serif

234-5 — half serif

(all lining) (top)

249

246, **259**-60, 266, 271, 304

265 — curl

258, **261**-2, 296, 298 — longer curl

295, **297** (base)

271

290

298 (lining) (top)

1

54, 58, 68, 77-80

16, 125, 139

82, 113, 123-4, 126

86 — pear

138

13, 45

75, 84, 98, 140 — pointed wedge serif

6 — angular

36

104 — curved, spiked serifs, flat

50, 128, 147

22

5

134

111, **135**, 141

112

9, 28 (bottom tail endings where different from top – curved top typefaces only)

12, **42**, 44, 108

17, 71

58, **68**

27

6, 20, 35, 38-9, 41, **52**-3, 55-6, 59, 61, 63, 70, 73, 87-8, 92, 94, 101, 105, 109, 125, 139

79-80

86

76

98

148 (non-lining)

65

14

78

32

8, **81** (all lining) (top)

182

159, 173, **181**

172, 186

173

158

152, **174**

165

'Special Earmarks'
The 'special earmarks' (or distinctive identifying features) are indicated on each letter. The general 'style' of typefaces with the same 'earmark' may vary. The figures refer to specimen numbers.

151, **166** *flat top*

214

(lining)

161, 167-8, 187 *curved top*

220, **222**, 240

155

223-5

157, 183

227

(all lining) *curved top*

236, 238

188

237

191, 202-3

219 *spiked serif*

201

226

205

233

3/61 *flat top*

229

190, 192

189

228 *flat top*

218

230

231

(non-lining)

235

232

234

(all lining) *curved top*

253, 259, 266

261, 265

284

285 *flat top*

246, **249**, 255, 260, 298

271, 304

296-7 *flat base*

303 *square*

(lining) (top)

8, 10, **84**-5, 94, 117, 125, 150

82

51, 113 *slight bowing*

23-4, 93, 147 *open*

28

104

(diagonal)

8, 57, 82, 85 *bowing*

1, 11-12, **29**-31, 42, 44, 82, 109, 128, 142

(crossbar terminal)

11, 36, **54**, 68 *full serif*

1, **7**, 12, 22, 26-7 *curled up*

135

44

17

(foot serif)

(non-lining) (top)

81, 143

14

(crossbar terminal)

14, 69

25, 81, **132** *turned up serif*

19, 77

(foot serif)

4

89

14 *turned foot*

(all lining)

158

182

172 *slight bowing*

153, **160**, 180

181 *'nib'*

160 *turned up serif*

166

182

(all lining)

190, 202

216 *bowing*

197

NB. *Bold figures indicate the specimen illustrated above.*

'Special Earmarks'
The 'special earmarks' (or distinctive identifying features) are indicated on each letter. The general 'style' of typefaces with the same 'earmark' may vary. The figures refer to specimen numbers.

(lining)
(top)

4
227

4
line serif
236, 238

4
↓
230

(diagonal)

slight bowing
4
226, 239-40

4
225, 237

(crossbar terminal)

4
full serif
218, 231, 236

4
turned up serif
228

4
221

4
230, **240**

(foot serif)

4
239-40

(non-lining)

4
232

4
234

4
235

(all lining)

4
272, 296

4
251, **274**

(diagonal)

4
303-4

4
247-8, **270**, 299-300

slight bowing
4
269, 297

(lining)
(top)

5
6, 117

5
12, 87, 125-6

5
turned down serif
2, 33, 82, 113, 128, 130

5
75, 134-5

5
turned up serif
27-8

5
gradual tapering
34

(base)

5
152, 155, 184

5
9, 28, 42, 45, 75, 84-5, 104

5
151, 165-6, 183

(all lining)

5
191, 194-5

5
201

(non-lining)

5
14

5
19

5
81

5
40, 107

5
60, 65

5
78

(all lining)

5
219, 240

5
189

ball
5
206-**9**, 211-7

(lining)
(top)

5
218, **224**

5
223, 226, 239

5
222, 225

turned up serif
5
219, 240

turned down serif
5
230, **233**, 237

↓
5
220, 227, **229**

(base)

5
220, 223-4

5
222, **225**, 240

5
230-1

5
239

(non-lining)

5
232, **235**

5
234

(all lining)

5
299

(base)

5
flat
290, 296-**7**, 303

5
304

(lining)
(top)

6
128

half serif
6
85

6
86, **101**, 147

6
vertical wedge serif
45, 104, 140

6
141

6
curl
5

(bowl)

6
open
13, 16, 18, 22, **44**, 83, 90, 108, 125, 135

(non-lining)

long top
6
46

(all lining)

6
166

6
open
181

(all lining)

6
189, **194**-5

'Special Earmarks'
The 'special earmarks' (or distinctive identifying features) are indicated on each letter. The general 'style' of typefaces with the same 'earmark' may vary. The figures refer to specimen numbers.

(6)
205

(6 ball)
206-9, **211-4**, 216-7

(lining)
(6 vertical serif)
224-5

(6)
219, 227

(6 hook serif)
231

(6)
228

(6)
236, 238

(6)
221, 229

(6)
240

(6 wedge serif)
230

(6 open)
222, 239

(non-lining)
(6)
232

(6)
215

(all lining)
(6)
251-2, **254**, 258-9, 262-4

(6)
265

(⌐)
303

(6)
295-6

(lining)
(top)
(7 turned up serif)
44

(7 wedge serif)
17, **134**

---

(7)
71, 92, 139

(7 short top)
7

(7)
92

(back)
(7 bowing)
15, **21**, 51, 82

(7 tapering)
31, **33**, 44

(𝟕)
142

(foot)
(7 long serif)
36

(7)
82, 85, 128

(7 bent)
108

(7 'nib')
12-13, **76**

(non-lining)
(7 wedge serif)
14

(7 turned down serif)
143

(7)
81, 97

(7)
4

(all lining)
(7 bowing)
156

(7 ball)
153

(7 full serif)
157, 165, 181

(all lining)
(7)
191, **203**

(lining)
(7)
240

(7 thickening)
228

(7 bend)
220

(7)
231

(7)
239-40

(all lining)
(7 vertical half serif)
273, 281, 290, 298, 303

(7)
298

(⌐)
303

(lining)
(8 open open)
22

(8 open)
104

(8 bottom heavy)
29, **34**, 47, 125, 128, 142, 150

(8 slightly square)
140

(non-lining)
(8)
14

(8)
65, 78

(8 stepped crossover)
8, **72**

(all lining)
(8)
151

(8 flattened)
169

(all lining)
(8 bottom heavy)
194-5

(lining)
(8 bottom heavy)
237

(8 open)
239

(non-lining)
(8 stepped crossover)
232

(8 stepped crossover)
266, **284**

(8 bottom heavy)
265, 296, **298**-300

(⌐)
303

(lining)
(9)
16, **18**, 22, 90, 104, 108, 125, 135

(9)
104, 140

(9)
5

(9)
9, 28

(9 pear)
54, 62, 77, **79**, 110, 117, 125, 130, 138, 150

NB. *Bold figures indicate the specimen illustrated above.*

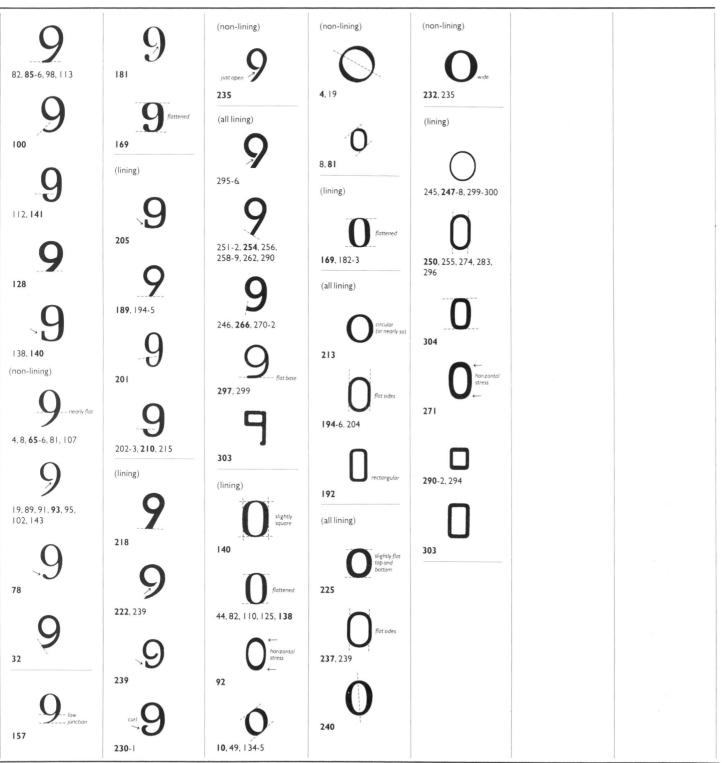

9
82, **85**-6, 98, 113

9
100

9
112, **141**

9
128

9
138, **140**

(non-lining)

9 — nearly flat
4, 8, **65**-6, 81, 107

9
19, 89, 91, **93**, 95, 102, 143

9
78

9
32

9 — low junction
157

9
181

9 flattened
169

(lining)

9
205

9
189, 194-5

9
201

9
202-3, **210**, 215

(lining)

9
218

9
222, 239

9
239

curl **9**
230-1

(non-lining)

9 just open
235

(all lining)

9
295-6

9
251-2, **254**, 256, 258-9, 262, 290

9
246, **266**, 270-2

9 — flat base
297, 299

9
303

(lining)

0 slightly square
140

0 flattened
44, 82, 110, 125, **138**

0 horizontal stress
92

0
10, 49, 134-5

(non-lining)

0
4, 19

0
8, **81**

(lining)

0 flattened
169, 182-3

(all lining)

0 circular (or nearly so)
213

0 flat sides
194-6, 204

0 rectangular
192

(all lining)

0 slightly flat top and bottom
225

0 flat sides
237, 239

0
240

(non-lining)

0 wide
232, 235

(lining)

0
245, **247**-8, 299-300

0
250, 255, 274, 283, 296

0
304

0 horizontal stress
271

0
290-2, 294

0
303

'Special Earmarks'
The 'special earmarks' (or distinctive identifying features) are indicated on each letter. The general 'style' of typefaces with the same 'earmark' may vary. The figures refer to specimen numbers.

NB. *Bold figures indicate the specimen illustrated above.*

pt.2:
(non-continuous text)

[Decorative]
typefaces

FLOWING
SCRIPTS

NON-FLOWING
SCRIPTS
(INCLUDING
BLACKLETTER & UNCIAL)

UNMODIFIED
(FORMAL TEXT SHAPE)

FAT FACE
& THIN FACE
(UNMODIFIED & MODIFIED)

ORNAMENTAL

MODIFIED
SERIF

MODIFIED
SANS SERIF

MODIFIED
SANS SERIF

MODIFIED
OUTRAGEOUS

DECORATIVE TYPEFACE CATEGORIES

THIS PART OF the book contains a cross-section of decorative typefaces, i.e. those not normally used for continuous text setting. Instead, they are used for headings and titling or in limited quantities and situations for display purposes. The characteristic features of each of the eight typeface categories are described below and are illustrated on the opposite page.

As with *Text* typefaces **the classification system and terminology is entirely new and does not follow established type classifications.** Categories are based on specific design features.

Each category is further divided into smaller groups according to more specific design features which are explained at the beginning of each section. Typeface specimens are then arranged alphabetically within each group and have an individual specimen number which is cross-referenced to the index.

NB. There is inevitably a small overlap between the *Text* and *Decorative* parts of the book. For instance, some *Decorative* typefaces in special circumstances may be used for continuous text setting and vice-versa.

Categories are as follows:

1. Flowing Scripts Nos. 305-322

This category includes script typefaces which, when typeset, give a 'joined up' script effect so that words appear to be 'flowing' as in handwriting. The category is divided into smaller groups of quill pen, felt or graphic pen and brush script effects. A further division is made into sloping, upright, rounded and angular forms.

2. Non-Flowing Scripts
(including Blackletter & Uncial)
Nos. 323-381

As the term describes, this category includes script typefaces in which the letters remain unjoined when typeset and are, therefore, 'non-flowing'. As in the 'flowing' category there are groups for quill pen, felt or graphic pen and brush. This category includes blackletter and uncial typefaces together with a small group of roman italic typefaces based on pen scripts.

3. Unmodified (Formal Text Shape)
Nos. 382-428

This category contains typefaces that generally adhere to the formal and traditional letter shapes normally associated with continuous text typefaces but which are usually used for decorative applications. However, it excludes those typefaces which, though conforming to this criteria, are either very bold or very thin. These will be found in the next category Fat & Thin Face. The category is arranged in groups according to whether the design is roman, slab, wedge or sans serif in origin and within each of these divisions there are separate groups for outline, inline, shaded, or with background versions.

4. Fat Face & Thin Face
(Unmodified & Modified)
Nos Fat 429-515, Thin 516-536

This category is divided into two parts and contains a selection of typefaces which represent the extremes in weight – very bold (Fat Face) and very light (Thin Face). As with the Unmodified Section, arrangement is by roman, slab, wedge and sans serif groups. The substantial roman serif group is further sub-divided depending on whether the typefaces have thin, medium or thick serifs. The sans serif group is also divided into typefaces of wide, medium or narrow design or of a special rounded shape. *NB. A small number of typefaces with Fat Face characteristics are to be found in the Modified Serif and Sans Serif categories as they were felt better placed there.*

5. Ornamental Nos. 537-563

Grouped here are typefaces of a particularly elaborate (often 'floriated') and highly decorated nature. In addition, those with 'swash style' characteristics or flourishes have been included. Consistent with the previous two sections, typefaces are arranged into roman, slab, wedge and sans serif groups. There is also a small group of script-based typefaces.

6. Modified Serif Nos. 564-603

The term 'modified' means non-formal or non-traditional letter shapes. Modification is by distortion, added or other subtracted elements (such as, for example, stencil letters) or by axis (sloping backwards). Arrangement is by roman, slab, wedge and sans serif groups. *NB. This category includes some typefaces with Fat Face characteristics that were felt better placed here.*

7. Modified Sans Serif Nos. 604-665

This section covers all 'modified' typefaces without serifs. Due to the varied and unusual nature of this typeface category new explanatory group headings have been created such as: vertical and horizontal thick and thin stress, electronic, cut, stencil or stencil effect, and striped or inline. *NB. This category includes some typefaces with Fat Face characteristics which were felt better placed here.*

8. Modified Outrageous Nos. 666-700

This final category includes both 'modified' serif and sans serif typefaces that are of a particularly unusual or 'way out' nature. They are highly stylised and often humorous and intended for special, very limited use only. Typeface groups include: heavy, inline or striped, dot-formed, shaded and 3D, with backgrounds and pictorial.

NB. A very small number of typeface specimens in this part of the book do not include an ampersand.

The Typefinding Process

1. To identify a typeface, first decide into which one of main categories shown opposite the typeface specimen you wish to identify belongs.

2. Using the thumb index on the edge of the page turn to the appropriate category introduction page.

3. From the listings there select the specific group within the category to which the specimen relates.

4. Read off the specimen numbers given for this group and find them in the following listings of typeface specimens.

5. Decide which of the typefaces in the group it equates to by 'scanning' the alphabetical listings until you find a typeface to which your specimen matches.

Type categories

General characteristics

1. Flowing Scripts. *Nos 305-322*

e.g. **310** Palace Script, **316** ITC Zapf Chancery, **319** Kaufmann and **322** Mistral.

Groups include:
quill pen — sloping and rounded | *quill pen — upright and rounded* | *felt or graphic pen — sloping* | *felt or graphic pen — upright* | *brush*

FLOWING SCRIPTS

2. Non-Flowing Scripts. (including Blackletter & Uncial) *Nos 323-381*

e.g. **323** Bernhard Tango, **333** Bologna, **372** Old English Text and **380** Blado Italic.

Groups include:
quill pen | *felt or graphic pen* | *brush* | *blackletter* | *uncial*

NON-FLOWING SCRIPTS (INCLUDING BLACKLETTER & UNCIAL)

3. Unmodified. *Nos 382-428*

e.g. **385** Engravers Roman, **392** Castellar, **412** Latin Antique No 9 and **422** Helvetica Outline.

roman serif | *slab serif* | *wedge serif* | *sans serif*

UNMODIFIED (FORMAL TEXT SHAPE)

4. Fat Face & Thin Face. *Nos 429-536* (Modified & Unmodified)

e.g. **434** Falstaff, **467** Cooper Black, **514** Harry Fat and **536** Harry Thin.

roman serif | *slab serif* | *wedge serif* | *sans serif*

FAT FACE & THIN FACE (UNMODIFIED & MODIFIED)

5. Ornamental. *Nos 537-563*

e.g. **540** Fry's Ornamented, **548** Lettres Ornées **554** Davida and **561** Ballé Initials.

roman serif | *slab serif* | *wedge serif* | *sans serif* | *script*

ORNAMENTAL

6. Modified Serif. *Nos 564-603*

e.g. **566** Belwe, **575** Stencil Bold, **579** Profil and **585** Charleston.

roman serif | *slab serif* | *wedge serif* | *wedge serif (sloping backwards)*

MODIFIED SERIF

7. Modified Sans Serif. *Nos 604-665*

e.g. **608** Peignot, **619** Frankfurter Medium, **626** Countdown and **646** Neon.

Groups include:
thick and thin stress (vertical) | *rounded* | *electronic* | *cut* | *shaded or 3D*

MODIFIED SANS SERIF

8. Modified Outrageous. *Nos 666-700*

e.g. **668** Litzenburg, **679** Shatter, **682** Pinball and **688** Calypso.

Groups include:
heavy distorted | *inline or striped* | *dot-formed* | *shaded or 3D* | *pictorial*

MODIFIED OUTRAGEOUS

I. FLOWING SCRIPTS

Specimen nos		Basic characteristics	Secondary characteristics	
305-315	*Flow*	quill pen	sloping and rounded	e.g. **310** Palace Script
316	*Flow*	,,	sloping and angular	e.g. **316** ITC Zapf Chancery
317-318	*Flow*	,,	upright	e.g. **318** Linoscript
319	*Flow*	felt pen or graphic pen	sloping	e.g. **319** Kaufmann
320	*Flow*	,,	upright	e.g. **320** Jiffy
321-322	*Flow*	brush		e.g. **322** Mistral

NB. *Typefaces in each group are arranged in alphabetical order.*

FLOWING SCRIPTS

Scr

Ariston Light Script
Bank Script
Commercial Script
Diskus
Künstler Schreibschrift
Palace Script
Park Avenue
Shelley Allegro Script
Shelley Andante Script
Snell Roundhand

quill pen sloping and rounded

305 Ariston Light Script

ABCDEFGHIJKLMNOPQRSTUVWXYZ&

306 Bank Script

ABCDEFGHIJKLMNOPQRSTUVWXYZ

307 Commercial Script

ABCDEFGHIJKLMNOPQRSTUVWXYZ

308 Diskus

ABCDEFGHIJKLMNOPQRSTUVWXYZ&

309 Künstler Schreibschrift

ABCDEFGHIJKLMNOPQRSTUVWXYZ&

310 Palace Script

ABCDEFGHIJKLMNOPQRSTUVWXYZ&

311 Park Avenue

ABCDEFGHIJKLMNOPQRSTUVWXYZ&

312 Shelley Allegro Script

ABCDEFGHIJKLMNOPQRSTUVWXYZ&

313 Shelley Andante Script

ABCDEFGHIJKLMNOPQRSTUVWXYZ&

314 Snell Roundhand

ABCDEFGHIJKLMNOPQRSTUVWXYZ&

Ariston Light Script **305**

abcdefghijklmnopqrstuvwxyz1234567890

Bank Script **306**

abcdefghijklmnopqrstuvwxyz1234567890

Commercial Script **307**

abcdefghijklmnopqrstuvwxyz 1234567890

Diskus **308**

abcdefghijklmnopqrstuvwxyz1234567890

Künstler Schreibschrift **309**

abcdefghijklmnopqrstuvwxyz1234567890

Palace Script **310**

abcdefghijklmnopqrstuvwxyz 1234567890

Park Avenue **311**

abcdefghijklmnopqrstuvwxyz1234567890

Shelley Allegro Script **312**

abcdefghijklmnopqrstuvwxyz1234567890

Shelley Andante Script **313**

abcdefghijklmnopqrstuvwxyz1234567890

Snell Roundhand **314**

abcdefghijklmnopqrstuvwxyz1234567890

FLOWING SCRIPTS

Scr

Yale Script
ITC Zapf Chancery
Gando Ronde Script
Linoscript
Kaufmann
Jiffy
Brush Script
Mistral

315 Yale Script

A B C D E F G H I J K L M N O P Q R S T U V W X Y Z

quill pen
sloping
and angular

316 ITC Zapf Chancery

ABCDEFGHIJKLMNOPQRSTUVWXYZ&

felt or
graphic pen
upright

317 Gando Ronde Script

A B C D E F G H I J K L M N O P Q R S T U V W X Y Z &

quill pen
upright
rounded

318 Linoscript

A B C D E F G H I J K L M N O P Q R S T U V W X Y Z &

felt or
graphic pen
sloping

319 Kaufmann

A B C D E F G H I J K L M N O P Q R S T U V W X Y Z &

320 Jiffy

A B C D E F G H I J K L M N O P Q R S T U V W X Y Z &

brush

321 Brush Script

A B C D E F G H I J K L M N O P Q R S T U V W X Y Z &

322 Mistral

ABCDEFGHIJKLMNOPQRSTUVWXYZ&

FLOWING SCRIPTS

Scr

Yale Script
ITC Zapf Chancery
Gando Ronde Script
Linoscript
Kaufmann
Jiffy
Brush Script
Mistral

Yale Script **315**

abcdefghijklmnopqrstuvwxyz 1234567890

ITC Zapf Chancery **316**

abcdefghijklmnopqrstuvwxyz1234567890

Gando Ronde Script **317**

abcdefghijklmnopqrstuvwxyz1234567890

Linoscript **318**

abcdefghijklmnopqrstuvwxyz1234567890

Kaufmann **319**

abcdefghijklmnopqrstuvwxyz1234567890

Jiffy **320**

abcdefghijklmnopqrstuvwxyz1234567890

Brush Script **321**

abcdefghijklmnopqrstuvwxyz1234567890

Mistral **322**

abcdefghijklmnopqrstuvwxyz1234567890

2. NON-FLOWING SCRIPTS
(INCLUDING BLACKLETTER & UNCIAL)

Specimen nos		Basic characteristics	Secondary characteristics	
323-326	*Nofl*	quill pen	sloping and rounded	e.g. **323** Bernhard Tango
327-331	*Nofl*	,,	sloping and angular	e.g. **330** Noris Script
332	*Nofl*	,,	upright and rounded	e.g. **332** Murray Hill Bold
333-336	*Nofl*	,,	upright and angular	e.g. **333** Bologna
337-338	**Nofl**	,,	'oriental'	e.g. **337** Auriol
339-343	*Nofl*	,,	decorative sloping	e.g. **343** Vivaldi
344-345	*Nofl*	,,	decorative upright	e.g. **344** Delphin No 1
346-352	*Nofl*	felt or graphic pen	sloping	e.g. **350** Sallwey Script
353-356	*Nofl*	,,	upright	e.g. **353** Artic
357-362	**Nofl**	brush		e.g. **359** Flash

NB. *Typefaces in each group are arranged in alphabetical order.*

continued on next page

Specimen nos

363-374	𝕹𝖔𝖋𝖑	blackletter	text	e.g. **372** Old English Text
375-376	𝕹𝖔𝖋𝖑	„	decorative	e.g. **376** St. Clair
377-378	nofl	uncial		e.g. **378** Libra
379-381	*Nofl*	roman italic (based on pen scripts)		e.g. **380** Blado Italic

NON-FLOWING SCRIPTS (INCLUDING BLACKLETTER & UNCIAL)

Scr

NB. *Typefaces in each group are arranged in alphabetical order.*

quill pen
sloping
and rounded

323 Bernhard Tango

ABCDEFGHIJKLMNOPQRSTUVWXYZ&

324 Dorchester Script

ABCDEFGHIJKLMNOP2RSTUVWXYZ&

325 Nuptial Script

ABCDEFGHIJKLMNOP2RSTUVWXYZ &

326 Stradivarius

ABCDEFGHIJKLMNOPQRSTUVWXYZ

quill pen
sloping
and angular

327 Cascade

ABCDEFGHIJKLMNOPQRSTUVWXYZ&

328 Klang

ABCDEFGHIJKLMNOPQRSTUVWXYZ&

329 Medici Script

ABCDEFGHIJKLMNOPQRSTUVWXYZ&

330 Noris Script

ABCDEFGHIJKLMNOPQRSTUVWXYZ&

331 Temple Script

ABCDEFGHIJKLMNOPQRSTUVWXYZ&

quill pen
upright
and rounded

332 Murray Hill Bold

ABCDEFGHIJKLMNOP2RSTUVWXYZ&

Bernhard Tango **323**

abcdefghijklmnopqrstuvwxyz 1234567890

Dorchester Script **324**

abcdefghijklmnopqrstuvwxyz1234567890

Nuptial Script **325**

abcdefghijklmnopqrstuvwxyz1234567890

Stradivarius **326**

abcdefghijklmnopqrstuvwxyz1234567890

Cascade **327**

abcdefghijklmnopqrstuvwxyz 1234567890

Klang **328**

abcdefghijklmnopqrstuvwxyz1234567890

Medici Script **329**

abcdefghijklmnopqrstuvwxyz1234567890

Noris Script **330**

abcdefghijklmnopqrstuvwxyz1234567890

Temple Script **331**

abcdefghijklmnopqrstuvwxyz1234567890

Murray Hill Bold **332**

abcdefghijklmnopqrstuvwxyz 1234567890

NON-FLOWING SCRIPTS
(INCLUDING BLACKLETTER & UNCIAL)

Scr

Bernhard Tango
Dorchester Script
Nuptial Script
Stradivarius
Cascade
Klang
Medici Script
Noris Script
Temple Script
Murray Hill Bold

NON-FLOWING SCRIPTS
(INCLUDING BLACKLETTER & UNCIAL)

Scr

Bologna
Codex
Lydian
Ondine
Auriol
Boutique
Crayonette
Kalligraphia
Le Griffe
Treasury Open

quill pen
upright
and angular

333 Bologna

ABCDEFGHIJKLMNOPQRSTUVWXYZ&

334 Codex

ABCDEFGHIJKLMNOPQRSTUVWXYZ&

335 Lydian

ABCDEFGHIJKLMNOPQRSTUVWXYZ&

336 Ondine

ABCDEFGHIJKLMNOPQRSTUVWXYZ

quill pen
'oriental'

337 Auriol

ABCDEFGHIJKLMNOPQRSTUVWXYZ&

338 Boutique

ABCDEFGHIJKLMNOPQRSTUVWXYZ&

quill pen
decorative
sloping

339 Crayonette

ABCDEFGHIJKLMNOPQRSTUVWXYZ&

340 Kalligraphia

ABCDEFGHIJKLMNOPQRSTUVWXYZ&

341 Le Griffe

ABCDEFGHIJKLMNOPQRSTUVWXYZ&

342 Treasury Open

ABCDEFGHIJKLMNOPQRSTUVWXYZ&

Bologna **333**

abcdefghijklmnopqrstuvwxyz1234567890

Codex **334**

abcdefghijklmnopqrstuvwxyz 1234567890

Lydian **335**

abcdefghijklmnopqrstuvwxyz 1234567890

Ondine **336**

abcdefghijklmnopqrstuvwxyz 1234567890

Auriol **337**

abcdefghijklmnopqrstuvwxyz 1234567890

Boutique **338**

abcdefghijklmnopqrstuvwxyz 1234567890

Crayonette **339**

abcdefghijklmnopqrstuvwxyz 1234567890

Kalligraphia **340**

abcdefghijklmnopqrstuvwxyz1234567890

Le Griffe **341**

abcdefghijklmnopqrstuvwxyz 1234567890

Treasury Open **342**

abcdefghijklmnopqrstuvwxyz1234567890

NON-FLOWING SCRIPTS (INCLUDING BLACKLETTER & UNCIAL)

Scr

Bologna
Codex
Lydian
Ondine
Auriol
Boutique
Crayonette
Kalligraphia
Le Griffe
Treasury Open

343 Vivaldi

ABCDEFGHIJKLMNOPQRSTUVWXYZ&

344 Delphin No 1

ABCDEFGHIJKLMNOPQRSTUVWXYZ&

345 Matura

ABCDEFGHIJKLMNOPQRSTUVWXYZ&

346 Balloon Extra Bold

ABCDEFGHIJKLMNOPQRSTUVWXYZ&

347 Caprice

ABCDEFGHIJKLMNOPQRSTUVWXYZ&

348 Gillies Extra Bold

ABCDEFGHIJKLMNOPQRSTUVWXYZ&

349 Lateinische Ausgangsschrift

ABCDEFGHIJKLMNOPQRSTUVWXYZ

350 Sallwey Script

ABCDEFGHIJKLMNOPQRSTUVWXYZ&

351 Venture

ABCDEFGHIJKLMNOPQRSTUVWXYZ&

352 Vertex

ABCDEFGHIJKLMNOPQRSTUVWXYZ&

NON-FLOWING SCRIPTS
(INCLUDING BLACKLETTER & UNCIAL)

Scr

Vivaldi
Delphin No 1
Matura
Balloon Extra Bold
Caprice
Gillies Extra Bold
Lateinische Ausgangsschrift
Sallwey Script
Venture
Vertex

Vivaldi **343**

abcdefghijklmnopqrstuvwxyz1234567890

Delphin No I **344**

abcdefghijklmnopqrstuvwxyz1234567890

Matura **345**

abcdefghijklmnopqrstuvwxyz1234567890

Balloon Extra Bold **346**

1234567890 no lower case

Caprice **347**

abcdefghijklmnopqrstuvwxyz1234567890

Gillies Extra Bold **348**

abcdefghijklmnopqrstuvwxyz1234567890

Lateinische Ausgangsschrift **349**

abcdefghijklmnopqrstuvwæyz1234567890

Sallwey Script **350**

abcdefghijklmnopqrstuvwxyz1234567890

Venture **351**

abcdefghijklmnopqrstuvwxyz1234567890

Vertex **352**

abcdefghijklmnopqrstuvwxyz1234567890

felt or graphic pen upright

353 Artic

ABCDEFGHIJKLMNOPQRSTUVWXYZ&

354 Dom Casual

ABCDEFGHIJKLMNOPQRSTUVWXYZ&

355 Present

ABCDEFGHIJJKLMNOPQRSTUVWXYZ&

356 Studio

ABCDEFGHIJKLMNOPQRSTUVWXYZ&

brush

357 Ashley Script

ABCDEFGHIJKLMNOPQRSTUVWXYZ&

358 Bison

ABCDEFGHIJJKLMNOPQRSTUVWXYZ&

359 Flash

ABCDEFGHIJKLMNOPQRSTUVWXYZ&

360 Forte

ABCDEFGHIJKLMNOPQRSTUVWXYZ&

361 Pepita

ABCDEFGHIJKLMNOPQRSTUVWXYZ&

362 Reporter No 2

ABCDEFGHIJKLMNOPQRSTUVWXYZ&

Artic **353**

abcdefghijklmnopqrstuvwxyz1234567890

Dom Casual **354**

abcdefghijklmnopqrstuvwxyz1234567890

Present **355**

abcdefghijklmnopqrstuvwxyz1234567890

Studio **356**

abcdefghijkl mnopqrstuvwxyz1234567890

Ashley Script **357**

abcdefghijklmnopqrstuvwxyz*1234567890*

Bison **358**

abcdefghijklmnopqrstuvwxyz1234567890

Flash **359**

abcdefghijklmnopqrstuvwxyz1234567890

Forte **360**

abcdefghijklmnopqrstuvwxyz1234567890

Pepita **361**

abcdefghijklmnopqrstuvwxyz1234567890

Reporter No 2 **362**

abcdefghijklmnopqrstuvwxyz1234567890

NON-FLOWING SCRIPTS (INCLUDING BLACKLETTER & UNCIAL)

Scr

blackletter
text

**NON-FLOWING
SCRIPTS
(INCLUDING
BLACKLETTER & UNCIAL)**

Scr

Caligra
Cloister Black
Fette Fraktur
Fraktur Bold
Gothique
Goudy Text
ITC Honda
Linotext
Luthersche Fraktur
Old English Text

363 Caligra

ABCDEFGHIJKLMNOPQRSTUVWXYZ

364 Cloister Black

ABCDEFGHIJKLMNOPQRSTUVWWXYZ&

365 Fette Fraktur

ABCDEFGHIJKLMNOPQRSTUVWXYZ&

366 Fraktur Bold

ABCDEFGHIJKLMNOPQRSTUVWXYZ&

367 Gothique

ABCDEFGHIJKLMNOPQRSTUVWXYZ&

368 Goudy Text

ABCDEFGHIJKLMNOPQRSTUVWXYZ&

369 ITC Honda

ABCDEFGHIJKLMNOPQRSTUVWXYZ&

370 Linotext

ABCDEFGHIJKLMNOPQRSTUVWXYZ&

371 Luthersche Fraktur

ABCDEFGHIJKLMNOPQRSTUVWXYZ&

372 Old English Text

ABCDEFGHIJKLMNOPQRSTUVWXYZ&

Caligra **363**

abcdefghijklmnopqrstuvwxyz1234567890

Cloister Black **364**

abcdefghijklmnopqrstubwxyz1234567890

Fette Fraktur **365**

abcdefghijklmnopqrstuvwxyz1234567890

Fraktur Bold **366**

abcdefghijklmnopqrstuvwxyz1234567890

Gothique **367**

abcdefghijklmnopqrstuvwxyz1234567890

Goudy Text **368**

abcdefghijklmnopqrstuvwxyz1234567890

ITC Honda **369**

abcdefghijklmnopqrstuvwxyz1234567890

Linotext **370**

abcdefghijklmnopqrstubwxyz1234567890

Luthersche Fraktur **371**

abcdefghijklmnopqrstuvwxyz1234567890

Old English Text **372**

abcdefghijklmnopqrstubwxyz1234567890

NON-FLOWING SCRIPTS (INCLUDING BLACKLETTER & UNCIAL)

Scr

Caligra
Cloister Black
Fette Fraktur
Fraktur Bold
Gothique
Goudy Text
ITC Honda
Linotext
Luthersche Fraktur
Old English Text

NON-FLOWING SCRIPTS
(INCLUDING BLACKLETTER & UNCIAL)

Scr

Venetian Text
Condensed

Wilhelm Klingspor
Gotisch

Pamela

St. Clair

American Uncial

Libra

Arrighi Italic
(Centaur Italic)

Blado Italic

Cancelleresca
Bastarda

373 Venetian Text Condensed

ABCDEFGHIJKLMNOPQRSTUVWXYZ&

374 Wilhelm Klingspor Gotisch

ABCDEFGHIJKLMNOPQRSTUVWXYZ&

blackletter
decorative

375 Pamela

ABCDEFGHIJKLMNOPQRSTUVWXYZ&

376 St. Clair

ABCDEFGHIJKLMNOPQRSTUVWXYZ&

uncial

377 American Uncial

abcdefghijklmnopqrstuvwxyz&

378 Libra

abcdefghijklmnopqrstuvwxyz

roman italic
(based on
pen scripts)

379 Arrighi Italic (Centaur Italic)

ABCDEFGHIJKLMNOPQRSTUVWXYZ&

380 Blado Italic

ABCDEFGHIJKLMNOPQRSTUVWXYZ&

381 Cancelleresca Bastarda

ABCDEFGHIJKLMNOPQRSTUVWXYZ

Venetian Text Condensed **373**

abcdefghijklmnopqrstuvwxyz **1234567890**

Wilhelm Klingspor Gotisch **374**

abcdefghijklmnopqrstuvwxyz1234567890

Pamela **375**

abcdefghijklmnopqrstuvwxyz *no figures*

St. Clair **376**

abcdefghijklmnopqrstuvwxyz1234567890

American Uncial **377**

1234567890 *no lower case*

Libra **378**

1234567890 *no lower case*

Arrighi Italic (Centaur Italic) **379**

abcdefghijklmnopqrstuvwxyz 1234567890

Blado Italic **380**

abcdefghijklmnopqrstuvwxyz 1234567890

Cancelleresca Bastarda **381**

abcdefghijklmnopqrstuvwxyz1234567890

NON-FLOWING SCRIPTS
(INCLUDING BLACKLETTER & UNCIAL)

Scr

Venetian Text Condensed
Wilhelm Klingspor Gotisch
Pamela
St. Clair
American Uncial
Libra
Arrighi Italic (Centaur Italic)
Blado Italic
Cancelleresca Bastarda

3. UNMODIFIED
(FORMAL TEXT SHAPE)

Specimen nos		Basic characteristics	Secondary characteristics	
382-390	R	roman serif		e.g. **385** Engravers Roman
391-399	R	,,	inline and outline	e.g. **392** Castellar
400-402	R	,,	shaded	e.g. **402** Thorne Shaded
403	SL	slab serif		e.g. **403** Hellenic Wide
404-405	SL	,,	inline and outline	e.g. **405** Egyptian Outline
406-408	SL	,,	shaded	e.g. **407** Gold Rush
409-415	W	wedge serif		e.g. **412** Latin Antique No 9
416-419	W	,,	inline	e.g. **417** Chisel
420-421	SA	sans serif		e.g. **420** Fleet
422	SA	,,	outline	e.g. **422** Helvetica Outline

NB. *Typefaces in each group are arranged in alphabetical order.*

continued on next page

UNMODIFIED
(FORMAL TEXT SHAPE)

UN

continued from previous page

423-426	SA	*(sans serif)*	*inline and outline shaded*	e.g. **425** Gill Sans Shadow 408
427-428	SA	,,	*with backgrounds*	e.g. **427** Gill Cameo

NB. *Typefaces in each group are arranged in alphabetical order.*

183

Bauer Classic Roman
Caslon Antique
Elizabeth Roman
Engravers Roman
Engravers Roman Bold
Felix Titling
Fleet Titling
Horizon
Victoria Titling
Caslon Open Face

roman serif

382 Bauer Classic Roman

ABCDEFGHIJKLMNOPQRSTUVWXYZ&

383 Caslon Antique

ABCDEFGHIJKLMNOPQRSTUVWXYZ&

384 Elizabeth Roman

ABCDEFGHIJKLMNOPQRSTUVWXYZ&

385 Engravers Roman

ABCDEFGHIJKLMNOPQRSTUVWXYZ&

386 Engravers Roman Bold

ABCDEFGHIJKLMNOPQRSTUVWXYZ&

387 Felix Titling

ABCDEFGHIJKLMNOPQRSTUVWXYZ

388 Fleet Titling

ABCDEFGHIJKLMNOPQRSTUVWXYZ&

389 Horizon

ABCDEFGHIJKLMNOPQRSTUVWXYZ&

390 Victoria Titling

ABCDEFGHIJKLMNOPQRSTUVWXYZ&

roman serif inline and outline

391 Caslon Open Face

ABCDEFGHIJKLMNOPQRSTUVWXYZ&

Bauer Classic Roman **382**

abcdefghijklmnopqrstuvwxyz1234567890

Caslon Antique **383**

abcdefghijklmnopqrstuvwxyz1234567890

Elizabeth Roman **384**

abcdefghijklmnopqrstuvwxyz 1234567890

small capitals (no lower case)

Engravers Roman **385**

ABCDEFGHIJKLMNOPQRSTUVWXYZ1234567890

small capitals (no lower case)

Engravers Roman Bold **386**

ABCDEFGHIJKLMNOPQRSTUVWXYZ1234567890

Felix Titling **387**

1234567890 *no lower case*

Fleet Titling **388**

1234567890 *no lower case*

Horizon **389**

abcdefghijklmnopqrstuvwxyz1234567890

Victoria Titling **390**

1234567890 *no lower case*

Caslon Open Face **391**

abcdefghijklmnopqrstuvwxyz1234567890

UNMODIFIED
(FORMAL TEXT SHAPE)

UN

Bauer Classic Roman
Caslon Antique
Elizabeth Roman
Engravers Roman
Engravers Roman Bold
Felix Titling
Fleet Titling
Horizon
Victoria Titling
Caslon Open Face

392 Castellar

ABCDEFGHIJKLMNOPQRSTUVWXYZ&

393 Cloister Open Face

ABCDEFGHIJKLMNOPQRSTUVWXYZ&

394 Goudy Handtooled

ABCDEFGHIJKLMNOPQRSTUVWXYZ

395 Hadriano Stonecut

ABCDEFGHIJKLMNOPQRSTUVWXYZ&

396 Old Style Bold Outline

ABCDEFGHIJKLMNOPQRSTUVWXYZ&

397 Times English Black Outline

ABCDEFGHIJKLMNOPQRSTUVWXYZ&

398 Windsor Bold Outline

ABCDEFGHIJKLMNOPQRSTUVWXYZ&

399 Windsor Elongated

ABCDEFGHIJKLMNOPQRSTUVWXYZ&

400 Bank Note

ABCDEFGHIJKLMNOPQRSTUVWXYZ&

401 Cheque

ABCDEFGHIJKLMNOPQRSTUVWXYZ&

UNMODIFIED
(FORMAL TEXT SHAPE)

UN

Castellar
Cloister Open Face
Goudy Handtooled
Hadriano Stonecut
Old Style Bold Outline
Times English
Black Outline
Windsor Bold Outline
Windsor Elongated
Bank Note
Cheque

roman serif
shaded

Castellar **392**

1234567890 *no lower case*

Cloister Open Face **393**

abcdefghijklmnopqrstuvwxyz1234567890

Goudy Handtooled **394**

abcdefghijklmnopqrstuvwxyz1234567890

Hadriano Stonecut **395**

1234567890 *no lower case*

Old Style Bold Outline **396**

abcdefghijklmnopqrstuvwxyz1234567890

Times English Black Outline **397**

abcdefghijklmnopqrstuvwxyz1234567890

Windsor Bold Outline **398**

abcdefghijklmnopqrstuvwxyz1234567890

Windsor Elongated **399**

abcdefghijklmnopqrstuvwxyz 1234567890

Bank Note **400**

1234567890 *no lower case*

Cheque **401**

1234567890 *no lower case*

UNMODIFIED
(FORMAL TEXT SHAPE)

UN

Castellar
Cloister Open Face
Goudy Handtooled
Hadriano Stonecut
Old Style Bold Outline
Times English
Black Outline
Windsor Bold Outline
Windsor Elongated
Bank Note
Cheque

402 Thorne Shaded

ABCDEFGHIJKLMNOPQRSTUVWXYZ

slab serif
inline and
outline

403 Hellenic Wide

ABCDEFGHIJKLMNOPQRSTUVWXYZ&

slab serif

404 ITC American Typewriter Bold Outline

ABCDEFGHIJKLMNOPQRSTUVWXYZ&

405 Egyptian Outline

ABCDEFGHIJKLMNOPQRSTUVWXYZ&

slab serif
shaded or 3D

406 Egyptienne Filette

ABCDEFGHIJKLMNOPQRSTUVWXYZ

407 Gold Rush

ABCDEFGHIJKLMNOPQRSTUVWXYZ&

408 Rockwell Shadow

ABCDEFGHIJKLMNOPQRSTUVWXYZ&

wedge serif

409 Augustea Nova

ABCDEFGHIJKLMNOPQRSTUVWXYZ&

410 Columna

ABCDEFGHIJKLMNOPQRSTUVWXYZ&

411 Jana

ABCDEFGHIJKLMNOPQRSTUVWXYZ&

UNMODIFIED
(FORMAL TEXT SHAPE)

UN

Thorne Shaded
Hellenic Wide
ITC American
Typewriter
Bold Outline
Egyptian Outline
Egyptienne Filette
Gold Rush
Rockwell Shadow
Augustea Nova
Columna
Jana

Thorne Shaded **402**

1234567890 *no lower case*

Hellenic Wide **403**

abcdefghijklmnopqrstuvwxyz 1234567890

ITC American Typewriter Bold Outline **404**

abcdefghijklmnopqrstuvwxyz 1234567890

Egyptian Outline **405**

1234567890 *no lower case*

Egyptienne Filette **406**

no lower case or figures

Gold Rush **407**

1234567890 *no lower case*

Rockwell Shadow **408**

1234567890 *no lower case*

Augustea Nova **409**

abcdefghijklmnopqrstuvwxyz1234567890

Columna **410**

1234567890 *no lower case*

Jana **411**

abcdefghijklmnopqrstuvwxyz 1234567890

UNMODIFIED
(FORMAL TEXT SHAPE)

UN

Thorne Shaded
Hellenic Wide
ITC American
Typewriter
Bold Outline
Egyptian Outline
Egyptienne Filette
Gold Rush
Rockwell Shadow
Augustea Nova
Columna
Jana

412 Latin Antique No 9

ABCDEFGHIJKLMNOPQRSTUVWXYZ&

413 Latin Condensed No 2

ABCDEFGHIJKLMNOPQRSTUVWXYZ&

414 Latin Wide

ABCDEFGHIJKLMNOPQRSTUVWXYZ&

415 Runic Condensed

ABCDEFGHIJKLMNOPQRSTUVWXYZ&

416 Augustea Inline

ABCDEFGHIJKLMNOPQRSTUVWXYZ&

417 Chisel

ABCDEFGHIJKLMNOPQRSTUVWXYZ&

418 Contura

ABCDEFGHIJKLMNOPQRSTUVWXYZ&

419 Crystal

ABCDEFGHIJKLMNOPQRSTUVWXYZ&

420 Fleet

ABCDEFGHIJKLMNOPQRSTUVWXYZ&

421 Hanseatic Bold

ABCDEFGHIJKLMNOPQRSTUVWXYZ&

UNMODIFIED
(FORMAL TEXT SHAPE)

UN

Latin Antique No 9
Latin Condensed No 2
Latin Wide
Runic Condensed
Augustea Inline
Chisel
Contura
Crystal
Fleet
Hanseatic Bold

wedge serif inline and outline

sans serif

Latin Antique No 9 **412**

abcdefghijklmnopqrstuvwxyz1234567890

Latin Condensed No 2 **413**

abcdefghijklmnopqrstuvwxyz1234567890

Latin Wide **414**

abcdefghijklmnopqrstuvwxyz 1234567890

Runic Condensed **415**

abcdefghijklmnopqrstuvwxyz1234567890

Augustea Inline **416**

1234567890 *no lower case*

Chisel **417**

abcdefghijklmnopqrstuvwxyz1234567890

Contura **418**

abcdefghijklmnopqrstuvwxyz1234567890

Crystal **419**

1234567890 *no lower case*

Fleet **420**

abcdefghijklmnopqrstuvwxyz1234567890

Hanseatic Bold **421**

abcdefghijklmnopqrstuvwxyz1234567890

UNMODIFIED
(FORMAL TEXT SHAPE)

UN

Latin Antique No 9
Latin Condensed No 2
Latin Wide
Runic Condensed
Augustea Inline
Chisel
Contura
Crystal
Fleet
Hanseatic Bold

UNMODIFIED
(FORMAL TEXT SHAPE)

UN

Helvetica Outline
Festival Titling
Gill Sans Shadow
Line 290
Gill Sans Shadow 408
Sans Serif Shaded
Gill Cameo
Gill Cameo Ruled

sans serif
outline

422 Helvetica Outline

ABCDEFGHIJKLMNOPQRSTUVWXYZ&

sans serif
inline and
outline
shaded

423 Festival Titling

ABCDEFGHIJKLMNOPQRSTUVWXYZ&

424 Gill Sans Shadow Line 290

ABCDEFGHIJKLMNOPQRSTUVWXYZ&

425 Gill Sans Shadow 408

ABCDEFGHIJKLMNOPQRSTUVWXYZ&

426 Sans Serif Shaded

ABCDEFGHIJKLMNOPQRSTUVWXYZ&

sans serif
with
backgrounds

427 Gill Cameo

ABCDEFGHIJKLMNOPQRSTUVWXYZ&

428 Gill Cameo Ruled

ABCDEFGHIJKLMNOPQRSTUVWXYZ&

Helvetica Outline **422**

abcdefghijklmnopqrstuvwxyz1234567890

Festival Titling **423**

1234567890 *no lower case*

Gill Sans Shadow Line 290 **424**

abcdefghijklmnopqrstuvwxyz1234567890

Gill Sans Shadow 408 **425**

1234567890 *no lower case*

Sans Serif Shaded **426**

1234567890 *no lower case*

Gill Cameo **427**

1234567890 *no lower case*

Gill Cameo Ruled **428**

1234567890 *no lower case*

UNMODIFIED
(FORMAL TEXT SHAPE)

UN

Helvetica Outline
Festival Titling
Gill Sans Shadow
Line 290
Gill Sans Shadow 408
Sans Serif Shaded
Gill Cameo
Gill Cameo Ruled

4. FAT & THIN FACE
(UNMODIFIED & MODIFIED)

FAT FACE

Specimen nos		Basic characteristics	Secondary characteristics	
429-443	**R**	roman serif	thin serifs	e.g. **434** Falstaff
444-449	**R**	,,	medium weight serifs	e.g. **445** Caslon Black
450-452	**R**	,,	heavy serifs	e.g. **451** Kompakt
453-458	**SL**	slab serif		e.g. **453** Figaro
459-466	**W**	wedge serif	thin/medium serifs	e.g. **459** Americana True
467-469	**W**	,,	heavy serifs	e.g. **467** Cooper Black
470-471	**W**	,,	heavy serifs and outline	e.g. **471** ITC Souvenir Bold Outline
472-481	**SA**	sans serif	wide	e.g. **472** Annonce Grotesque
482	**SA**	,,	wide outline	e.g. **482** Gill Kayo Outline
483-498	**SA**	,,	medium width	e.g. **493** Helvetica Heavy

NB. *Typefaces in each group are arranged in alphabetical order.*

continued on next page

continued from previous page

499-506	**SA** *(sans serif)*	*narrow*	e.g. **501** Compacta Bold
507-509	SA ,,	*narrow outline*	e.g. **508** Impact Outline
510-514	SA ,,	*rounded shape*	e.g. **514** Harry Fat
515	SA ,,	*rounded shape outline*	e.g. **515** ITC Bauhaus Heavy Outline

THIN FACE

516-519	LS *slab serif*		e.g. **519** ITC Stymie Hairline
520-521	W *wedge serif*		e.g. **520** ITC Newtext Light
522-533	SA *sans serif*		e.g. **530** Helvetica Ultra Light
534-536	SA ,,	*rounded shape*	e.g. **535** Churchward 70 Hairline

NB. *Typefaces in each group are arranged in alphabetical order.*

FAT FACE
& THIN FACE
(UNMODIFIED & MODIFIED)

roman serif with thin serifs

429 Annlie Extra Bold

ABCDEFGHIJKLMNOPQRSTUVWXYZ&

430 Brace Condensed

ABCDEFGHIJKLMNOPQRSTUVWXYZ&

431 Carousel

ABCDEFGHIJKLMNOPQRSTUVWXYZ&

432 ITC Didi

ABCDEFGHIJKLMMNOPQRSTUVWWXYZ&

° **FAT FACE
& THIN FACE
(UNMODIFIED & MODIFIED)**

Annlie Extra Bold
Brace Condensed
Carousel
ITC Didi
Elongated Roman
Falstaff
ITC Firenze
Normande
Orator
Perpetua Black

433 Elongated Roman

ABCDEFGHIJKLMNOPQRSTUVWXYZ&

434 Falstaff

ABCDEFGHIJKLMNOPQRSTUVWXYZ&

435 ITC Firenze

ABCDEFGHIJKLMNOPQRSTUVWXYZ&

436 Normande

ABCDEFGHIJKLMNOPQRSTUVWXYZ&

437 Orator

ABCDEFGHIJKLMNOPQRSTUVWXYZ&

438 Perpetua Black

ABCDEFGHIJKLMNOPQRSTUVWXYZ&

Annlie Extra Bold **429**

abcdefghijklmnopqrstuvwxyz **1234567890**

Brace Condensed **430**

abcdefghijklmnopqrstuvwxyz 1234567890

Carousel **431**

abcdefghijklmnopqrstuvwxyz**1234567890**

ITC Didi **432**

abcdefghijklmnopqrstuvwxyz1234567890

Elongated Roman **433**

1234567890 *no lower case*

Falstaff **434**

abcdefghijklmnopqrstuvwxyz**1234567890**

ITC Firenze **435**

abcdefghijklmnopqrstuvwxyz**1234567890**

Normande **436**

abcdefghijklmnopqrstuvwxyz**1234567890**

Orator **437**

abcdefghijklmnopqrstuvwxyz**1234567890**

Perpetua Black **438**

abcdefghijklmnopqrstuvwxyz1234567890

**FAT FACE
& THIN FACE**
(UNMODIFIED & MODIFIED)

Annlie Extra Bold
Brace Condensed
Carousel
ITC Didi
Elongated Roman
Falstaff
ITC Firenze
Normande
Orator
Perpetua Black

439 Pistilli Roman

ABCDEFGHIJKLMNOPQRSTUVWXYZ&

440 Poster Bodoni

ABCDEFGHIJKLMNOPQRSTUVWXYZ&

441 Thorowgood

ABCDEFGHIJKLMNOPQRSTUVWXYZ&

442 ITC Tiffany Heavy

ABCDEFGHIJKLMNOPQRSTUVWXYZ&

443 ITC Zapf Book Heavy

ABCDEFGHIJKLMNOPQRSTUVWXYZ&

roman serif with medium thickness serifs 444 Aetna

ABCDEFGHIJKLMNOPQRSTUVWXYZ&

445 Caslon Black

ABCDEFGHIJKLMNOPQRSTUVWXYZ&

446 ITC Century Ultra

ABCDEFGHIJKLMNOPQRSTUVWXYZ&

447 ITC Galliard Ultra

ABCDEFGHIJKLMNOPQRSTUVWXYZ&

448 ITC Garamond Ultra

ABCDEFGHIJKLMNOPQRSTUVWXYZ&

**FAT FACE
& THIN FACE
(UNMODIFIED & MODIFIED)**

Pistilli Roman
Poster Bodoni
Thorowgood
ITC Tiffany Heavy
ITC Zapf Book Heavy
Aetna
Caslon Black
ITC Century Ultra
ITC Galliard Ultra
ITC Garamond Ultra

Pistilli Roman **439**

abcdefghijklmnopqrstuvwxyz1234567890

Poster Bodoni **440**

abcdefghijklmnopqrstuvwxyz1234567890

Thorowgood **441**

abcdefghijklmnopqrstuvwxyz1234567890

ITC Tiffany Heavy **442**

abcdefghijklmnopqrstuvwxyz1234567890

ITC Zapf Book Heavy **443**

abcdefghijklmnopqrstuvwxyz1234567890

Aetna **444**

1234567890 *no lower case*

Caslon Black **445**

abcdefghijklmnopqrstuvwxyz1234567890

ITC Century Ultra **446**

abcdefghijklmnopqrstuvwxyz1234567890

ITC Galliard Ultra **447**

abcdefghijklmnopqrstuvwxyz1234567890

ITC Garamond Ultra **448**

abcdefghijklmnopqrstuvwxyz1234567890

**FAT FACE
& THIN FACE**
(UNMODIFIED & MODIFIED)

Pistilli Roman
Poster Bodoni
Thorowgood
ITC Tiffany Heavy
ITC Zapf Book Heavy
Aetna
Caslon Black
ITC Century Ultra
ITC Galliard Ultra
ITC Garamond Ultra

449 ITC Grouch

ABCDEFGHIJKLMNOPQRSTUVWXYZ&

roman serifs with heavy serifs

450 ITC Cheltenham Ultra

ABCDEFGHIJKLMNOPQRSTUVWXYZ&

451 Kompakt

ABCDEFGHIJKLMNOPQRSTUVWXYZ&

452 Whitin Black

ABCDEFGHIJKLMNOPQRSTUVWXYZ&

slab serif

453 Figaro

ABCDEFGHIJKLMNOPQRSTUVWXYZ&

454 Hidalgo

ABCDEFGHIJKLMNOPQRSTUVWXYZ&

455 Karnak Black

ABCDEFGHIJKLMNOPQRSTUVWXYZ&

456 Memphis Extra Bold

ABCDEFGHIJKLMNOPQRSTUVWXYZ&

457 Playbill

ABCDEFGHIJKLMNOPQRSTUVWXYZ&

458 Rockwell Extra Bold

ABCDEFGHIJKLMNOPQRSTUVWXYZ&

**FAT FACE
& THIN FACE
(UNMODIFIED & MODIFIED)**

ITC Grouch
ITC Cheltenham Ultra
Kompakt
Whitin Black
Figaro
Hidalgo
Karnak Black
Memphis Extra Bold
Playbill
Rockwell Extra Bold

ITC Grouch **449**

abcdefghijklmnopqrstuvwxyz1234567890

ITC Cheltenham Ultra **450**

abcdefghijklmnopqrstuvwxyz1234567890

Kompakt **451**

abcdefghijklmnopqrstuvwxyz1234567890

Whitin Black **452**

abcdefghijklmnopqrstuvwxyz1234567890

Figaro **453**

abcdefghijklmnopqrstuvwxyz1234567890

Hidalgo **454**

1234567890 *no lower case*

Karnak Black **455**

abcdefghijklmnopqrstuvwxyz1234567890

Memphis Extra Bold **456**

abcdefghijklmnopqrstuvwxyz1234567890

Playbill **457**

abcdefghijklmnopqrstuvwxyz1234567890

Rockwell Extra Bold **458**

abcdefghijklmnopqrstuvwxyz1234567890

**FAT FACE
& THIN FACE
(UNMODIFIED & MODIFIED)**

ITC Grouch
ITC Cheltenham Ultra
Kompakt
Whitin Black
Figaro
Hidalgo
Karnak Black
Memphis Extra Bold
Playbill
Rockwell Extra Bold

wedge serif with thin or medium serifs

459 Americana True

ABCDEFGHIJKLMNOPQRSTUVWXYZ&

460 Hawthorn

ABCDEFGHIJKLMNOPQRSTUVWXYZ&

461 Hess Neobold

ABCDEFGHIJKLMNOPQRSTUVWXYZ&

462 Las Vegas

ABCDEFGHIJKLMNOPQRSTUVWXYZ&

**FAT FACE
& THIN FACE
(UNMODIFIED & MODIFIED)**

Americana True
Hawthorn
Hess Neobold
Las Vegas
Macbeth
ITC Novarese Ultra
ITC Serif Gothic Heavy
Trooper Black
Cooper Black
Pabst

463 Macbeth

ABCDEFGHIJKLMNOPQRSTUVWXYZ&

464 ITC Novarese Ultra

ABCDEFGHIJKLMNOPQRSTUVWXYZ&

465 ITC Serif Gothic Heavy

ABCDEFGHIJKLMNOPQRSTUVWXYZ&

466 Trooper Black

ABCDEFGHIJKLMNOPQRSTUVWXYZ&

wedge serif with heavy serifs

467 Cooper Black

ABCDEFGHIJKLMNOPQRSTUVWXYZ&

468 Pabst

ABCDEFGHIJKLMNOPQRSTUVWXYZ&

Americana True **459**

abcdefghijklmnopqrstuvwxyz1234567890

Hawthorn **460**

abcdefghijklmnopqrstuvwxyz1234567890

Hess Neobold **461**

1234567890 *no lower case*

Las Vegas **462**

abcdefghijklmnopqrstuvwxyz1234567890

Macbeth **463**

abcdefghijklmnopqrstuvwxyz1234567890

ITC Novarese Ultra **464**

abcdefghijklmnopqrstuvwxyz1234567890

ITC Serif Gothic Heavy **465**

abcdefghijklmnopqrstuvwxyz1234567890

Trooper Black **466**

abcdefghijklmnopqrstuvwxyz1234567890

Cooper Black **467**

abcdefghijklmnopqrstuvwxyz1234567890

Pabst **468**

abcdefghijklmnopqrstuvwxyz1234567890

FAT FACE
& THIN FACE
(UNMODIFIED & MODIFIED)

Americana True
Hawthorn
Hess Neobold
Las Vegas
Macbeth
ITC Novarese Ultra
ITC Serif Gothic Heavy
Trooper Black
Cooper Black
Pabst

469 ITC Souvenir Bold

ABCDEFGHIJKLMNOPQRSTUVWXYZ&

wedge serif with heavy serifs and outline

470 Cooper Black Outline

ABCDEFGHIJKLMNOPQRSTUVWXYZ&

471 ITC Souvenir Bold Outline

ABCDEFGHIJKLMNOPQRSTUVWXYZ&

sans serif wide

472 Annonce Grotesque

ABCDEFGHIJKLMNOPQRSTUVWXYZ&

473 Antique Olive Nord

ABCDEFGHIJKLMNOPQRSTUVWXYZ&

474 ITC Bolt Bold

ABCDEFGHIJKLMNOPQRSTUVWXYZ&

475 Fehrle Display

ABCDEFGHIJKLMNOPQRSTUVWXYZ&

476 Gill Kayo

ABCDEFGHIJKLMNOPQRSTUVWXYZ&

477 Helvetica Bold Extended

ABCDEFGHIJKLMNOPQRSTUVWXYZ&

478 Information Black Extended

ABCDEFGHIJKLMNOPQRSTUVWXYZ&

**FAT FACE
& THIN FACE
(UNMODIFIED & MODIFIED)**

ITC Souvenir Bold
Cooper Black Outline
ITC Souvenir Bold Outline
Annonce Grotesque
Antique Olive Nord
ITC Bolt Bold
Fehrle Display
Gill Kayo
Helvetica Bold Extended
Information Black
Extended

ITC Souvenir Bold **469**

abcdefghijklmnopqrstuvwxyz**1234567890**

Cooper Black Outline **470**

abcdefghijklmnopqrstuvwxyz1234567890

ITC Souvenir Bold Outline **471**

abcdefghijklmnopqrstuvwxyz1234567890

Annonce Grotesque **472**

abcdefghijklmnopqrstuvwxyz1234567890

Antique Olive Nord **473**

abcdefghijklmnopqrstuvwxyz1234567890

ITC Bolt Bold **474**

abcdefghijklmnopqrstuvwxyz1234567890

Fehrle Display **475**

abcdefghijklmnopqrstuvwxyz1234567890

Gill Kayo **476**

abcdefghijklmnopqrstuvwxyz1234567890

Helvetica Bold Extended **477**

abcdefghijklmnopqrstuvwxyz1234567890

Information Black Extended **478**

abcdefghijklmnopqrstuvwxyz1234567890

**FAT FACE
& THIN FACE**
(UNMODIFIED & MODIFIED)

ITC Souvenir Bold
Cooper Black Outline
ITC Souvenir Bold Outline
Annonce Grotesque
Antique Olive Nord
ITC Bolt Bold
Fehrle Display
Gill Kayo
Helvetica Bold Extended
Information Black
Extended

479 Koloss

ABCDEFGHIJKLMNOPQRSTUVWXYZ&

480 Spartan Extra Black

ABCDEFGHIJKLMNOPQRSTUVWXYZ&

481 Univers 83

ABCDEFGHIJKLMNOPQRSTUVWXYZ&

sans serif wide outline

482 Gill Kayo Outline

ABCDEFGHIJKLMNOPQRSTUVWXYZ&

sans serif medium width

483 Antique Olive Compact

ABCDEFGHIJKLMNOPQRSTUVWXYZ&

484 Broadway

ABCDEFGHIJKLMNOPQRSTUVWXYZ&

485 Broadway Engraved

ABCDEFGHIJKLMNOPQRSTUVWXYZ&

486 Bullion Solid

ABCDEFGHIJKLMNOPQRSTUVWXYZ &

487 Dynamo

ABCDEFGHIJKLMNOPQRSTUVWXYZ&

488 Folio Extra Bold

ABCDEFGHIJKLMNOPQRSTUVWXYZ&

**FAT FACE
& THIN FACE**
(UNMODIFIED & MODIFIED)

Koloss
Spartan Extra Black
Univers 83
Gill Kayo Outline
Antique Olive Compact
Broadway
Broadway Engraved
Bullion Solid
Dynamo
Folio Extra Bold

Koloss **479**

abcdefghijklmnopqrstuvwxyz1234567890

Spartan Extra Black **480**

abcdefghijklmnopqrstuvwxyz1234567890

Univers 83 **481**

abcdefghijklmnopqrstuvwxyz1234567890

Gill Kayo Outline **482**

abcdefghijklmnopqrstuvwxyz1234567890

Antique Olive Compact **483**

abcdefghijklmnopqrstuvwxyz1234567890

Broadway **484**

abcdefghijklmnopqrstuvwxyz1234567890

Broadway Engraved **485**

abcdefghijklmnopqrstuvwxyz1234567890

Bullion Solid **486**

1234567890 *no lower case*

Dynamo **487**

abcdefghijklmnopqrstuvwxyz1234567890

Folio Extra Bold **488**

abcdefghijklmnopqrstuvwxyz1234567890

FAT FACE
& THIN FACE
(UNMODIFIED & MODIFIED)

Koloss
Spartan Extra Black
Univers 83
Gill Kayo Outline
Antique Olive Compact
Broadway
Broadway Engraved
Bullion Solid
Dynamo
Folio Extra Bold

489 Frutiger 75 Black

ABCDEFGHIJKLMNOPQRSTUVWXYZ&

490 Gothic No 16

ABCDEFGHIJKLMNOPQRSTUVWXYZ&

491 ITC Grizzly

ABCDEFGHIJKLMNOPQRSTUVWXYZ&

492 Haas Unica Black

ABCDEFGHIJKLMNOPQRSTUVWXYZ&

493 Helvetica Heavy

ABCDEFGHIJKLMNOPQRSTUVWXYZ&

494 Helvetica No 2 Bold

ABCDEFGHIJKLMNOPQRSTUVWXYZ&

495 Neil Bold

ABCDEFGHIJKLMNOPQRSTUVWXYZ&

496 Plak Heavy

ABCDEFGHIJKLMNOPQRSTUVWXYZ&

497 Syntax Ultra Black

ABCDEFGHIJKLMNOPQRSTUVWXYZ&

498 Univers 75

ABCDEFGHIJKLMNOPQRSTUVWXYZ&

**FAT FACE
& THIN FACE
(UNMODIFIED & MODIFIED)**

Frutiger 75 Black
Gothic No 16
ITC Grizzly
Haas Unica Black
Helvetica Heavy
Helvetica No 2 Bold
Neil Bold
Plak Heavy
Syntax Ultra Black
Univers 75

Frutiger 75 Black **489**

abcdefghijklmnopqrstuvwxyz1234567890

Gothic No 16 **490**

abcdefghijklmnopqrstuvwxyz1234567890

ITC Grizzly **491**

abcdefghijklmnopqrstuvwxyz1234567890

Haas Unica Black **492**

abcdefghijklmnopqrstuvwxyz1234567890

Helvetica Heavy **493**

abcdefghijklmnopqrstuvwxyz1234567890

Helvetica No 2 Bold **494**

abcdefghijklmnopqrstuvwxyz1234567890

Neil Bold **495**

abcdefghijklmnopqrstuvwxyz1234567890

Plak Heavy **496**

abcdefghijklmnopqrstuvwxyz1234567890

Syntax Ultra Black **497**

abcdefghijklmnopqrstuvwxyz1234567890

Univers 75 **498**

abcdefghijklmnopqrstuvwxyz1234567890

**FAT FACE
& THIN FACE
(UNMODIFIED & MODIFIED)**

Frutiger 75 Black
Gothic No 16
ITC Grizzly
Haas Unica Black
Helvetica Heavy
Helvetica No 2 Bold
Neil Bold
Plak Heavy
Syntax Ultra Black
Univers 75

sans serif narrow

499 Anzeigen Grotesque

ABCDEFGHIJKLMNOPQRSTUVWXYZ&

500 Block Black Condensed

ABCDEFGHIJKLMNOPQRSTUVWXYZ&

501 Compacta Bold

ABCDEFGHIJKLMNOPQRSTUVWXYZ&

502 Futura Display

ABCDEFGHIJKLMNOPQRSTUVWXYZ&

503 Headline Bold

ABCDEFGHIJKLMNOPQRSTUVWXYZ&

504 Impact

ABCDEFGHIJKLMNOPQRSTUVWXYZ&

505 ITC Machine

ABCDEFGHIJKLMNOPQRSTUVWXYZ&

506 Placard Extra Bold Condensed

ABCDEFGHIJKLMNOPQRSTUVWXYZ&

sans serif narrow outline or inline

507 Compacta Bold Outline

ABCDEFGHIJKLMNOPQRSTUVWXYZ&

508 Impact Outline

ABCDEFGHIJJKLMNOPQRSTUVWXYZ&

FAT FACE
& THIN FACE
(UNMODIFIED & MODIFIED)

Anzeigen Grotesque
Block Black Condensed
Compacta Bold
Futura Display
Headline Bold
Impact
ITC Machine
Placard Extra Bold
Condensed
Compacta Bold Outline
Impact Outline

Anzeigen Grotesque **499**

abcdefghijklmnopqrstuvwxyz1234567890

Block Black Condensed **500**

abcdefghijklmnopqrstuvwxyz1234567890

Compacta Bold **501**

abcdefghijklmnopqrstuvwxyz1234567890

Futura Display **502**

abcdefghijklmnopqrstuvwxyz1234567890

Headline Bold **503**

abcdefghijklmnopqrstuvwxyz1234567890

Impact **504**

abcdefghijklmnopqrstuvwxyz1234567890

ITC Machine **505**

1234567890 *no lower case*

Placard Extra Bold Condensed **506**

abcdefghijklmnopqrstuvwxyz1234567890

Compacta Bold Outline **507**

1234567890 *no lower case*

Impact Outline **508**

abcdefghijklmnopqrstuvwxyz1234567890

**FAT FACE
& THIN FACE
(UNMODIFIED & MODIFIED)**

Anzeigen Grotesque
Block Black Condensed
Compacta Bold
Futura Display
Headline Bold
Impact
ITC Machine
Placard Extra Bold
Condensed
Compacta Bold Outline
Impact Outline

509 Superstar

ABCDEFGHIJKLMNOPQRSTUVWXYZ&

sans serif rounded shape

510 ITC Bauhaus Heavy

ABCDEFGHIJKLMNOPQRSTUVWXYZ&

511 Blippo Black

ABCDEFGHIJKLMNOPQRSTUVWXYZ&

512 Cable Heavy (Klingspor)

ABCDEFGHIJKLMNOPQRSTUVWXYZ&

513 Churchward 70 Ultra Black

ABCDEFGHIJKLMNOPQRSTUVWXYZ&

514 Harry Fat

ABCDEFGHIJKLMNOPQRSTUVWXYZ&

sans serif rounded shape outline

515 ITC Bauhaus Heavy Outline

ABCDEFGHIJKLMNOPQRSTUVWXYZ&

slab serif

516 ITC American Typewriter Light

ABCDEFGHIJKLMNOPQRSTUVWXYZ&

517 Glypha 35 Thin

ABCDEFGHIJKLMNOPQRSTUVWXYZ&

518 Serifa 35 Thin

ABCDEFGHIJKLMNOPQRSTUVWXYZ&

**FAT FACE
& THIN FACE
(UNMODIFIED & MODIFIED)**

Superstar
ITC Bauhaus Heavy
Blippo Black
Cable Heavy (Klingspor)
Churchward 70
Ultra Black
Harry Fat
ITC Bauhaus
Heavy Outline
ITC American
Typewriter Light
Glypha 35 Thin
Serifa 35 Thin

Superstar **509**

1234567890 *no lower case*

ITC Bauhaus Heavy **510**

abcdefghijklmnopqrstuvwxyz1234567890

Blippo Black **511**

abcdefghijklmnopqrstuvwxyz1234567890

Cable Heavy (Klingspor) **512**

abcdefghijklmnopqrstuvwxyz1234567890

Churchward 70 Ultra Black **513**

abcdefghijklmnopqrstuvwxyz1234567890

Harry Fat **514**

abcdefghijklmnopqrstuvwxyz1234567890

ITC Bauhaus Heavy Outline **515**

abcdefghijklmnopqrstuvwxyz1234567890

ITC American Typewriter Light **516**

abcdefghijklmnopqrstuvwxyz1234567890

Glypha 35 Thin **517**

abcdefghijklmnopqrstuvwxyz1234567890

Serifa 35 Thin **518**

abcdefghijklmnopqrstuvwxyz1234567890

**FAT FACE
& THIN FACE**
(UNMODIFIED & MODIFIED)

Superstar
ITC Bauhaus Heavy
Blippo Black
Cable Light (Klingspor)
Churchward 70
Ultra Black
Harry Fat
ITC Bauhaus
Heavy Outline
ITC American
Typewriter Light
Glypha 35 Thin
Serifa 35 Thin

519 ITC Stymie Hairline

ABCDEFGHIJKLMNOPQRSTUVWXYZ&

wedge serif

520 ITC Newtext Light

ABCDEFGHIJKLMNOPQRSTUVWXYZ&

521 Virgin Roman

ABCDEFGHIJKLMNOPQRSTUVWXYZ&

sans serif

522 ITC Avant Garde Gothic Extra Light

ABCDEFGHIJKLMNOPQRSTUVWXYZ&

**FAT FACE
& THIN FACE
(UNMODIFIED & MODIFIED)**

ITC Stymie Hairline
ITC Newtext Light
Virgin Roman
ITC Avant Garde Gothic
Extra Light
Cable Light (Klingspor)
Empire
ITC Eras Light
Futura Light
Gill Sans Light
Grotesque 126

523 Cable Light (Klingspor)

ABCDEFGHIJKLMNOPQRSTUVWXYZ&

524 Empire

ABCDEFGHIJKLMNOPQRSTUVWXYZ&

525 ITC Eras Light

ABCDEFGHIJKLMNOPQRSTUVWXYZ&

526 Futura Light

ABCDEFGHIJKLMNOPQRSTUVWXYZ&

527 Gill Sans Light

ABCDEFGHIJKLMNOPQRSTUVWXYZ&

528 Grotesque 126

ABCDEFGHIJKLMNOPQRSTUVWXYZ&

ITC Stymie Hairline **519**

abcdefghijklmnopqrstuvwxyz1234567890

ITC Newtext Light **520**

abcdefghijklmnopqrstuvwxyz1234567890

Virgin Roman **521**

abcdefghijklmnopqrstuvwxyz1234567890

ITC Avant Garde Gothic Extra Light **522**

abcdefghijklmnopqrstuvwxyz1234567890

Cable Light (Klingspor) **523**

abcdefghijklmnopqrstuvwxyz1234567890

Empire **524**

1234567890 *no lower case*

ITC Eras Light **525**

abcdefghijklmnopqrstuvwxyz1234567890

Futura Light **526**

abcdefghijklmnopqrstuvwxyz1234567890

Gill Sans Light **527**

abcdefghijklmnopqrstuvwxyz1234567890

Grotesque 126 **528**

abcdefghijklmnopqrstuvwxyz1234567890

**FAT FACE
& THIN FACE**
(UNMODIFIED & MODIFIED)

ITC Stymie Hairline
ITC Newtext Light
Virgin Roman
ITC Avant Garde Gothic
Extra Light
Cable Light (Klingspor)
Empire
ITC Eras Light
Futura Light
Gill Sans Light
Grotesque 126

529 Helvetica Thin

ABCDEFGHIJKLMNOPQRSTUVWXYZ&

530 Helvetica Ultra Light

ABCDEFGHIJKLMNOPQRSTUVWXYZ&

531 L & C Hairline

ABCDEFGHIJKLMNOPQRSTUVWXYZ &

532 Penny Bee

ABCDEFGHIJKLMNOPQRSTUVWXYZ&.

533 Stark Debonair

ABCDEFGHIJKLMNOPQRSTUVWXYZ&.

sans serif rounded shape

534 ITC Busorama Light

ABCDEFGHIJKLMNOPQRSTUVWXYZ&

535 Churchward 70 Hairline

ABCDEFGHIJKLMNOPQRSTUVWXYZ&

536 Harry Thin

ABCDEFGHIJKLMNOPQRSTUVWXYZ&

**FAT FACE
& THIN FACE
(UNMODIFIED & MODIFIED)**

Helvetica Thin
Helvetica Ultra Light
L & C Hairline
Penny Bee
Stark Debonair
ITC Busorama Light
Churchward 70
Hairline
Harry Thin

Helvetica Thin **529**

abcdefghijklmnopqrstuvwxyz1234567890

Helvetica Ultra Light **530**

abcdefghijklmnopqrstuvwxyz1234567890

L & C Hairline **531**

abcdefghijklmnopqrstuvwxyz1234567890

Penny Bee **532**

1234567890 *no lower case*

Stark Debonair **533**

abcdefghijklmnopqrstuvwxyz1234567890

ITC Busorama Light **534**

1234567890 *no lower case*

Churchward 70 Hairline **535**

abcdefghijklmnopqrstuvwxyz1234567890

Harry Thin **536**

abcdefghijklmnopqrstuvwxyz1234567890

**FAT FACE
& THIN FACE
(UNMODIFIED & MODIFIED)**

Helvetica Thin
Helvetica Ultra Light
L & C Hairline
Penny Bee
Stark Debonair
ITC Busorama Light
Churchward 70
Hairline
Harry Thin

5. ORNAMENTAL

Specimen nos		Basic characteristics	Secondary characteristics	
537-546	R	roman serif		e.g. **540** Fry's Ornamented
547	R	,,	sloping	e.g. **547** Goudy Fancy
548-551	SL	slab serif		e.g. **548** Lettres Ornées
552-559	W	wedge serif		e.g. **554** Davida
560	SA	sans serif		e.g. **560** Abramesque
561-563	SCR	script		e.g. **561** Ballé Initials

NB. *Typefaces in each group are arranged in alphabetical order.*

roman serif

537 Flirt

ABCDEFGHIJKLMNOPQRSTUVWXYZ&

538 Floriated Capitals

ABCDEFGHIJKLMNOPQRSTUVWXYZ

539 Fontanesi

ABCDEFGHIJKLMNOPQRSTUVWXYZ&

540 Fry's Ornamented

ABCDEFGHIJKLMNOPQRSTUVWXYZ &

541 Gallia

ABCDEFGHIJKLMNOPQRSTUVWXYZ&

542 Lexington

ABCDEFGHIJKLMNOPQRSTUVWXYZ&

543 Modernistic

ABCDEFGHIJKLMNOPQRSTUVWXYZ&

544 Mole Foliate

ABCDEFGHIJKLMNOPQRSTUVWXYZ&

545 Nymphic

ABCDEFGHIJKLMNOPQRSTUVWXYZ&

546 Sapphire

ABCDEFGHIJKLMNOPQRSTUVWXYZ&

ORNAMENTAL

OR

Flirt
Floriated Capitals
Fontanesi
Fry's Ornamented
Gallia
Lexington
Modernistic
Mole Foliate
Nymphic
Sapphire

Flirt **537**

abcdefghijklmnopqrstuvwxyz1234567890

Floriated Capitals **538**

no lower case or figures

Fontanesi **539**

1234567890 *no lower case*

Fry's Ornamented **540**

no lower case or figures

Gallia **541**

1234567890 *no lower case*

Lexington **542**

1234567890 *no lower case*

Modernistic **543**

1234567890 *no lower case*

Mole Foliate **544**

1234567890 *no lower case*

Nymphic **545**

abcdefghijklmnopqrstuvwxyz 1234567890

Sapphire **546**

1234567890 *no lower case*

ORNAMENTAL

Flirt
Floriated Capitals
Fontanesi
Fry's Ornamented
Gallia
Lexington
Modernistic
Mole Foliate
Nymphic
Sapphire

roman serif
sloping

547 Goudy Fancy

ABCDEFGHIJKLMNOPQRSTUVWXYZ&

slab serif

548 Lettres Ornées

ABCDEFGHIJKLMNOPQRSTUVWXYZ

549 Quentin

ABCDEFGHIJKLMNOPQRSTUVWXYZ&

550 Romantiques No 5

ABCDEFGHIJKLMNOPQRSTUVWXYZ&

551 Trocadero

ABCDEFGHIJKLMNOPQRSTUVWXYZ&

wedge serif

552 Aesthetic Ornamented

ABCDEFGHIJKLMNOPQRSTUVWXYZ&

553 Arnold Böcklin

ABCDEFGHIJKLMNOPQRSTUVWXYZ&

554 Davida

ABCDEFGHIJKLMNOPQRSTUVWXYZ&

555 Karnac

ABCDEFGHIJKLMNOPQRSTUVWXYZ&

556 Kismet

ABCDEFGHIJKLMNOPQRSTUVWXYZ&

ORNAMENTAL

Goudy Fancy
Lettres Ornées
Quentin
Romantiques No 5
Trocadero
Aesthetic
Ornamented
Arnold Böcklin
Davida
Karnac
Kismet

Goudy Fancy **547**

abcdefghijklmnopqrstuvwxyz1234567890

Lettres Ornées **548**

no lower case or figures

Quentin **549**

1234567890 *no lower case*

Romantiques No 5 **550**

1234567890 *no lower case*

Trocadero **551**

1234567890 *no lower case*

Aesthetic Ornamented **552**

ABCDEFGHIJKLMNOPQRSTUVWXYZ1234567890 *small capitals (no lower case)*

Arnold Böcklin **553**

abcdefghijklmnopqrstuvwxyz1234567890

Davida **554**

1234567890 *no lower case*

Karnac **555**

abcdefghijklmnopqrstuvwxyz1234567890

Kismet **556**

abcdefghijklmnopqrstuvwxyz1234567890

ORNAMENTAL

Goudy Fancy
Lettres Ornées
Quentin
Romantiques No 5
Trocadero
Aesthetic
Ornamented
Arnold Böcklin
Davida
Karnac
Kismet

557 Recherche

ABCDEFGHIJKLMNOPQRSTUVWXYZ&

558 Ringlet

ABCDEFGHIJKLMNOPQRSTUVWXYZ

559 Victorian

ABCDEFGHIJKLMNOPQRSTUVWXYZ&

sans serif

560 Abramesque

ABCDEFGHIJKLMNOPQRSTUVWXYZ &

script

561 Ballé Initials

ABCDEFGHIJKLMNOPQRSTUVWXYZ

562 Lilith

ABCDEFGHIJKLMNOPQRSTUVWXYZ&

563 Raffia Initials

ABCDEFGHIJKLMNOPQRSTUVWXYZ

ORNAMENTAL

Recherche
Ringlet
Victorian
Abramesque
Ballé Initials
Lilith
Raffia Initials

Recherche **557**

abcdefghijklmnopqrstuvwxyz1234567890

Ringlet **558**

abcdefghijklmnopqrstuvwxyz1234567890

Victorian **559**

abcdefghijklmnopqrstuvwxyz1234567890

Abramesque **560**

no lower case or figures

Ballé Initials **561**

no lower case or figures

Lilith **562**

abcdefghijklmno pqrstuvwxyz1234567890

Raffia Initials **563**

1234567890 *no lower case*

6. MODIFIED SERIF

Specimen nos	Basic characteristics	Secondary characteristics	
564-574	R	roman serif	e.g. **566** Belwe
575-576	R	,,	stencil or stencil effect	e.g. **575** Stencil Bold
577-579	SL	slab serif	e.g. **579** Profil
580-601	W	wedge serif	e.g. **585** Charleston
602-603	W	,,	sloping backwards	e.g. **602** Alfereta

NB. Typefaces in each group are arranged in alphabetical order.

MODIFIED
SERIF

MS

roman serif

564 Abbott Old Style

ABCDEFGHIJKLMNOPQRSTUVWXYZ&

565 Antikva Margaret

ABCDEFGHIJKLMNOPQRSTUVWXYZ&

566 Belwe

ABCDEFGHIJKLMNOPQRSTUVWXYZ&

567 Bernhard Antique

ABCDEFGHIJKLMNOPQRSTUVWXYZ&

568 Greco Bold

ABCDEFGHIJKLMNOPQRSTUVWXYZ&

569 Koch Antiqua

ABCDEFGHIJKLMNOPQRSTUVWXYZ&

570 Milton

ABCDEFGHIJKLMNOPQRSTUVWXYZ&

571 Packhard

ABCDEFGHIJKLMNOPQRSTUVWXYZ&

572 Richmond

ABCDEFGHIJKLMNOPQRSTUVWXYZ&

573 Skyjald

ABCDEFGHIJKLMNOPQRSTUVWXYZ&

MODIFIED SERIF

Abbott Old Style
Antikva Margaret
Belwe
Bernhard Antique
Greco Bold
Koch Antiqua
Milton
Packhard
Richmond
Skyjald

Abbott Old Style **564**

abcdefghijklmnopqrstuvwxyz1234567890

Antikva Margaret **565**

abcdefghijklmnopqrstuvwxyz1234567890

Belwe **566**

abcdefghijklmnopqrstuvwxyz 1234567890

Bernhard Antique **567**

abcdefghijklmnopqrstuvwxyz1234567890

Greco Bold **568**

abcdefghijklmnopqrstuvwxyz1234567890

Koch Antiqua **569**

abcdefghijklmnopqrstuvwxyz1234567890

Milton **570**

abcdefghijklmnopqrstuvwxyz1234567890

Packhard **571**

abcdefghijklmnopqrstuvwxyz1234567890

Richmond **572**

abcdefghijklmnopqrstuvwxyz1234567890

Skyjald **573**

abcdefghijklmnopqrstuvwxyz1234567890

MODIFIED SERIF

MS

Abbott Old Style
Antikva Margaret
Belwe
Bernhard Antique
Greco Bold
Koch Antiqua
Milton
Packhard
Richmond
Skyjald

574 University Roman

ABCDEFGHIJKLMNOPQRSTUVWXYZ&

roman serif
stencil or
stencil effect

575 Stencil Bold

ABCDEFGHIJKLMNOPQRSTUVWXYZ&

576 Teachest

ABCDEFGHIJKLMNOPQRSTUVWXYZ&

slab serif

577 Antiqua Pointed

ABCDEFGHIJKLMNOPQRSTUVWXYZ

578 Nubian

ABCDEFGHIJKLMNOPQRSTUVWXYZ&

579 Profil

ABCDEFGHIJKLMNOPQRSTUVWXYZ&

wedge serif

580 Algerian

ABCDEFGHIJKLMNOPQRSTUVWXYZ&

581 Blackfriars Roman

ABCDEFGHIJKLMNOPQRSTUVWXYZ&

582 Brutus

ABCDEFGHIJKLMNOPQRSTUVWXYZ&

583 Bullfinch

ABCDEFGHIJKLMNOPQRSTUVWXYZ&

MODIFIED
SERIF

University Roman
Stencil Bold
Teachest
Antiqua Pointed
Nubian
Profil
Algerian
Blackfriars Roman
Brutus
Bullfinch

University Roman **574**

abcdefghijklmnopqrstuvwxyz1234567890

Stencil Bold **575**

abcdefghijklmnopqrstuvwxyz1234567890

Teachest **576**

1234567890 *no lower case*

Antiqua Pointed **577**

1234567890 *no lower case*

Nubian **578**

abcdefghijklmnopqrstuvwxyz1234567890

Profil **579**

1234567890 *no lower case*

Algerian **580**

1234567890 *no lower case*

Blackfriars Roman **581**

abcdefghijklmnopqrstuvwxyz1234567890

Brutus **582**

abcdefghijklmnopqrstuvwxyz1234567890

Bullfinch **583**

abcdefghijklmnopqrstuvwxyz1234567890

MODIFIED SERIF

MS

University Roman
Stencil Bold
Teachest
Antiqua Pointed
Nubian
Profil
Algerian
Blackfriars Roman
Brutus
Bullfinch

233

584 Chantrey

ABCDEFGHIJKLMNOPQRSTUVWXYZ&

585 Charleston

ABCDEFGHIJKLMNOPQRSTUVWXYZ&

586 Columbus

ABCDEFGHIJKLMNOPQRSTUVWXYZ&

587 Croydon

ABCDEFGHIJKLMNOPQRSTUVWXYZ&

588 Desdemona

ABCDEFGHIJKLMNOPQRSTUVWXYZ&

589 Eckmann

ABCDEFGHIJKLMNOPQRSTUVWXYZ&

590 Edda

ABCDEFGHIJKLMNOPQRSTUVWXYZ&

591 Fantail

ABCDEFGHIJKLMNOPQRSTUVWXYZ&

592 Hermosa

ABCDEFGHIJKLMNOPQRSTUVWXYZ

593 Hobo

ABCDEFGHIJKLMNOPQRSTUVWXYZ&

MODIFIED
SERIF

MS

Chantrey
Charleston
Columbus
Croydon
Desdemona
Eckmann
Edda
Fantail
Hermosa
Hobo

Chantrey **584**

abcdefghijklmnopqrstuvwxyz1234567890

Charleston **585**

abcdefghijklmnopqrstuvwxyz1234567890

Columbus **586**

abcdefghijklmnopqrstuvwxyz1234567890

Croydon **587**

1234567890 *no lower case*

Desdemona **588**

1234567890 *no lower case*

Eckmann **589**

abcdefghijklmnopqrstuvwxyz1234567890

Edda **590**

1234567890 *no lower case*

Fantail **591**

abcdefghijklmnopqrstuvwxyz1234567890

Hermosa **592**

abcdefghijklmnopqrstuvwxyz1234567890

Hobo **593**

abcdefghijklmnopqrstuvwxyz1234567890

MODIFIED SERIF

MS

594 Hogarth

ABCDEFGHIJKLMNOPQRSTUVWXYZ&

595 Lafayette

ABCDEFGHIJKLMNOPQRSTUVWXYZ&

596 Mikado Black

ABCDEFGHIJKLMNOPQRSTUVWXYZ&

597 Neptune

ABCDEFGHIJKLMNOPQRSTUVWXYZ&

598 Pretorian

ABCDEFGHIJKLMNOPQRSTUVWXYZ&

599 Tango

ABCDEFGHIJKLMNOPQRSTUVWXYZ&

600 Thalia

ABCDEFGHIJKLMNOPQRSTUVWXYZ&

601 Tip Top

ABCDEFGHIJKLMNOPQRSTUVWXYZ&

602 Alfereta

ABCDEFGHIJKLMNOPQRSTUVWXYZ&

603 Blanchard

ABCDEFGHIJKLMNOPQRSTUVWXYZ&

MODIFIED SERIF

Hogarth
Lafayette
Mikado Black
Neptune
Pretorian
Tango
Thalia
Tip Top
Alfereta
Blanchard

wedge serif
sloping
backwards

Hogarth **594**

abcdefghijklmnopqrstuvwxyz1234567890

Lafayette **595**

abcdefghijklmnopqrstuvwxyz1234567890

Mikado Black **596**

abcdefghijklmnopqrstuvwxyz1234567890

Neptune **597**

abcdefghijklmnopqrstuvwxyz1234567890

Pretorian **598**

abcdefghijklmnopqrstuvwxyz1234567890

Tango **599**

abcdefghijklmnopqrstuvwxyz1234567890

Thalia **600**

abcdefghijklmnopqrstuvwxyz1234567890

Tip Top **601**

abcdefghijklmnopqrstuvwxyz1234567890

Alfereta **602**

abcdefghijklmnopqrstuvwxyz1234567890

Blanchard **603**

abcdefghijklmnopqrstuvwxyz1234567890

MODIFIED SERIF

MS

Hogarth
Lafayette
Mikado Black
Neptune
Pretorian
Tango
Thalia
Tip Top
Alfereta
Blanchard

7. MODIFIED SANS SERIF

Specimen nos		Basic characteristics	
604-609	TH	thick and thin stress (vertical)	e.g. **608** Peignot
610	TH	thick and thin stress (horizontal)	e.g. **610** Sintex I
611-612	B	heavy bow-shaped	e.g. **611** Becket
613-614	SQ	square-shaped	e.g. **613** Tamil
615	SL	sloping	e.g. **615** Condensa
616-623	RO	rounded shape	e.g. **619** Frankfurter Medium
624	RO	rounded shape outline	e.g. **624** Helvetica Rounded Outline
625-629	EL	electronic	e.g. **626** Countdown
630-633	CU	cut	e.g. **632** Neuland
634-642	ST	stencil or stencil effect	e.g. **636** Futura Black

NB. Typefaces in each group are arranged in alphabetical order.

continued on next page

MODIFIED
SANS SERIF

MSS

continued from previous page

643-654 INL *inline or striped* e.g. **646** Neon

655-662 SH *shaded or 3D* e.g. **659** Superstar Shadow

663-665 SH *shaded or 3D
inline or patterned* e.g. **663** Baby Arbuckle

NB. *Typefaces in each group are arranged in alphabetical order.*

MODIFIED
SANS SERIF

MSS

thick and thin stress (vertical)

604 Britannic

ABCDEFGHIJKLMNOPQRSTUVWXYZ&

605 Florentine

ABCDEFGHIJKLMNOPQRSTUVWXYZ&

606 Inga

ABCDEFGHIJKLMNOPQRSTUVWXYZ&

607 Parisian

ABCDEFGHIJKLMNOPQRSTUVWXYZ&

608 Peignot

ABCDEFGHIJKLMNOPQRSTUVWXYZ&

609 Radiant

ABCDEFGHIJKLMNOPQRSTUVWXYZ&

Britannic
Florentine
Inga
Parisian
Peignot
Radiant
Sintex I
Becket
Revue
Tamil

thick and thin stress (horizontal)

610 Sintex I

ABCDEFGHIJKLMNOPQRSTUVWXYZ&

heavy bow-shaped

611 Becket

ABCDEFGHIJKLMNOPQRSTUVWXYZ&

MODIFIED SANS SERIF

MSS

612 Revue

ABCDEFGHIiJKLMNOPQRSTUVWXYZ&

square-shaped

613 Tamil

ABCDEFGHIJKLMNOPQRSTUVWXYZ&

Britannic **604**

abcdefghijklmnopqrstuvwxyz1234567890

Florentine **605**

abcdefghijklmnopqrstuvwxyz1234567890

Inga **606**

abcdefghijklmnopqrstuvwxyz1234567890

Parisian **607**

abcdefghijklmnopqrstuvwxyz1234567890

Peignot **608**

AbcdefGhijklmnopqrstuvwxyz1234567890

Radiant **609**

abcdefghijklmnopqrstuvwxyz1234567890

Sintex I **610**

abcdefghijklmnopqrstuvwxyz1234567890

Becket **611**

abcdefghijklmnopqrstuvwxyz1234567890

Revue **612**

abcdefghijklmnopqrstuvwxyz1234567890

Tamil **613**

abcdefghijklmnopqrstuvwxyz1234567890

Britannic
Florentine
Inga
Parisian
Peignot
Radiant
Sintex I
Becket
Revue
Tamil

MODIFIED
SANS SERIF

MSS

614 Topic

ABCDEFGHIJKLMNOPQRSTUVWXYZ&

sloping

615 Condensa

ABCDEFGHIJKLMNOPQRSTUVWXYZ&

rounded shape

616 Capone

ABCDEFGHIJKLMNOPQRSTUVWXYZ&

617 Dempsey Medium

ABCDEFGHIJKLMNOPQRSTUVWXYZ&

618 Formula I

ABCDEFGHIJKLMNOPQRSTUVWXYZ&

619 Frankfurter Medium

ABCDEFGHIJKLMNOPQRSTUVWXYZ&

620 Helvetica Rounded

ABCDEFGHIJKLMNOPQRSTUVWXYZ&

621 Horatio Medium

ABCDEFGHIJKLMNOPQRSTUVWXYZ&

622 Octopuss

ABCDEFGHIJKLMNOPQRSTUVWXYZ&

623 Pump

ABCDEFGHIJKLMNOPQRSTUVWXYZ&

Topic
Condensa
Capone
Dempsey Medium
Formula I
Frankfurter Medium
Helvetica Rounded
Horatio Medium
Octopuss
Pump

**MODIFIED
SANS SERIF**

Topic **614**

abcdefghijklmnopqrstuvwxyz**1234567890**

Condensa **615**

*abcdefghijklmnopqrstuvwxyz***1234567890**

Capone **616**

abcdefghijklmnopqrstuvwxyz1234567890

Dempsey Medium **617**

abcdefghijklmnopqrstuvwxyz1234567890

Formula I **618**

abcdefghijklmnopqrstuvwxyz**1234567890**

Frankfurter Medium **619**

abcdefghijklmnopqrstuvwxyz**1234567890**

Helvetica Rounded **620**

abcdefghijklmnopqrstuvwxyz**1234567890**

Horatio Medium **621**

abcdefghijklmnopqrstuvwxyz1234567890

Octopuss **622**

abcdefghijklmnopqrstuvwxyz1234567890

Pump **623**

abcdefghijklmnopqrstuvwxyz1234567890

Topic
Condensa
Capone
Dempsey Medium
Formula I
Frankfurter Medium
Helvetica Rounded
Horatio Medium
Octopuss
Pump

MODIFIED
SANS SERIF

rounded
shape
outline

624 Helvetica Rounded Outline

ABCDEFGHIJKLMNOPQRSTUVWXYZ&

electronic

625 Amelia

ABCDEFGHIJKLMNOPQRSTUVWXYZ&

626 Countdown

ABCDEFGHIJKLMNOPQRSTUVWXYZ&

627 Data 70

ABCDEFGHIJKLMNOPQRSTUVWXYZ&

628 Digital

ABCDEFGHIJKLMNOPQRSTUVWXYZ

629 Russell Square

ABCDEFGHIJKLMNOPQRSTUVWXYZ&

cut

630 Ad Lib

ABCDEFGHIJKLMNOPQRSTUVWXYZ&

631 Kino

ABCDEFGHIJKLMNOPQRSTUVWXYZ

632 Neuland

ABCDEFGHIJKLMNOPQRSTUVWXYZ&

633 Othello

ABCDEFGHIJKLMNOPQRSTUVWXYZ&

Helvetica Rounded
Outline
Amelia
Countdown
Data 70
Digital
Russell Square
Ad Lib
Kino
Neuland
Othello

**MODIFIED
SANS SERIF**

MSS

Helvetica Rounded Outline **624**

abcdefghijklmnopqrstuvwxyz1234567890

Amelia **625**

abcdefghijklmnopqrstuvwxyz1234567890

Countdown **626**

abcdefghijklmnopqrstuvwxyz1234567890

Data 70 **627**

abcdefghijklmnopqrstuvwxyz1234567890

Digital **628**

1234567890 *no lower case*

Russell Square **629**

abcdefghijklmnopqrstuvwxyz1234567890

Ad Lib **630**

abcdefghijklmnopqrstuvwxyz1234567890

Kino **631**

abcdefghijklmnopqrstuvwxyz1234567890

Neuland **632**

1234567890 *no lower case*

Othello **633**

1234567890 *no lower case*

Helvetica Rounded
Outline
Amelia
Countdown
Data 70
Digital
Russell Square
Ad Lib
Kino
Neuland
Othello

MODIFIED
SANS SERIF

MSS

stencil or stencil effect

634 Braggadocio

ABCDEFGHIJKLMNOPQRSTUVWXYZ&

635 Folio Stencil

ABCDEFGHIJKLMNOPQRSTUVWXYZ&

636 Futura Black

ABCDEFGHIJKLMNOPQRSTUVWXYZ&

637 Glaser Stencil Bold

ABCDEFGHIJKLMNOPQRSTUVWXYZ&

638 Glyphic

ABCDEFGHIJKLMNOPQRSTUVWXYZ

639 Motter Tektura

ABCDEFGHIJKLMNOPQRSTUVWXYZ&

640 Stop

ABCDEFGHIJKLMNOPQRSTUVWXYZ&

641 Tabasco

ABCDEFGHIJKLMNOPQRSTUVWXYZ&

642 Traffic

no capital letters

inline or striped

643 Fatima

ABCDEFGHIJKLMNOPQRSTUVWXYZ&

Braggadocio
Folio Stencil
Futura Black
Glaser Stencil Bold
Glyphic
Motter Tektura
Stop
Tabasco
Traffic
Fatima

MODIFIED SANS SERIF

Braggadocio **634**

abcdefghijklmnopqrstuvwxyz1234567890

Folio Stencil **635**

1234567890 *no lower case*

Futura Black **636**

abcdefghijklmnopqrstuvwxyz1234567890

Glaser Stencil Bold **637**

123-4567890 *no lower case*

Glyphic **638**

1234567890 *no lower case*

Motter Tektura **639**

abcdefghijklmnopqrstuvwxyz1234567890

Stop **640**

1234567890 *no lower case*

Tabasco **641**

abcdefghijklmnopqrstuvwxyz1234567890

Traffic **642**

abcdefghijklmnopqrstuvwxyz1234567890

Fatima **643**

1234567890 *no lower case*

Braggadocio
Folio Stencil
Futura Black
Glaser Stencil Bold
Glyphic
Motter Tektura
Stop
Tabasco
Traffic
Fatima

**MODIFIED
SANS SERIF**

644 French Flash

ABCDEFGHIJKLMNOPQRSTUVWXYZ

645 Michel

ABCDEFGHIJKLMNOPQRSTUV W X Y Z &

646 Neon

ABCDEFGHIJKLMNOPQRSTUVWXYZ &

647 Optex

ABCDEFGHIJKLMNOPQRSTUVWXYZ &

648 Oxford

no capital letters

649 Piccadilly

ABCDEFGHIJKLMNOPQRSTUVWXYZ&

650 Pluto

ABCDEFGHIJKLMNOPQRSTUVWXYZ&

651 Prisma

ABCDEFGHIJKLMNOPQRSTUVW XYZ &

652 Pump Triline

ABCDEFGHIJKLMNOPQRSTUVWXYZ&

653 ITC Uptight Neon

ABCDEFGHIJKLMNOPQRSTUVWXYZ&

French Flash
Michel
Neon
Optex
Oxford
Piccadilly
Pluto
Prisma
Pump Triline
ITC Uptight Neon

**MODIFIED
SANS SERIF**

MSS

French Flash **644**

1234567890 *no lower case*

Michel **645**

abcdefghijklmnopqrstuvwxyz1234567890

Neon **646**

1234567890 *no lower case*

Optex **647**

abcdefghijklmnopqrstuvwxyz1234567890

Oxford **648**

abcdefghijklmnopqrstuvwxyz1234567890

Piccadilly **649**

1234567890 *no lower case*

Pluto **650**

abcdefghijklmnopqrstuvwxyz1234567890

Prisma **651**

1234567890 *no lower case*

Pump Triline **652**

abcdefghijklmnopqrstuvwxyz1234567890

ITC Uptight Neon **653**

abcdefghijklmnopqrstuvwxyz1234567890

French Flash
Michel
Neon
Optex
Oxford
Piccadilly
Pluto
Prisma
Pump Triline
ITC Uptight Neon

MODIFIED
SANS SERIF

MSS

654 Zeppelin

ABCDEFGHIJKLMNOPQRSTUVWXYZ&

shaded or 3D

655 Bullion Shadow

ABCDEFGHIJKLMNOPQRSTUVWXYZ&

656 Old Bowery

ABCDEFGHIJKLMNOPQRSTUVWXYZ&

657 Pioneer Shadow

ABCDEFGHIJKLMNOPQRSTUVWXYZ&

658 Premier Shaded

ABCDEFGHIJKLMNOPQRSTUVWXYZ&

659 Superstar Shadow

ABCDEFGHIJKLMNOPQRSTUVWXYZ &

660 Tintoretto

ABCDEFGHIJKLMNOPQRSTUVWXYZ &

661 Umbra

ABCDEFGHIJKLMNOPQRSTUVWXYZ &

662 Uncle Bill

ABCDEFGHIJKLMNOPQRSTUVWXYZ&

663 Baby Arbuckle

ABCDEFGIHJKLMNOPQRSTUVXWYZ&

Zeppelin
Bullion Shadow
Old Bowery
Pioneer Shadow
Premier Shaded
Superstar Shadow
Tintoretto
Umbra
Uncle Bill
Baby Arbuckle

MODIFIED
SANS SERIF

MSS

shaded or 3D
inline or
patterned

Zeppelin **654**

abcdefghijklmnopqrstuvwxyz1234567890

Bullion Shadow **655**

1234567890 *no lower case*

Old Bowery **656**

no lower case or figures

Pioneer Shadow **657**

1234567890 *no lower case*

Premier Shaded **658**

1234567890 *no lower case*

Superstar Shadow **659**

1234567890 *no lower case*

Tintoretto **660**

abcdefghijklmnopqrstuvwxyz 1234567890

Umbra **661**

1234567890 *no lower case*

Uncle Bill **662**

1234567890 *no lower case*

Baby Arbuckle **663**

1234567890 *no lower case*

Zeppelin
Bullion Shadow
Old Bowery
Pioneer Shadow
Premier Shaded
Superstar Shadow
Tintoretto
Umbra
Uncle Bill
Baby Arbuckle

MODIFIED
SANS SERIF

664 Jim Crow

ABCDEFGHIJKLMNOPQRSTUWVXYZ

665 Quicksilver

ABCDEFGHIJKLMNOPQRSTUVWXYZ &

Jim Crow
Quicksilver

Jim Crow **664**

1234567890 *no lower case*

Quicksilver **665**

1234567890 *no lower case*

Jim Crow
Quicksilver

**MODIFIED
SANS SERIF**

MSS

8. MODIFIED OUTRAGEOUS

Specimen nos		Basic characteristics	
666-671	**HE**	heavy / distorted	e.g. **668** Litzenburg
672-678	**INL**	inline or striped	e.g. **672** ITC Aki Lines
679	**BR**	broken-surfaced and distorted	e.g. **679** Shatter
680-684	**DOT**	dot-formed	e.g. **682** Pinball
685-694	**SH**	shaded or 3D	e.g. **688** Calypso
695-698	**B**	with backgrounds	e.g. **697** Process
699-700	**Z**	pictorial	e.g. **700** Zip

NB. *Typefaces in each group are arranged in alphabetical order.*

MODIFIED
OUTRAGEOUS

heavy/ distorted

666 Bottleneck

ABCDEFGHIJKLMNOPQRSTUVWXYZ &

667 Florist

ABCDEFGHIJKLMNOPQRSTUVWXYZ&

668 Litzenburg

ABCDEFGHIJKLMNOPQRSTUVWXYZ&

669 Pierrot

ABCDEFGHIJKLMNOPQRSTUVWXYZ&

670 Starvation

ABCDEFGHIJKLMNOPQRSTUVWXYZ&

671 Talbot

ABCDEFGHIJKLMNOPQRSTUVWXYZB

inline or striped

672 ITC Aki Lines

ABCDEFGHIJKLMNOPQRSTUVWXYZ&

673 Groove

674 Horseman Sidesaddle

ABCDEFGHIJKLMNOPQRSTUVWXYZ&

675 Matra

ABCDEFGHIJKLMNOPQRSTUVWXYZ

Bottleneck
Florist
Litzenburg
Pierrot
Starvation
Talbot
ITC Aki Lines
Groove
Horseman Sidesaddle
Matra

MODIFIED OUTRAGEOUS

Bottleneck **666**

abcdefghijklmnopqrstuvwxyz 1234567890

Florist **667**

1234567890 *no lower case*

Litzenburg **668**

1234567890 *no lower case*

Pierrot **669**

abcdefghijklmnopqrstuvwxyz1234567890

Starvation **670**

1234567890 *no lower case*

Talbot **671**

1234567890 *no lower case*

ITC Aki Lines **672**

1234567890 *no lower case*

Groove **673**

1234567890 *no lower case*

Horseman Sidesaddle **674**

1234567890 *no lower case*

Matra **675**

1234567890 *no lower case*

Bottleneck
Florist
Litzenburg
Pierrot
Starvation
Talbot
ITC Aki Lines
Groove
Horseman Sidesaddle
Matra

MODIFIED
OUTRAGEOUS

676 Old Glory

677 Sinaloa

678 Stripes

broken surfaced and distorted

679 Shatter

ABCDEFGHIJKLMNOPQRSTUVWXYZ &

dot-formed

680 Astra

681 Chequered

ABCDEFGHIJKLMNOPQRSTUVWXYZ&

682 Pinball

ABCDEFGHIJKLMNOPQRSTUVWXYZ&

683 Spangle

ABCDEFGHIJKLMNOPQRSTUVWXYZ

684 Spotty Face

ABCDEFGHIJKLMNOPQRSTUVWXYZ&

shaded or 3D

685 Block up

Old Glory
Sinaloa
Stripes
Shatter
Astra
Chequered
Pinball
Spangle
Spotty Face
Block up

**MODIFIED
OUTRAGEOUS**

Old Glory **676**

1234567890 *no lower case*

Sinaloa **677**

1234567890 *no lower case*

Stripes **678**

1234567890 *no lower case*

Shatter **679**

abcdefghijklmnopqrstuvwxyz 1234567890

Astra **680**

1234567890 *no lower case*

Chequered **681**

1234567890 *no lower case*

Pinball **682**

abcdefghijklmnopqrstuvwxyz1234567890

Spangle **683**

1234567890 *no lower case*

Spotty Face **684**

1234567890 *no lower case*

Block up **685**

1234567890 *no lower case*

MODIFIED
OUTRAGEOUS

686 Bombere

ABCDEFGHIJKLMNOPQRSTUVWXYZ &

687 Buster

ABCDEFGHIJKLMNOPQRSTUVWXYZ&

688 Calypso

ABCDEFGHIJLLMNOPRSTUVWXYZ

689 Italiennes Ombrees

ABCDEFGHIJKLMNOPQRSTUVWXYZ&

690 Perspective Italic

ABCDEFGHIJKLMNOPQRSTUVWXYZ

691 Speed Caps

ABCDEFGHIJKLMNOPQRSTUVWXYZ&

692 Stack

ABCDEFGHIJKLMNOPQRSTUVWXYZ&

693 Sunshine

no capitals

694 Talbot's Rocky Mountain

ABCDEFGHIJKLMNOPQRSTUVWXYZ

with backgrounds

695 Good Vibrations

ABCDEFGHIJKLMNOPQRSTUVWXYZ&

Bombere
Buster
Calypso
Italiennes Ombrees
Perspective Italic
Speed Caps
Stack
Sunshine
Talbot's
Rocky Mountain
Good Vibrations

**MODIFIED
OUTRAGEOUS**

Bombere **686**

 no lower case

Buster **687**

 no lower case

Calypso **688**

no lower case or figures

Italiennes Ombrees **689**

1234567890 *no lower case*

Perspective Italic **690**

no lower case or figures

Speed Caps **691**

1234567890 *no lower case*

Stack **692**

1234567890 *no lower case*

Sunshine **693**

abcdefghijklmnopqrstuvwxyz1234567890

Talbot's Rocky Mountain **694**

1234567890 *no lower case*

Good Vibrations **695**

1234567890 *no lower case*

Bombere
Buster
Calypso
Italiennes Ombrees
Perspective Italic
Speed Caps
Stack
Sunshine
Talbot's
Rocky Mountain
Good Vibrations

MODIFIED
OUTRAGEOUS

696 Phase Two

ABCDEFGHIJKLMNOPQRSTUVWXYZ&

697 Process

ABCDEFGHIJKLMNOPQRSTUVWXYZ&

698 Tonal

ABCDEFGHIJKLMNOPQRSTUVWXYZ&

pictorial

699 Via Face Don Black

ABCDEFGHIJKLMNOPQRSTUVWXYZ

700 Zip

ABCDEFGHIJKLMNOPQRSTUVWXYZ&

Phase Two
Process
Tonal
Via Face Don Black
Zip

MODIFIED
OUTRAGEOUS

Phase Two **696**

abcdefghijklmnopqrstuvwxyz 1234567890

Process **697**

1234567890 *no lower case*

Tonal **698**

1234567890 *no lower case*

Via Face Don Black **699**

no lower case or figures

Zip **700**

1234567890 *no lower case*

Phase Two
Process
Tonal
Via Face Don Black
Zip

MODIFIED
OUTRAGEOUS

'TYPEFINDER' CLASSIFICATION SYSTEM

TEXT TYPEFACE CATEGORIES

I. Sloping e-Bar (Venetian Serif). *Nos 1-34*

Includes all roman, slab and wedge serif faces with a sloping bar on the lower case e, a traditional feature of 'Venetian' typefaces. The mixture of serif-style typefaces in this category means that other characteristics are mixed – for example, typefaces may have either vertical or angled stress and oblique or straight serifs.

e.g. Kennerley, Centaur, ITC Souvenir.

2. Angled Stress/Oblique Serifs (Old Style Serif). *Nos 35-53*

Includes 'Old Style' or 'Old Face' typefaces providing they have the above characteristics and do not possess a sloping bar on the lower case e.

e.g. Bembo, Plantin, Times New Roman.

3. Vertical Stress/Oblique Serifs (Transitional Serif). *Nos 54-110*

Includes 'Transitional' typefaces providing they have these characteristics and do not have a sloping bar on the lower case e. 'Transitional' typefaces with horizontal serifs or abrupt contrast will be found in either Categories 4 or 5.

e.g. Caslon Old Face, Baskerville 169 (Monotype), Garamond (Stempel).

4. Vertical Stress/Straight Serifs (New Transitional Serif). *Nos 111-150*

Contains 'Transitional' typefaces which have straight (horizontal) serifs or nearly so, as well as 'Twentieth Century Roman' typefaces with the same characteristics.

e.g. Joanna, Century Schoolbook, Cheltenham

5. Abrupt Contrast/Straight Serifs (Modern Serif). *Nos 151-187*

Contains 'Modern', 'Transitional' and 'Twentieth Century Romans' with good contrast and straight (horizontal) serifs.

e.g. Bauer Bodoni, Caledonia, Scotch Roman.

6. Slab Serif. *Nos 188-217*

Typefaces of a generally heavy appearance, either with square or bracketed slab serifs. Also includes rounded slab typefaces (typewriter designs).

e.g. Rockwell, Clarendon, ITC American Typewriter

7. Wedge Serif (Hybrid Serif). *Nos 218-240*

Includes some 'Glyphic' typefaces used for continuous text setting plus typefaces with wedge-ended, or wedge-shaped serifs. The category also includes 'hybrid' typefaces which are neither clearly serif nor sans serif in origin.

e.g. Albertus, Meridien, Copperplate Gothic

BRITISH STANDARDS CLASSIFICATION OF TYPEFACES (BS 2961: 1967)

Category		Description	Examples
No.	**Name**		
I	Humanist	Typefaces in which the cross stroke of the lower case e is oblique; the axis of the curves is inclined to the left; there is no great contrast between thin and thick strokes; the serifs are bracketed; the serifs of the ascenders in the lower case are oblique. NOTE. This was formerly known as 'Venetian', having been derived from the 15th century minuscule written with a varying stroke thickness by means of an obliquely-held broad pen.	Verona, Centaur, Kennerley
II	Garalde	Typefaces in which the axis of the curves is inclined to the left; there is generally a greater contrast in the relative thickness of the strokes than in Humanist designs; the serifs are bracketed; the bar of the lower case e is horizontal; the serifs of the ascenders in the lower case are oblique. NOTE. These are types in the Aldine and Garamond tradition and were formerly called 'Old Face' and 'Old Style'.	Bembo, Garamond, Caslon, Vendôme
III	Transitional	Typefaces in which the axis of the curves is vertical or inclined slightly to the left; the serifs are bracketed, and those of the ascenders in the lower case are oblique. NOTE. This typeface is influenced by the letterforms of the copperplate engraver. It may be regarded as a transition from Garalde to Didone, and incorporates some characteristics of each.	Fournier, Baskerville, Bell, Caledonia, Columbia
IV	Didone	Typefaces having an abrupt contrast between thin and thick strokes; the axis of the curves is vertical; the serifs of the ascenders of the lower case are horizontal; there are often no brackets to the serifs. NOTE. These are typefaces as developed by Didot and Bodoni. Formerly called 'Modern'.	Bodoni, Corvinus, Modern Extended
V	Slab-serif	Typefaces with heavy, square-ended serifs, with or without brackets.	Rockwell, Clarendon, Playbill

Extracts from BS 2961:1967. Reproduced by permission of the British Standards Institutions, 2 Park Street, London W1A 2BS from whom complete copies of the Standard can be obtained.
'Typefinder' Classification System devised by Christopher Perfect & Eiichi Kono.

'TYPEFINDER' CLASSIFICATION SYSTEM

TEXT TYPEFACE CATEGORIES *continued*

8. Sans Serif. *Nos 245-304*

Includes 'Lineale' designs used for continuous text setting arranged according to the width of the capital G and whether or not it has a spur. There are additional groups for square, sloping, rounded and electronic designs.

e.g. Futura, Gill Sans, Unvers.

DECORATIVE (NON-CONTINUOUS TEXT) TYPEFACE CATEGORIES

3. Unmodified (Formal Text Shape). *Nos 382-428*

'Glyphic' typefaces not usually used for continuous text setting will be found here. The category contains serif or sans serif typefaces of a traditional letter shape normally used for titling or headings but not for continuous text setting.

e.g. Engravers Roman, Castellar, Latin Antique No. 9

1. Flowing Scripts *Nos 305-322* and
2. Non-Flowing Scripts *Nos 323-381*

'Script' and 'Graphic' typefaces are to be found in one of these two categories according to whether their letters are joined when typeset and therefore appear 'flowing' like handwriting. The Non-Flowing category includes blackletter and uncial typefaces as well as roman italic typefaces based on pen scripts.

e.g. **1.** Palace Script, Kaufmann, Mistral.
e.g. **2.** Bernhard Tango, Old English Text, Libra.

4. Fat & Thin Face (Modified & Unmodified).
Nos. 429-536

Includes serif or sans serif typefaces of the extremes in weight – very bold or very light.

e.g. Falstaff, Cooper Black, Harry Thin.

5. Ornamental. *Nos 537-563*

Serif, sans serif or script typefaces of a very elaborately patterned or 'floriated' design.

e.g. Fry's Ornamented, Lettres Ornées, Ballé Initials.

6. Modified Serif. *Nos 564-603*

Serif typefaces of a 'non-formal/traditional' shape.
e.g. Belwe, Profil, Charleston.

7. Modified Sans Serif. *Nos 604-665*

Sans serif typefaces of a 'non-formal/traditional' shape.
e.g. Peignot, Frankfurter Medium, Countdown.

8. Modified Outrageous. *Nos 666-700*

Serif and sans serif typefaces of a highly unusual or 'way out' nature.
e.g. Shatter, Pinball, Calypso.

BRITISH STANDARDS CLASSIFICATION OF TYPEFACES (BS 2961: 1967)

Category No.	Category Name	Description	Examples
VI	Lineale	Typefaces without serifs. NOTE. Formerly called 'Sans-serif'.	
	a Grotesque	Lineale typefaces with 19th century origins. There is some contrast in thickness of strokes. They have squareness of curve, and curling close-set jaws. The R usually has a curled leg and the G is spurred. The ends of the curved strokes are usually horizontal.	SB Grot. No. 6, Cond. Sans No. 7, Monotype Headline Bold
	b Neo-grotesque	Lineale typefaces derived from the grotesque. They have less stroke contrast and are more regular in design. The jaws are more open than in the true grotesque and the g is often open-tailed. The ends of the curved strokes are usually oblique.	Edel/Wotan, Univers, Helvetica
	c Geometric	Lineale typefaces constructed on simple geometric shapes, circle or rectangle. Usually monoline, and often with single-storey a.	Futura, Erbar, Eurostyle
	d Humanist	Lineale typefaces based on the proportions of inscriptional Roman capitals and Humanist or Garalde lower-case, rather than on early grotesques. They have some stroke contrast, with two-storey a and g.	Optima, Gill Sans, Pascal
VII	Glyphic	Typefaces which are chiselled rather than calligraphic in form.	Latin, Albertus, Augustea
VIII	Script	Typefaces that imitate cursive writing.	Palace Script, Legend, Mistral
IX	Graphic	Typefaces whose characters suggest that they have been drawn rather than written.	Libra, Cartoon, Old English (Monotype)

BIOGRAPHICAL NOTES ON LEADING TYPE DESIGNERS
by Sarah Rookledge

The information that makes up this section has been compiled from sources too numerous to list here. Major ones include D.B. Updike; *Printing Types, Their History, Forms, and Use*, Sebastian Carter; *Twentieth Century Type Designers*, and Geoffrey Dowding; *An Introduction to the History of Printing Types.*

Ludovico degli Arrighi da Vincenzia, d.c1527
Blado italic, 380

Ludovico degli Arrighi, who lived in Rome, was a professional calligrapher, and later a printer of fine editions, who also designed type. In 1524 he started a small press with Lautitius Perusinus, a printer but also an engraver and as such probably the cutter of the types. They printed fine editions of short contemporary works using type based on Arrighi's formal cursive script. The type was later acquired by Antonio Blado who gives his name to its contemporary version.

Richard Austin and John Bell, 1746-1831
Bell, 172

Scotch Roman, 185/186

In 1788, inspired by Fournier's types, John Bell, a newspaper publisher and pioneer of cheap editions of the classics, started The British Letter Foundry and issued his first type specimen, cut by Richard Austin. A skilful cutter, Austin produced a very sharp letter which Stanley Morison called the first English modern face. Actually the type retains some old style characteristics and should more properly be called a late transitional. Austin went on to cut true moderns, though in 1819 when he had started a foundry of his own he outlined the dangers of such designs being taken to extremes.

The British Letter Foundry closed in 1798. Between this date and Austin's setting up The Imperial Letter Foundry in Worship Street, London he cut types for the Wilson Foundry in Glasgow and for William Miller in Edinburgh. The Miller & Richards types known as the Scotch Romans are probably his work. Austin also worked as a cutter of typographical ornaments.

John Baskerville, 1706-1775
Baskerville, 77-80

John Baskerville's contribution to printing is enormous. He adapted the old face roman to produce highly influential new types; he recognised the important role of typography in book design; he modified inks and the printing press to give blacker, sharper letters on the page and may also be responsible for the introduction of wove paper (though he sold it for writing not printing). Baskerville's work influenced Continental printers like Didot and Bodoni but in his native England it was frequently derided.

Like Caslon, John Baskerville was born in Worcestershire but in 1725 he moved to Birmingham where he worked as a writing master and did some stone engraving. He cut inscriptions on gravestones. Later, when he was to design his own types, he could use the knowledge of lettering he acquired in this period. He taught writing for ten years, then decided to take advantage of the fashion for japanned ornaments (japanning is a method of decorating which gives a glossy finish). The business prospered and made Baskerville a prominent figure in Birmingham society.

In 1750, he set up a printing press but the pace of work and the exacting standards he set himself were such that it was to take him seven years before that press produced its first book. Existing types, inks and presses did not meet his standards. Despite lacking any printing background he determined to create his own. By 1752 he had cut fourteen letters. By 1753 he had enough type to produce an advertisement for his first book, a fine edition of Virgil. The book itself appeared in 1757, as did another specimen sheet, this time showing four sizes of roman.

Baskerville's type was much criticised in England and compared unfavourably to Caslon's. People said it was difficult to read, even that it would damage the sight, but it also had its advocates, notably Benjamin Franklin. The Bible which Baskerville printed (on special dispensation from the Cambridge University Press) brought him great acclaim on the Continent. The appearance of Baskerville's books, unlike those of most of his contemporaries, did not depend on illustrations. He achieved his effects through good types cleanly printed, and a judicious use of leading and letter spacing. Other printers, most notably Bodoni, followed his lead in this.

Baskerville died in 1775 and his wife Sarah sold his remaining stock to Beaumarchais for an edition of the works of Voltaire. His punches eventually came into the hands of Deberny & Peignot who made new matrices from them for their version of Baskerville. In 1953 they presented the punches to the Cambridge University Press.

John Bell, see Richard Austin

Morris Fuller Benton, 1872-1948
Century Schoolbook, 119

Franklin Gothic, 276

News Gothic, 287

Morris Fuller Benton was the son of Linn Boyd Benton, inventor of the pantographic punchcutting machine and cutter of Century for Theodore De Vinne's magazine *The Century*. Like his father, Morris Benton worked for American Typefounders (ATF); he joined Linn Boyd Benton as his assistant in ATF's type design department. This was the first department of its kind in a foundry and had been set up by his father at the instigation of ATF's director Robert Nelson. Benton has been credited with inventing the concept of the type family, and although this is not the case he did do his best work expanding faces into families and adapting existing type styles. Between 1900 and 1928 he designed eighteen variations on Century, including the popular Century Schoolbook (1924). Other Benton types include: Franklin Gothic (1903) and News Gothic (1980).

Giovanni Battista Bodoni, 1740-1813
Bodoni, 154/162/163

Bodoni is one of the first cutters of a modern face; that is, a typeface which has hairline serifs at right angles to the uprights, vertical stress and abrupt contrast between thick and thin strokes. He took French types, such as Fournier's and those of the Didot's as his models. Bodoni was, in his day, the best known printer in Europe.

Bodoni was born in Saluzzo in Piedmont in the north of Italy in 1740, the son of a printer. He was apprenticed to be a compositor at the press of Properganda Fide in Rome but left after the suicide of the Director. At 28 he was made Director of the press of the Duke of Parma, the last of the Ducal private presses.

His early types are based on those of Pierre Simon Fournier, whose work he admired, but he experimented with these letter forms to create his own. The roman letter he cut in 1798 is what we generally mean by a Bodoni. The contrast of light and shade in his types can produce a sparkling effect on the page. The books which he printed reveal a taste for large sizes of type, generous use of white space and few ornaments. In addition to his romans Bodoni also produced a great many script types.

Bodoni set out his principles of typography (although stated in vague and general terms) in his *Manual Tipographico*. This book was completed by his wife and she published it in 1818, five years after his death.

Bodoni's faces appear today in two main recuttings: American Typefounders' and Bauer. The ATF version was cut by M. F. Benton and copied with minor variations by The Monotype Corporation, Haas, Linotype, Intertype, and Ludlow. The more delicate Bauer version is used by Bauer alone.

Margaret Calvert, see Jock Kinneir

Ron Carpenter, b.1950
Calisto, 53A
Cantoria, 240A

Ron Carpenter joined Monotype in 1968 where he trained as a type draftsman. His first experience of typeface design was working on the italic for Nimrod with Robin Nicholas. Since becoming Senior Type Designer in 1984 he has been responsible for designing Cantoria and Calisto and new weights for Times New Roman.

Matthew Carter, b.1937
Auriga, 151
Bell Centenial, 284
Galliard, 74
Olympian, 71
Video, 283

Matthew Carter is the son of printing historian Harry Carter who was archivist to the Oxford University Press. He was taught by Jan Van Krimpen's assistant and worked for Crossfield Electronics and Mergenthaler Linotype, designing Bell Centenial for the latter in 1978. Also in 1978, he designed Galliard with Mike Parker and in 1981 they set up Bitstream to supply new type designs in digital form. Bitstream Charter is the first new design they have issued.

William Caslon, 1692-1766
Caslon, 59-61/99/383/391/445

Worcestershire-born William Caslon began his career engraving and chasing gun barrels (occasionally also cutting brass letters for bookbinders) until a printer called William Bowyer who had seen some of his letters encouraged him to try punchcutting. Bowyer was so confident Caslon would succeed at it he, and two other printers, lent him £500 to start his own foundry which opened in about 1716.

Caslon was the first British typefounder of any reknown. Previously British printers were dependent mainly on imported types, chiefly Dutch and French. In 1722 he produced his second type, a roman based on Dutch models. With the publication of his first specimen sheet in 1734 he became immediately successful. Unlike those of John Baskerville Caslon's designs were not innovative; similar types were in use a hundred years earlier; but it was his skills as an engraver that distinguished him. His roman quickly established itself as a popular book face.

In 1766 the Oxford University Press bought Caslon type to supplement the Fell types. He published further sheets and, later, books of his types. His work found particular favour in America and Caslon type was used by Mary Katherine Goddard of Baltimore for the printing of the Declaration of Independence.

The Caslon foundry continued under the directorship of successive William Caslons until the death of the last male Caslon in 1873. The company remained in existence, for much of the time in the same Chiswell Street premises in London, until 1936. Its stock was bought up by Stephenson Blake and Company.

Thomas J. Cobden Sanderson, 1840-1922, and Emery Walker, 1851-1933

Thomas Cobden Sanderson, an important member of the Arts and Crafts movement in the late nineteenth and early twentieth centuries founded The Doves Press in 1901, with the typographer Emery Walker. Emery Walker had also worked for William Morris, as his typographical consultant. (The name Doves came from a local inn.)

Unfortunately an initially productive relationship degenerated into bitter quarrels, mainly over Doves, the press's own type, which was based on a Jenson type of 1476. Both partners had worked on Doves and each claimed authorship for himself. In 1912 as a result of this dispute, Cobden Sanderson smashed the matrices and dropped the type into the River Thames over Hammersmith Bridge.

François-Ambroise Didot, 1730-1804
Pierre-François Didot, 1732-95
and Firmin Didot, 1766-1836
Didot, 156

The Didot family of Paris dominated the French book world in the late eighteenth and early nineteenth centuries. Its members were involved in printing, publishing, type-founding, punchcutting and paper manufacture. Among their contributions were what is generally agreed to be the first modern face and a reform of the point system of type measurement.
Its most notable members are François-Ambroise, Pierre-François and François-Ambroise's younger son Firmin. Didot's roman types were the standard book types used in France during the nineteenth century and are still in general use today.

F-A Didot initially printed with Garamond types but began to produce his own in about 1775. In 1784 the first modern face appeared in an edition of Tasso's *Gerusalemme Liberata*. It is characterised by thin serifs, vertical stress and abrupt shading from thick strokes to thin. By this time the Didots were using wove paper and an improved printing press which allowed the fine details of such type to be reproduced. This important type was cut in 1783 by F. A. Didot's son Firmin, then 19. Firmin took over from his father's

previous punchcutter Pierre Louis Wafflard. François-Ambroise was also the Director of the *Imprimerie National* and in this capacity he revised Fournier's point system. His name survives in the Continental didot point.

William Addison Dwiggins, 1880-1956
Caledonia, 174
Electra, 148
Metro, 263

Dwiggins had a varied career that took in illustration, printing, advertising and book design. He began designing types when he was 44 at the invitation of Mergenthaler Linotype. His first type was a sans serif, Metro. His best known face is Caledonia which fuses aspects of the Scotch Romans and the types cut for Bulmer by William Martin.

He wrote widely on design matters; Mergenthaler Linotype's idea for a Dwiggins sans serif came from reading him on sans serif faces in one of his books *Layout in Advertising* (Harper, 1928). In 1929 he was awarded the American Institute of Graphic Arts Gold Medal.

Dr. John Fell, 1625-86

Dr Fell was Bishop of Oxford, Dean of Christ Church and Vice Chancellor of Oxford University. With three others (and for an annual payment of £200) he took over the management of the University Press in 1671. Between 1667 and 1672 he imported types, punches and matrices which were bought in Holland on his behalf by Thomas Marshall. These included some Granjon types and some supplied by Van Dijck. In 1676 he set up a type foundry attached to the press and employed a Dutch typecutter, Peter Walpergen. A specimen sheet was issued by the press in 1693, and the types became known as the Fell Types.

Pierre Simon Fournier, 1712-1768
Barbou, 89
Fournier, 90

Pierre Simon Fournier, also known as Fournier le jeune, made several important contributions to the field of type design. He set up his own foundry in Paris where he cut and founded all the types himself, pioneered the concept of the type family and is said to have cut 60,000 punches for 147 alphabets of his own design. He created new printers flowers and ornaments that caught the mood of his age. He invented a point system for standardising type sizes and published it in its first version when he was only 25. (The Didot system used on the Continent today was developed from Fournier's and retained the name of his unit, the point, while fractionally increasing its size). Not surprisingly perhaps Fournier's death at 56 was attributed to overwork. He is probably best remembered as the designer of one of the earliest transitional faces. His St. Augustine Ordinair served as the model for Monotype's Fournier of 1925. Another, version, Barbou, was issued in 1968, the bicentenary of his death.

Adrian Frutiger, b.1928

Adrian Frutiger is one of the most important type designers to emerge since World War II. Now living just outside Paris, he was born near Interlaken in Switzerland. He was apprenticed as a compositor and later studied wood-cutting and calligraphy before coming to the attention of Charles Peignot of Deberny and Peignot who asked him to adapt Futura.

Finding Futura too geometric, and wanting to design a sans serif with a large, matched, family of weights, Frutiger designed the twenty-one weights of Univers which was issued in 1955. Many founders and designers have followed this idea and have since produced large sans serif families of their own.

Frutiger's other designs do not confine themselves to sans serifs. Apollo is new transitional, Serifa is a slab serif, and OCR-B could be termed experimental.

The face, named after him, Frutiger, was developed from a design he used at Roissy Airport near Paris. While its weights follow the numbered form of Univers, it is much more humanistic in feel.

Aside from type design, Frutiger also designs books and periodicals, and lectures. Among his writings is *Type, Sign, Symbol* (ABE Editions, Zurich).

In 1986 he received the Gutenberg Prize for technical and aesthetic achievement in type.

Joseph Fry; 1728-1787, and Isaac Moore

Joseph Fry was a Birmingham man by birth who, like Baskerville, came to typefounding relatively late in his career and was also successful in other fields (among his numerous business ventures he started Fry's chocolates).

In 1764, while living in Bristol, Fry decided to go into partnership with a local printer, William Pine, and set up a foundry attached to Pine's print works. Isaac Moore, previously a whitesmith (that is, a metal finisher) was taken on to cut types for them and later became a partner. Moore cut his types after Baskerville's (though they're not close copies) and the foundry's early types are all of this kind.

In 1770 they published their second specimen sheet which shows a much more extensive selection of type sizes than their first and a number of ornaments. In 1776 Moore retired and the foundry produced Caslon style types in preference to Baskerville's.

Claude Garamond, c1480-1561

Claude Garamond was the first person to specialise in the design and cutting of type on a large scale. The roman letters he designed at his Paris foundry took the Aldine (see Aldus Manutius, and the introduction to category 2, p24) roman as their model, but improved upon it; the 'fit' of the letters together was better and the capitals, lower case and italic were better balanced to give a comprehensive and harmonious fount of type.

These types were much copied; by the end of the sixteenth century they had become the standard European type and they were still in use in the eighteenth century. Garamond cut the Grecs du roi letters for Francois I of France but other printers could use them with the King's permission. He is credited with the roman types used by the publishers Estienne from 1532 onwards. Three other French publishers also used related founts around this time. The *caractères de l'université* at the *Imprimerie Royale* were attributed to him until Beatrice Warde proved them to be a later type in the Garamond style cut by Jean Jannon.

In 1545 Garamond began publishing on his own account using types of his own design including a new italic cut in two sizes. His first book was the *Pia et religiosa meditatio* of David Chambellan. After Garamond's death in 1561 his stock was sold off. Among those buying type from the foundry was Christopher Plantin of Antwerp.

Arthur Eric Rownton Gill, 1882-1940

Gill was born in Brighton, the son of a nonconformist minister. He studied at Chichester School of Art before being apprenticed to the ecclesiastical architect W. D. Caröe in London. While in London he attended classes taught by the calligrapher Edward Johnston at the Central School of Arts and Crafts. Gill was greatly inspired by Johnston's work and the two men became good friends. Gill cut inscriptions for Caröe but also fulfilled commissions from members of the Art Workers Guild and eventually ended his apprenticeship to pursue this work. During his career he also created woodcuts and engravings for Harry Kessler's Cranach Press in Weimar, the St Dominic's Press, owned by Hilary Peplar, and Robert and Moira Gibbins's Golden Cockerel Press.

Gill left London in 1907 to live in Ditchling, Sussex; later he moved to Capel-y-Ffin in the Welsh mountains and finally Piggotts near High Wycombe.

He designed his first typeface at the invitation of Stanley Morison of the Monotype Corporation. The drawings for this type, Perpetua, were begun in 1925. Morison had made the request because he felt Gill's background in cutting stone inscriptions would give him an understanding of serifs. Charles Malin, punchcutter of the French foundry Deberny and Peignot converted Gill's drawings into type.

Gill Sans was influenced by Edward Johnston's Railway Type though Gill distinguished the two faces by saying that his own was designed to be read as a text face whereas Johnston's was intended purely for signs. Gill had used sans serif lettering for signs at Capel-y-Ffin and for the lettering on a Bristol bookshop owned by Douglas Cleverdon, which Gill painted in 1927. It was this bookshop sign which suggested the idea of a Gill sans serif to Morison.

Joanna, a much praised face, was named after his daughter Joan and designed for Hague and Gill, the printing partnership formed by Gill himself and Joan's husband René Hague. It was first used in 1931. In 1938 J. M. Dent bought the exclusive rights to Joanna and the face was not issued to the trade until 1958.

Bunyan, 1934, was Gill's last roman face. An adaptation by American Linotype was issued in 1953 and called Pilgrim.

In 1935 Gill was made an Associate of the Institute of British Architects. Two years later he was made an Associate of the Royal Academy. In 1939 he was among the first group to be given the title Royal Designer for Industry. He died at home the following year after a lung operation.

Frederick W. Goudy, 1865-1947

Frederick Goudy, one of the best known and most prolific of type designers, was born in Bloomington, Illinois in 1865. He became interested in type through the work of the English private presses.

His Kennerly Old Style, produced for New York publishers Mitchell Kennerly in 1911 and a set of titling, Forum, produced at the same time established his reputation and were particularly popular in England. American Type Founders commissioned him to design a face for them and the result was Goudy Old Style. In 1920 Lanston Monotype appointed Goudy as Art Advisor and it was in this capacity that he worked on the revival Garamond.

Goudy had a particular interest in blackletter. His best known such type is Goudy Text. He designed over 100 faces, by his own reckoning (though he counts each italic as a separate face).

and perhaps as a result his output was uneven in quality. One of his favourite faces was his last major one; California Old Style (now Berkley Old Style). Goudy died at his home, a water-mill on the Hudson River, in 1947.

Phillippe Grandjean, 1666-1714

Philippe Grandjean de Fouchy was born of an old Mâcon family, and became interested in type design after a chance visit to a Parisian printers. He was recommended to Louis XIV and began working for the Royal Printing Office, the *Imprimerie Royal*, under its director Jean Anisson.

In 1792 Louis XIV appointed a committee from the *Académie des Sciences* to draw up plans for a new typeface which would be the exclusive property of the *Imprimerie Royal*. The committee studied types then in current use, historical manuscripts and principles of geometry. The letter designs it then drew up were based on divisions of the circle. The type was to be called the Romains du Roi (the King's roman). Philippe Grandjean was assigned as punch-cutter and created types which were based on the drawings but did not follow them rigidly.

The Romains du Roi is a significant development in the history of typography because it was the first real departure from the old style faces in use in Europe at the time of its creation. It is thus the first transitional face.

Robert Granjon, 1513-1589

Robert Granjon was the son of Jean Granjon, a Paris printer. His principal work was the design and supply of type but he also printed, going into partnership with Michael Fezendat in 1549.

Granjon began supplying types while in Paris in the 1540s; moved to Lyon in 1557; later to Antwerp and finally to Rome where his clients included the New Vatican Press.

Many of Granjon's types were adopted enthusiastically by European printers, most notably Christopher Plantin. In recent times they have provided the model for Monotype's Plantin 1913 and Times New Roman 1932 as well as Matthew Carter's Galliard, however Granjon, the face that was named after him in a 1924 Linotype revival, is based on a Garamond type.

Chauncey H. Griffiths, 1879-1956
Bell Gothic, 285
Corona, 120
Excelsior, 115
Paragon, 144

In his position as Vice-President of Typographic Development for the Mergenthaler Company of New York, Chauncey H. Griffith was responsible for instigating many new designs. He is best known for the Legibility Group: Ionic, Excelsior, Paragon, Opticon and Corona, all newspaper types. Ionic, designed in 1922, was the first of the series and in 1930 it was adopted by the restyled *Daily Herald*. Excelsior has been described as one of the most influential newspaper faces of all time.

Two designers who worked under his direction were W. A. Dwiggins and Rudolph Ruzicka.

During his time with the company it issued revivals of Granjon, Baskerville, and Janson, and Griffiths also helped prepare Bell Gothic for the Bell Telephone Company. He retired in 1949 but continued to work for Linotype as a consultant.

Francesco Griffo, see Aldus Manutius

Johann Gutenberg, c 1394-1468

Johann Gutenberg of Mainz in Germany is generally believed to be the first European printer, though there are those who credit the invention to Laurents Coster of Haarlem. The invention, which probably took place around 1450, would have involved bringing together several existing techniques: the screw press, oil based pigments, the metal working skills of punch-cutting, and casting.

The principal work produced by Gutenberg's Mainz press was the *Forty-two-line Bible* in 1455, a Latin Bible which gets its name from the number of lines to a page.

The Textura typeface used in the Forty-two-line Bible was later the inspiration for Goudy's Goudy Text.

Jean Jannon, 1580-1658

Jean Jannon was a printer and punchcutter who worked in Sedan and Paris in the seventeenth century. He was the cutter of the *Imprimerie Nationale* Caractères de l'université which were once attributed to Garamond.

Nicholas Jenson, 1420-1480
Jenson, 16

Nicholas Jenson was one of the first printers to use type based on the model of traditional roman letter rather than the dark gothic type used in earlier German printed books.

Although known for his work in Venice, Nicholas Jenson was a Frenchman, born in Sommevoire in the district of Champagne around 1420. He served an apprenticeship in the Paris Mint and was promoted to be Master of the Mint at Tours. Apparently Charles VII sent Jenson to Mainz in 1458 in order that he should discover more about the new invention of printing. From his return to France in 1461 and his first publications in Venice in 1470, nothing is known of him.

In his first year of publishing, Jenson published Eusebius' *De evangelica praeparatione*, Justinus *Epitomata*, Cicero *Epistole ad atticum* and Cicero *Rheorica & De Inventione*. He continued to publish regularly until his death in September 1480. Around 155 editions exist known to be printed by Jenson or attributed to his press.

Jenson's faces had a great influence when a revival of interest in printing and typography took place in the late nineteenth and early twentieth centuries. Among the faces that took his as a model were Morris's Golden, Doves (of the Doves Press), Centaur, Cloister Old Style, Eusebius and Italian Old Style.

Edward Johnston, 1872-1944
Imprint, 67

Edward Johnston came to type designing from a background in calligraphy. He became interested in calligraphy as a young man, rapidly became a central figure in the Arts and Craft movement at the turn of the century and was instrumental in the revival of calligraphy. Among his notable designs are the initial capitals for the Doves Press Folio Bible.

In 1899 he began teaching writing and illuminating at the Central School of Arts and Crafts in London. Among his pupils were type designers Ernst F. Detterer and Eric Gill. In 1915 Johnston was commissioned by Pick to design what has become his best known face: Johnston's Railway Type, for the exclusive use of London Underground. It is a sans serif face based on classical Roman forms rather than on the nineteenth century grotesques. This face was later to provide the inspiration for Gill's Gill Sans.

George W. Jones, 1860-1942
Granjon, 66

English Linotype made G.W. Jones their printing advisor in 1921 to help them plan a series of type revivals. They were the first British foundry to create such a position (Monotype were to follow with the appointment of Stanley Morison). Jones designed Granjon (1924) as a rival to Monotype Garamond, and named it in honour of Robert Granjon, the sixteenth century punchcutter. He also designed Venezia in 1928 and Estienne in 1930.

Jones lectured on letterpress in Britain and the United States. He was a founder of the British Typographia – an association for printing education, and helped found the journal, *British Printer*.

Jock Kinneir, b.1917, and Margaret Calvert, b.1936
Transport, 282

Jock Kinneir worked for the Design Research Unit and was involved with the Festival of Britain. In 1956 he began working alone and took on one of his students, Margaret Calvert, who became a partner in 1964.

They designed the sign system and lettering at Gatwick Airport in the mid 1950's using a highly legible sans serif face which they refined and used on the motorway and road networks, British Rail and the British Airports Authority.

Margaret Calvert designed the typeface that bears her name in the late 1970's, a slab-serif, it developed from lettering designed for the Tyne and Wear Metro.

Gunter Gerhard Lange, b.1921
Concorde, 100
Concorde Nova, 64
Imago, 274

Gunter Gerhard Lange, born in 1921, is artistic director of the foundry of H. Berthold AG. Under his direction the company has issued original typefaces at a rate as high as one new face a month. Many of those designs are by Lange himself and those he does not design he still corrects by hand. Lange has also adapted classic typefaces such as Baskerville, Caslon, Walbaum, Bodoni and Garamond for film setting.

Aldus Manutius; 1450-1515, and Francesco Griffo; d.1519
Bembo, 35
Poliphilus, 40

Aldus Manutius, the great Renaissance printer and publisher, was born in 1450 in the Duchy of Sermoneta. He spent the early part of his career working under the patronage of the Count Alberto Pio, Prince of Carpi, but left Carpi for Venice in 1489 to further his ambition of publishing Greek classics in the original. While the market for Latin editions in Italy was overcrowded the opposite was true of Greek works and in Venice he had access to collections of fine manuscripts. His types were cut and (it is now generally believed) designed for him by Francesco Griffo. His first publications came out in 1484: an edition of the *Galyeomyomachia* and Musaeus' *De Herone et Leandro*.

The first Aldine roman is the type used in Cardinal Bembo's *De Aetna*, published in 1495. Stanley Morison demonstrated that Claude Garamond used it as the basis for his types, and this makes it the first of the old face types. Monotype have produced two faces based on Manutius' designs. Poliphilus (1923) is a facsimile revival of the type used in the *Hypnerotomachia Poliphili* of 1499 whilst Bembo (1929) is based on the *De Aetna* type.

Aldus published on a large scale (a letter of his refers to a thousand or more volumes a month) and amassed a considerable fortune, aided by a number of copyrights and monopolies which the College of Venice had granted him. He helped to popularise many works by using an octavo format which made his books cheaper and more portable. Francesco Griffo had a dispute with Aldus, whom he claimed had not given him sufficient credit for the types and this dispute over authorship of the so-called Aldine types was later taken up by type scholars.

Aldus died at 65 in his house in the Venetian printing quarter of San Paternian and his body lay in state there surrounded by copies of his books. Francesco Griffo died some time around 1518/19. The cause and exact date of his death are not known but it seems likely that he was hanged as a punishment for killing his brother-in-law, which he did with an iron bar in May 1518 during a fight.

Dr. Hans (also Giovanni) Mardersteig, 1892-1977
Dante, 102
Fontana, 65

Hans Mardersteig was both a scholar and a printer. He researched in Renaissance printing, focusing particularly on the work of Francesco Griffo. He is best known for the work of the private press which he founded, the *Officina Bodoni*, but after World War II he added a commercial press, the *Stamparia Valdonega*.

Many of the types used at the Officina were of Mardersteig's design. They were cut for him by the Paris punchcutter Charles Malin, a productive collaboration, and although Mardersteig continued working until he was 86 his type designing ceased with Malin's death in 1955. Mardersteig's best known type are Fontana and Dante. The first was designed not for the Officina but for the publishers William Collins of Glasgow.

William Martin, d.1815
Bulmer, 58

William Martin was the brother of Robert Martin, Baskerville's punchcutter. William too trained under Baskerville, whose types clearly influenced his own. William Martin's types are cut more sharply than his teacher's and more closely approach the modern face. He is said to have cut the last of the transitionals.

Martin's types were cut for the printer William Bulmer (1757-1830), and being sharply cut were a good choice, since they combined well with engravings and appeared to advantage in the large formats he favoured.

M. F. Benton cut a replica of a Martin type cut for the Shakespeare Press around 1790. This replica, Bulmer, was cut for A.T.F. in 1928.

Max Miedinger,
Neu Haas Grotesque/Helvetica, 279/422/477/493-4/529-530/620/624

Max Miedinger of Zurich was an in-house designer with the Haas Foundry in Munchenstein, Switzerland. In 1956 he was asked to adapt the existing Haas Grotesk and bring it up to date, but the type which was produced from his china ink drawings seemed like a new design. Originally New Haas Grotesque, it became known as Helvetica when released by Stempel A.G. in 1961. It is the most widely available sans serif.

Isaac Moore, see Joseph Fry

Stanley Morison, 1889-1967
Times New Roman, 52/53

Morison was the typographical consultant to the Monotype Corporation and directed its programme of revivals. Monotype was not alone among foundries in reviving historic types and it had already begun to do so before Morison joined the Corporation. Nonetheless Morison, a largely self-taught scholar of printing and typographic history, brought an informed enthusiasm to the work. His interest in types also embraced contemporary designs and he was responsible for commissioning original faces from Eric Gill (whom he introduced to type design) and Jan Van Krimpen.

Stanley Morison designed only one type but that face, which he called Times New Roman, is more commonly used today than any other. It rose rapidly to this position after its launch in the redesigned *Times* newspaper which first appeared on 3rd October 1932.

William Morris, 1834-1896

William Morris was a key figure in the Arts and Crafts movement of the late nineteenth century but did not involve himself in printing and typography until he was approaching the end of his career. In 1890 Morris founded the Kelmscott Press and in 1891 it became established in its own premises. It was always intended as a small private press; he used type which was cut by a hand punchcutter and hand set; hand presses, and he also printed on dampened handmade paper.

Morris designed two types for the press. Golden was the result of his early drawings of Venetian types and it was the more influential. He planned to use it for an edition of *The Golden Legend*, hence the name. Golden sparked off the interest in Jenson revivals.

His other face is a Fere-humanistica (an informal blackletter) for the Kelmscott Chaucer. This face came in two sizes known as Troy and Chaucer. Morris's punchcutter for the types was E. P. Prince, and Emery Walker, later of the Doves Press, worked as Morris's typographic consultant.

Robin Nicholas, b.1947
Nimrod, 122

Robin Nicholas has been the manager of the Monotype Corporation's type drawing office since 1982. Between 1978 and 1980 he designed Nimrod, a group of related roman faces designed for newspaper text, headlines and small ads. Nimrod has been widely praised for its legibility and is used by *The Guardian*, *Daily Telegraph* and *Today*. He has also supervised the redesign of many Monotype faces such as Bell, Centaur and Janson for the Lasercomp system.

Aldo Novarese, b.1920
Augustea, 171/409/416
Eurostile, 291-2
Microgramma, 294
Novarese, 226/264

Aldo Novarese has designed most of his types for the Nebolio Art Studio in Turin which he joined at 16. Augustea and Microgramma are among those he designed in partnership with Alessandro Butti (1893-1959), while the type that bears his name, Novarese, was designed for Haas. In Italy he is also known as a writer on type and he contributes to a number of design and graphics publications.

George Peignot, d.1914, and Charles Peignot, 1897-1983

George and Charles Peignot were father and son. George took over the Paris type foundry Deberny and Peignot from his father Gustave, and Charles took over in his turn when George and his brothers died in World War I. Both men had a policy of commissioning types from contemporary graphic artists. The Swiss designer Adrian Frutiger worked for Charles Peignot. The type that bears their name, Peignot (1936), was designed for the foundry by the poster artist A.M. Cassandre.

Charles Peignot was extremely active in the cause of typeface copyright and to this end he helped found the *Association Typographique International*.

Charles' son Remy is a type designer. He designed Cristal, a titling face, in 1957.

Frank Hinman Pierpont, 1860-1937
Plantin, 39

Although American, Frank Hinman Pierpont spent most of his career working for English Monotype as the manager of their Salford works in Surrey. He adapted existing type designs to suit Monotype machines, aided by the German Fritz Steltzer. In 1913 they designed Plantin which is based on a face from the Plantin Moretus Museum (although this face was never used by the great Antwerp printer of that name). Pierpont and Steltzer wanted a large-bodied face and they designed Plantin with ink-spread in mind so that it would print well on smooth and coated papers.

Pierpont, a founder executive of Monotype, had reservations about the Corporation's revivals programme. After Morison's appointment by Monotype as their advisor there was a certain amount of friction between the two men. Pierpont regarded the Salford works as his domain and he resented what he saw as Morison's interference.

Christopher Plantin, 1514/20-1589
Plantin, 39

Although Christopher Plantin was born in France it is his work in the Netherlands that made him famous. He began his working life as a bookbinder, first in Caen and then in Paris. It was probably during his time in Paris that he learnt how to print.

In 1548/9 he settled in Antwerp and was soon established as one of the foremost North European publishers and printers.

Although Plantin himself did not design type he was very interested in its selection. He collected type, punches and matrices, buying from, among others, Robert Granjon and Claude Garamond. He has given his name to Plantin, a face designed for Monotype by F. H. Pierpont.

Friedrich Poppl, 1923-1982
Poppl Laudatio, 227
Poppl Pontifex, 85

Friedrich Poppl became known as a calligrapher in the 1960's, when his work was shown in several important exhibitions, but not until the release of Poppl-Pontifex in 1976-9 did he achieve recognition as a type designer. His types were commissioned by Berthold at the instigation of its artistic director Gunter Gerhard Lange.

Paul Renner, 1878-1956
Futura, 254/502/526
Futura Black, 636
Topic, 614

Paul Renner was the designer of Futura: issued by the Bauer foundry in Frankfurt. It was the leading sans serif face for 25 years and still remains popular. Futura was conceived on geometrical principles which Renner modified as the design developed. It was originally cut with a number of experimental forms for some letters which were cut as alternative sorts. Their unfamiliar shapes were not taken up by the trade and were abandoned in later cuttings although Futura retains a single-bowled a.

Bruce Rogers, 1870-1957
Centaur, 19

Born in Lafayette, Indiana, Bruce Rogers was a book designer who occasionally designed type. His early work was influenced by William Morris's Kelmscott Press style, although he then developed his own.

At the Riverside Press, Boston, he designed his first type, the Jenson-based Montaigne, for a three-volume edition of the essays of Montaigne, published by the Press 1902-4. He is best known for Centaur which takes as its model the Jenson type used in Eusebius *De evangelica praeparatione* (1470).

A critical report Rogers prepared for Cambridge University on the use of type in the University Press led to their eventual appointment of a type consultant – Stanley Morison.

Sumner Stone, b.1945

Sumner Stone is Director of Typography at Adobe Systems Incorporated in California. At college he studied mathematics and calligraphy (learning the latter from the calligrapher Lloyd Reynolds in Oregon). He has worked as lettering artist for Hallmark Cards but joined Adobe in 1984. Adobe are the originators of the computer page description language Postscript and it was for Adobe he designed Stone, a family consisting of a roman, a sans serif and an informal.

George Trump, 1896-1985
City, 192
Codex, 334
Schadow Antiqua, 203
Trump Mediaeval, 44

George Trump was a teacher of graphics and a type designer with a particular interest in script types. He taught at the Advanced School of Book Printing in Berlin and just before World War II began designing type for the Weber Foundry in Stuttgart. He retired from teaching in 1953 but continued to design type. His most important typeface, Trump Mediaeval dates from this period.

Jan Tschichold, 1902-1974
Sabon, 88

The son of a sign writer, Jan Tschichold spent his teenage years studying calligraphy, typography and engraving. His work at this time was influenced by the types of the Italian Renaissance and blackletter but in 1923 he saw the Bauhaus Exhibition at Weimar. He became the best known publicist and practitioner of the 'new typography' that developed in Europe between the wars. He advocated assymmetric layouts and sans serif typefaces and rejected revivals of historic styles of type as 'fancy dress'.

Later in his career he was to revise such pronouncements, finding them too doctrinaire. Tschichold designed only one widely used type, Sabon. His views were popularised by his writings, particularly *Die neue Typographie* (The New Typography) and *Typographische Gestaltung* (Assymmetric Typography).

Later in his career he was to revise such pronouncements, finding them too doctrinaire. He worked for Penguin Books in London between 1947 and 1949 and was responsible for establishing design guidelines and series styles. In the 1960's he designed the Garamond-derived Sabon.

In 1958 he was awarded the Institute of Graphic Arts Gold Medal and was made an Honorary Royal Designer for Industry by the Royal Society of Arts in 1965.

Cristoffel Van Dijck, 1601-1672
Van Dijck, 107

Cristoffel Van Dijck (also Dyck) was a celebrated Dutch type founder whose work is associated with the golden age of Dutch printing. His type foundry was established in 1648. In 1937 Stanley Morison and Van Krimpen designed a face called Van Dijck for Monotype. This is based on a type used in a 1671 Ovid attributed to his foundry.

Jan Van Krimpen, 1892-1958
Cancelleresca Bastarda, 381
Lutetia, 25
Romulus, 105
Spectrum, 97

After studying at the Academy of Art in the Hague Jan Van Krimpen worked as a freelance designer and illustrator. At 31 his work was spotted by Dr Johannes Enschedé of the Joh. Enschedé en Zohen in Haarlem, Holland. Enschedé asked him to design a new type for his company, and was so pleased with the result he invited Van Krimpen to join them as one of their house designers. He was to stay with the company until his retirement.

Van Krimpen was a skilled calligrapher but believed calligraphy and type design to be essentially different and his types show little calligraphic influence. His letter forms have been described as 'austerely restrained'. Although beautiful and influential they are not widely used.

Van Krimpen did not confine himself to type design but was also a notable book designer, working for Enschedé and fulfilling commissions from other presses.

Justus Erich Walbaum, 1768-1839
Walbaum, 161/167/168/187

Justus Erich Walbaum had his own letter foundry, first based in Goslar and later in Weimar. His faces were neo-classical, derived from the Didot roman.

The founders Berthold still own his original matrices which they bought (from F.H. Brockhaus) in 1918. Berthold's Walbaum was cast from these. Walbaum's types became available in Britain through the Curwen Press in 1925 and some Continental sizes of Monotype Walbaum were available after 1930.

Frederic Warde, 1894-1939
Arrighi, 379

Frederic Warde was the husband of Beatrice Warde, the type publicist and (as Paul Beaujon) type scholar.

In 1926 he published *The Calligraphic Models of Ludovico Degli Arrighi* a complete facsimile of a book by the sixteenth century writing master. The introduction to this book, by Stanley Morison, was set in a new italic modelled on Arrighi's and cut by Georges Plumet. The design of this italic, Arrighi, is generally attributed to Warde although James Moran, in his book on Morison, disputes this. He adapted this first Arrighi italic for Monotype to use with Bruce Rodger's Centaur in 1929, this version is called Centaur Italic.

Emery Walker, see Thomas J. Cobden Sanderson, p.269

Emil Rudolf Weiss, 1875-1943
Weiss, 98

Professor Emil Rudolf Weiss was interested in many aspects of art and design and had already established himself in other areas before the Bauer foundry encouraged him to turn his attention to typefaces. Bauer had a policy of commissioning types from graphic artists and all three of Weiss's types (plus a number of ornaments) were designed for them. The best known, Weiss Antiqua, evolved very slowly. It can be identified by its distinctive 'upside-down' S.

Alexander Wilson, 1714-1784

In 1742 Alexander Wilson set up a type foundry in St Andrews. This foundry, which later moved to Glasgow, ended the dependence of Scottish printers on types brought in from London and the Netherlands, indeed it was to become a serious rival to London foundries. While Alexander Wilson ran the foundry (originally with a partner) it produced types which were influenced by the work of Caslon and Baskerville.

Notable cutters to work for the Wilson foundry include Richard Austin, who cut a modern face for them, and Johann Bauer who was later to start his own foundry in Frankfurt. The Miller Foundry in Edinburgh was started by an ex-manager of Wilson's, and The Wilson Foundry itself was to open an Edinburgh branch (Bauer trained here and Alexander's grandson kept this branch open when he transferred the foundry's main operation to London in 1834).

In this century English Roman No. 1, a Wilson Foundry type though possibly not designed by Alexander Wilson himself, served as the model for Hans Mardersteig's Fontana, designed for Collins of Glasgow in 1936.

Berthold Wolpe, 1905-1989
Albertus, 218
Pegasus, 235

Berthold Wolpe, born in Offenbach near Frankfurt in 1905, spent the greater part of his working life in England. From 1941-1975 he designed book-jackets for the publishers Faber & Faber, creating as many as 1500 designs. His best known type is Albertus which was commissioned by Stanley Morison of the Monotype Corporation. He taught lettering to students at Camberwell College of Art and the Royal College of Art, London. A retrospective exhibition of his work was held at the Victoria and Albert Museum in London in 1980 to mark his 75th birthday.

Hermann Zapf, b.1918
Aldus, 75
Comenius, 125
Kompact, 451
Melior, 138
Optima, 268
Orion, 139
Palatino, 84
Sapphire, 546
Zapf Book, 169/443
Zapf Chancery, 316
Zapf International, 150

Hermann Zapf is a prolific type designer and a notable writer on type. He spent the early part of his career working for the Stempel foundry in Germany and his work helped to fill the shortage of designs for roman typefaces that existed in West Germany after the war (the main source of such types, Leipzig, having gone to the East).

Although he was to resign this post in 1956 to spend more time on other work this was to be a particularly productive time for him. Zapf faces of this period include Palatino, a design based on Renaissance forms which was much admired and quickly taken up by other foundries.

In 1958 Zapf designed Optima, at that time an unclassifiable face but one which Zapf himself called a serifless roman. It was inspired by inscriptional lettering he had seen in Florence, and is probably his best known typeface.

Since leaving Stempel Zapf has created typefaces for a number of other companies including Berthold, Hell Digiset, Mergenthaler Linotype, Hallmark Cards, and ITC. He has designed new faces for filmsetting and digitisation as well as overseeing the transfer of many of his older designs to the new systems. In 1977 he was made Professor of Typographic Computer Programming at Rochester Institute of Technology in New York.

Bibliography/Further reading

Biggs, *An approach to type.* Blandford Press, 1949
British Standards Institution, *Typeface nomenclature and classification.* (BS 2961), 1967
Carter, *Twentieth century type designers.* Trefoil, 1987
Dowding, *An introduction to the history of printing types.* Wace & Company Limited, 1961
Gates, *Type.* Watson-Guptill Publications, 1973
Gottschall, *Typographic communications today.* MIT Press, 1989
Haley, *A guide to in-house typography & design.* Robert Hale Limited, 1981
Jaspert, Berry & Johnson, *Encyclopaedia of typefaces.* Blandford Press, 1962, 1970 and 1983 editions
Jongejans, *Typefaces.* Wolters-Noordhoff/steen drukkerij de Jong & Co. Hilversum, c. 1980
Karch, *How to recognise typefaces.* McKnight & McKnight, 1959
Lieberman, *Types of typefaces and how to recognise them.* Sterling Publishing Co. Inc., 1967
McClean, *Typography.* Thames and Hudson, 1980
Merriman, *Type comparison book.* The Advertising Typographers Association of America, Inc., 1965
Monotype Corporation, *Students type study leaflets*
Rosen, *Type and typography.* Van Nostrand Reinhold, 1976
Sutton & Bartram, *An atlas of typeforms.* Lund Humphries, 1967

Catalogues & typeface information of the following companies were also referred to:
Alphatype Systems Limited
American Type Foundry
AM International Inc.
Amsterdam Foundry
Association Typographique Internationale (A. Typ. I)
H. Berthold AG
Bobst SA (Bobstgraphic Division)
Compugraphic Corporation
Harris Communications
International Typeface Corporation (ITC)
ITEK Corporation
Linotype-Paul Limited
Letraset UK Limited
Mecanorma
Mergenthaler, Linotype, Stempel, Haas
The Monotype Corporation
Mouldtype Foundry Limited
Stephenson, Blake & Company Limited
Tetterode-Nederland (*Lettertypen*)
Yendall & Company Limited (Riscatype)

INDEX

'Bastard' names listed are cross-referenced to the appropriate typeface.

NB. *Bold figures refer to specimen numbers.*

'Bastard' names listed are cross-referenced to the appropriate typeface.

NB. Bold figures refer to specimen numbers.

Feb 2/06